# SUNDAY'S WOMEN

# SUNDAY'S WOMEN

## A Report on Lesbian Life Today

**SASHA GREGORY LEWIS**

BEACON PRESS / BOSTON

Beacon Press books are published under the auspices
of the Unitarian Universalist Association
Published simultaneously in Canada by
Fitzhenry & Whiteside Limited, Toronto
Printed in the United States of America

(hardcover) 9 8 7 6 5 4 3 2 1


Library of Congress Cataloging in Publication Data

Lewis, Sasha Gregory.
    Sunday's women.
    Includes bibliographical references and index.
    1.   Lesbians—United States.   2.   Lesbianism—
    United States.     I.   Title.
HQ75.6.U5L4   1979              301.41'57         78-53655
ISBN   0−8070−3794−X

For
**Mary and Hansel**
for their years of encouragement
and to
**Loretta**
who proved I could write
(and also live)
without drinking

Monday's child is fair of face
Tuesday's child is full of grace
Wednesday's child is full of woe
Thursday's child has far to go
Friday's child is loving and giving
Saturday's child has to work for its living
But a child that's born on the Sabbath day
          is fair and wise, and good and gay.

# Acknowledgments

This book would have been impossible without the generosity of the two dozen lesbians who gave so freely of their time discussing some of their most intimate experiences. Unfortunately, many of them cannot be named here because their professional lives might be put in jeopardy. Ten women, however, felt it important to make a statement about the pride they take in their lifestyles by having their names listed here. They are Sydney Barrett, Cheryl Brandeberry, Barbara M. Fellman, Corrine E. Gearhart, Karen Koehler, Sharon Mills, Maureen Oddone, Barbara Root, Helen L. Snyder, and Carole L. Weidner. I extend my deep gratitude to all these women, named and unamed.

I am also indebted to Marilyn G. Fleener for sharing the results of her study of 162 lesbians with me for this book and to Mary E. Lewis who made our interviews much more rewarding.

A good share of the credit for this book also goes to editor Charlotte Cecil Raymond of Beacon Press who gave it, through its several revisions, her patient and thoughtful assistance.

Errors, misstatements, and general blunders are, of course, solely my responsibility.

# Contents

**SUNDAY'S WOMEN**

# Introduction

The contemporary lesbian experience cannot be separated from its historical and social context. Lesbians have endured through several eras: pre-Christian times of acceptance; seventeen centuries of Christian rule when they were repressed as individuals, and when even the notion that their lifestyle was possible was also repressed; and the last quarter-century, a time when lesbians rebelled openly against both personal oppression and their invisibility as a group—a rebellion countered by a reaction that would try to make lesbians once again pariahs, women outcast and unmentionable. Today thousands of lesbians have come out from hiding, out from the underground, to face their oppression head on in a battle that can be either won or lost but not compromised. As lesbians, reactionaries, and those on the sidelines experience this battle they are forced to face serious questions about some of the basic assumptions underlying our culture and social institutions.

Whether the American mainstream accepts some of the lessons learned from this conflict and uses them to improve the quality of human experience for all people, or whether it chooses instead to avoid the challenges of the lesbian revolt—challenges posed by self-defined women who are free from many of the constraints imposed on most members of our society—is a question for the future.

The lesbian movement of the last quarter-century has special significance when viewed in context with the much more explosive revolution that is transforming the mainstay of American social policies and interactions—the patriarchal family. This institution has long been tied to the American national identity. Imported with the Puritan colonists who brought with them the English common-law-assumption that women were the property of their husbands, the patriarchal family seemed to blossom in the post-World War II era when it became increasingly possible for many families in a growing (white) middle class to subsist on the earnings of one worker. This worker was, of course, the father of the family, the patriarch, the one to whom law and custom allowed the highest wage. The mother, meanwhile, was expected to service the needs of her husband-provider and to care for their children.

But this lifestyle was a boomtime economic luxury that is fast vanishing from the American scene. A 1978 Census Bureau profile, for example, found that one white child in eight under eighteen, and two black children in five under eighteen, live in families without a father present. And, of the children born in 1978, a Bureau expert predicted, only 55 percent will grow up in a traditional two-parent family. Forty-five percent, according to Bureau experts, will spend a substantial part of their lives with only one parent.[1]

No longer is the father his family's sole provider. In 30.4 million families—more than half of all U.S. families—both adults work. Mothers no longer spend their days at home caring for their children; economic necessity prevents it. They are joining the workforce in increasing numbers in both full- and part-time capacities. In mid-1978 slightly less than half of all adult American women, many of them mothers, worked at salaried jobs.[2] This number was expected to increase to more than half by the end of the year. Fourteen percent, or about eight million American families, are headed by a single woman, with no father present to contribute to his children's lives either emotionally or financially.[3] In recognition of these facts a few American companies and municipalities are providing day-care centers to enable the large number of working mothers to continue their much needed employment.

Although the mass media occasionally try boosting the idea that the traditional American family is far from obsolete—especially among the economically privileged—the cold facts tell a different story. Even what survives of the traditional family is in severe crisis. Statistics on alcoholism and drug abuse among American nonworking wives are just beginning to be accumulated. The FBI considers domestic violence to be the most common and the most underreported crime in the country. About one-fourth of all murders and the U.S. occur within the family and half of these are husband-wife killings. One in three families is said to have experienced "at least one instance of domestic battery," and one in ten reported that domestic violence was a regular occurrence.[4] Children, supposedly the beneficiaries of the traditional family, are often the victims of this domestic violence, a national tragedy that has spawned hundreds of organizations to work with parental child-batterers. Yet *sexually* abused children, according to a study of sex crimes against children in Brooklyn performed by the Children's Division of the American Humane Association, are statistically more prevalent than the physically abused or battered child. More than a quarter of the cases studied by the association involved incest—until recently a taboo enshrined crime that still remains underreported. The rate of incest, so far untabulated, is also said to be staggering.

Those institutions that buttressed and grew out of the patriarchal nuclear family are also ailing, crippled by an increasingly transient America. One of three families move each year, leaving children (and their parents) with little chance to make lifelong friends or to develop roots in any community. It is these rootless Americans, as researcher Harvey Cox suggests, who join religious cults and street gangs in search of "simple friendship . . . Many seekers who drift into such movements looking for intimacy quickly learn to express their reasons in the group argot. But the need for plain friendship is clearly their chief motivation. They are looking for warmth, affection, and close ties of feeling. They don't find it at work, at school, in the churches they attend, or even at home."[5]

Public schools, originally designed to supplement the moral and spiritual education children received at home during a time when parents were there to provide it, now often must carry the whole burden of their students' development. It is a task the schools were not designed for and daily they are turning into armed camps surrounded by barbed-wire-topped fences, their hallways patrolled by armed guards.

Neighborhoods and small towns, once communities of extended families which looked after all their members, have all but disappeared as residents move in and out of mass-produced suburbs and apartment complexes, seldom even learning a next-door neighbor's name, much less keeping an eye out for her or his children or property. Police must now try to do the job neighbors once did, and crime rates increase while rootless and increasingly isolated Americans look the other way.

Rootlessness and isolation came upon America gradually, were whispered about in sociologists' studies and doctoral theses, or discussed in books soon forgotten. They came without announcement, caused no immediate trauma, and developed no easily diagnosable symptoms. Rootlessness and human isolation were nonproblems, facts of existence much like a few pounds of excess weight which did not seem to warrant drastic remedy. Rather than create new institutions and alternatives to accommodate the needs of the nontraditional family and the mobile, uprooted, quarantined American, we ignored these needs. Rather than attack the debilitating effects of the disease by making fundamental changes in our economic and social systems— changes that could have made possible healthier environments for children, less stress for their parents, schools that would be places of learning rather than prisons, and neighborhoods that would fight crime rather than hide from it—we did nothing.

Thus, we left an open door for demagogues who attacked what they defined as symptoms of an ailing people—prostitution, pornography, crime, abortion—anything that seemed to threaten what they believed America should be. Their most vicious attacks were leveled at what they considered threats to the patriarchal family, the presumed God-given cornerstone of the nation. First in their rifle sights was the women's liberation movement, heralded as the newest enemy of one-hundred-percent Americanism. Jacquie Davison, in 1970, was apparently the first to successfully capitalize on this target. Locating a convenient symbolic issue, the Equal Rights Amendment, she founded Happiness of Womanhood (HOW) with two immediate objectives:

To aid in the attempt to stop the passage by the United States Congress of the "Equal Rights Amendment" . . . to stress femininity, to help women be happy in marriage.[6]

Davison's full program, explained an early manifesto, presaged the goals of the Pro-Family movement that developed several years after she dropped out of the crusade:

HOW is an organization that is dedicated to the preservation of the masculine role as guide, protector and provider, and preservation of the feminine role as wife, mother and homemaker . . . Preservation of the Family . . . Remove Women's liberation teachings from our schools: Our tax dollars are paying some teachers whose intent it is to destroy the family structure . . . Teach our young daughters the joys of womanhood: and teach them to take on the role of Housewife with the pride and dignity it deserves.[7]

In 1972 Phyllis Schlafly, a more politically experienced activist, took up Davison's crusade, launching a multifaceted attack on both ERA and the women's movement as the ultimate enemies of the American family. Wrote Schlafly in 1972:

There are two very different types of women lobbying for the Equal Rights Amendment. One group is the women's liberationists. Their motive is totally radical. They hate men, marriage, and children. They are out to destroy morality and the family. They look upon husbands as the exploiters, children as an evil to be avoided (by abortion if necessary), and the family as an institution which keeps women in "second-class citizenship" or even "slavery." . . . There is another type of woman supporting the Equal Right Amendment from the most sincere motives.[8]

Schlafly was more forceful in her advocacy of the preservation of the patriarchal family and its significance for America in her 1977 book, *The Power of the Positive Women:*

To reject the obligation to take whatever action is necessary to safeguard the moral, social, and economic integrity of the family is to abandon the future [of the nation] to a bunch of marital misfits who are . . . mistaken about morals, misinformed about history . . . and who want to remake our laws, revise the marriage contract, restructure society and mold our children to conform to lib values instead of God's values . . . It is the task of the Positive Woman to keep America good.[9]

## THE LESBIAN MENACE

Assertive women within the women's movement had always been branded "lesbians" whether they were or not, just as earlier reformers had been uniformly branded "communists," whatever their political affiliation. In the face of such branding the women's movement began to debate whether it should ostracize the lesbians within it or take up the cause of lesbian rights as one of its own. After protracted and sometimes bitter controversy, the movement decided to support its lesbian sisters, realizing that to do otherwise would lead only to continued lesbian-baiting and to the ultimate destruction of the movement. This phenomenon gave Schlafly and her followers a new weapon in the arsenal aimed at saving the patriarchal family: a scapegoat— lesbians. Looming large among the dangers Schlafly now found in the "women's lib" and ERA movements was the fact that they supported "lesbians' right to teach in schools & adopt children."[10]

Antilesbian arguments such as these had been relatively low-key in the Schlafly repertoire until early in 1977, when Florida orange juice promoter Anita Bryant made the whispered word one of the most discussed topics in the nation as she launched an all-out attack against a Dade County gay rights ordinance. Bryant had finally pointed out the ultimate enemy of the patriarchal family and the American way of life—homosexuals. As she explained after her successful crusade:

Our country was strong for so long because we claimed we were one nation under God and God blessed us. I believe that right now, God has removed himself from America. If we'll look through history, we're in the same situation as were Greece and Rome, when homosexuality and other sins were so rampant they became the norm . . . I didn't even come to the realization that America was so far gone until the time of the referendum, when I got letters from groups all over the country describing the fights they were in and how they were fighting some of the same things and it looked to me like a big octopus that had its tentacles around America and was squeezing our country to death.[11]

Teaming up with Bryant in her 1977 campaign were a variety of political conservatives including many from the American Conservative Union (ACU) and several from the radical right fringe including such unwanted groups as the Ku Klux Klan. Joining a crusade that soon dominated the front pages of newspapers that had never before printed the word *homosexual* were ultraright evangelists who also at first had difficulty uttering the previously unmentionable word. With top-notch political advice from leaders of the ACU and such new right organizations as the National Conservative Political Action Committee, the Bryant team masterminded a political campaign that brought together for the first time the divided segments of the Miami area voting public. A surprising majority voted against what Bryant strategists labeled "homosexual privilege"—the right to equal opportunity in employment and housing. Christians voted with Jews; Catholics voted with born-again fundamentalists; Cubans voted with Anglos; Democrats voted with Republicans. The victory was heralded in the ACU's *Battle Line* as a new era for conservative politics. "Issues," said the magazine, "can be couched in the phraseology of 'moral issues' and [successfully] fought in the political arena."[12]

Schlafly, an ACU leader, was not going to fall behind the new politics in her anti-ERA crusade. Capitalizing on the Dade County gay rights furor, her troops were again successful in defeating the state legislature's attempt to ratify the amendment. A few Florida legislators, prepared to vote in favor of ratification, were, some observers said, persuaded to change their votes by anti-ERA lobbyists, who emphasized the argument that ERA would allegedly legalize homosexual marriages. Meanwhile, Schlafly's own literature became more and more antilesbian. While her earliest newsletters had made only the barest mention of the word, claiming only that "radicals" and "libbers" were out to destroy American womanhood, her post-Bryant-victory materials took a new tone, emphasizing the dangers of "privileges for lesbians to teach in the schools and have child custody."[13]

The new era of attack on lesbians peaked later that year at the Houston International Women's Year Conference. Women's liberation opponents were so grossly outnumbered at the official conclave that they held their own unofficial rally at the Houston Astrodome. There they began a new coalition, the Pro-Family Movement. The three key planks of the movement forged in Houston were opposition to the ERA, to abortion, and to homosexual privilege (gay civil rights).

The Pro-Family group, aided by Anita Bryant and her followers, took the antigay campaign nationwide and managed to overturn existing gay rights protections in St. Paul, Minnesota, Wichita, Kansas, and Eugene, Oregon. Oklahoma, which had earlier enacted a commendation for Bryant—Miss Oklahoma before her orange juice career—passed legislation banning homosexuals from teaching in the state's schools.

But by late 1978 something had gone wrong for Pro-Family activists; antigay campaigns began to lose. Fewer than 100 people turned out in Madison, Wisconsin, to hear the Reverend Carl McIntire denounce homosexuals. Bryant could draw so few people to a rally in Boston that it was canceled. And two referendums—one to overturn Seattle's gay rights law, and one to ban all teachers who advocated gay rights (whether gay or straight) from California schools—were overwhelmingly defeated in November elections.

Schlafly's antilesbian ploys also began to backfire. As evidence of the supposed vileness of the women's liberation movement, a group of Schlaflyites had collected commercial lesbian materials from the Houston International Women's Year Conference. Among these privately produced materials were descriptions, in both words and drawings, of lesbian sex acts. Also included were copies of literature advertising vibrators to be used for sexual stimulation and masturbation. Schlaflyites packaged these materials and, indicating that they were government-financed literature, distributed them to state legislators considering ERA-related action in Alabama, Kentucky, Indiana, and Oklahoma. Rather than becoming angry at Women's Year promoters, or women's movement activists, or even at lesbians, the legislators took umbrage at the Schlaflyites, accusing them of distributing pornography.

## MYTH, THREAT, REALITY

The 1977 Bryant and Pro-Family assaults on lesbian rights were successful largely because lesbians were still invisible to mainstream Americans. A survey at the beginning of 1978 in California reported that only 52 percent of the state's voters, most of them in San Francisco and Los Angeles, personally knew a homosexual of either gender.[14] Similar surveys in other states would doubtlessly have shown vastly lower percentages. Although lesbians had been organizing in California, New York, and a few isolated cities to assert their rights as American citizens for more than two decades, their existence rarely rated even back-page mention save for occasional lurid articles boasting of the arrest of so many "perverts" at one bar or another. Although no study of the subject has been undertaken, it is doubtful that even 10 percent of America's news media had ever used the word *lesbian* in print or on the air prior to the Bryant crusade. Thus, when Bryant began her assault, the subject of lesbianism was enveloped in distasteful myths that provided an amorphously evil target for her campaign—as they had for campaigns preceding it from the Inquisition to the McCarthy period.

The myths were many and their origins old—nearly two thousand years old. The development of ancient tales about lesbianism paralleled the demise of the stature of women in Western society. Researcher Dolores Klaich, in her book *Woman + Woman,* describes the concurrent demise of women's stature and the rise of a mythologized lesbian ethos in her discussion of Sappho and her work. Sappho lived during the sixth century B.C. in a nonpatriarchal Asian Greek culture. Here aristocratic women were the legal, spiritual, and social equals of their male counterparts and here homosexuals were treated no differently from other citizens. In this milieu the lesbian poet came to be acclaimed as one of the greatest lyricists of all time.

Klaich explains in *Woman + Woman:*

In Sappho's day (c. 612–588 B.C.) her poems were read and sung throughout the Greek world. No woman of the time was more celebrated. Coins were minted in her honor, statues erected in tribute. She was pretty much a household word, with no opprobrium [for her love of women] attached; when she died, she was given a noble burial.[15]

By Aristotle's time, however, the male supremacist axiom ruled in the Greek world, changing the situation both for women and for Sappho's reputation. Women were no longer citizens, but servants. And Sappho, who was still difficult to completely ignore despite her gender, was a figure of history honored, according to Aristotle's report, *"although* she was a woman." Sappho was on her way to oblivion.

During the second century A.D., reports Klaich, Sappho's love of women was made a target of ridicule. Historical fantasies were fabricated about her life by comedic writers of the era. Lesbos, the island of Sappho's birth, was identified with her love of women. (During Sappho's own time, the word *lesbian* referred simply to a resident of Lesbos, male or female, hetero- or homosexual.) Lesbians, according to one comedic writer, were semifemale creatures who looked and acted like men, and who merely imitated men in their lovemaking. And lesbianism, in an even more farcical deviation from the historic reality of Sappho's life, became synonymous with sexual depravity. None of these fallacies finds justification in Sappho's work or in the facts of her life (or in the lives of most contemporary lesbians), but they became dogma nonetheless.

Under Christian rule in 380 A.D., when the first death penalty laws for homosexuals were enacted—ridicule apparently having failed to eliminate the supposedly pagan practices—Sappho's lyrics were collected and burned. The songs that survived this first burning were again condemned to the fires by Christian leaders in the eleventh century: this second burning almost succeeding in obliterating the works of the famed lyricist (if not lesbianism) from history.

When fragments of Sappho's work were uncovered centuries later and translated into English, scholars attempted another eradication of her essence from history, again condemning to invisibility a lifestyle that by then could not be mentioned by name: all references to Sappho's female lovers were changed to the masculine gender.

9

Scholars continued their efforts to hide Sappho's affectional preference and the joy she took in her loves by creating the myth that she
ended her life by suicide after losing a man's love. As late as 1963,
Klaich reports, some scholars were still attempting to deny Sappho her
lesbian identity by proving that her poems were too pure to have been
written by someone as depraved as a lesbian.[16]

After more than seventeen centuries of such fabrication, all of it
shoring up a male supremacist axiom that equated men with the source
of all female pleasure, it is no wonder that those listening to Anita
Bryant and Phyllis Schlafly had little evidence of their own with which
to counter the sexually titillating fantasies originating in the second
century.

Chief among the centuries-old myths still dominating many
people's thinking about lesbians is one that gained currency through
Lucian of Samosata's second-century *Dialogues of the Courtesans*.
Here the lesbian is portrayed as an essentially sexual creature, one
whose personality is dominated by a masculine-type lust for the
physical attractions of other women. It is interesting to speculate why
this myth has been so pervasive. The lesbian alone may be written off
as simply a woman deluded about her identity. But when she enters a
sexual relationship with another woman which cannot be reasonably
described in terms of male-female intercourse, she somehow comes
alive as someone out of the ordinary who must be dealt with, one way
or another. More importantly, she becomes a threat to male
hegemony. That women can provide each other, without the assistance of masculine interventions, with that most valued and expensive
commodity of the patriarchal universe—sexual gratification—is the
ultimate assault on the macho heritage.

The degree of threat perceived in lesbian sexuality is made clear in
the paradox of Anita Bryant's and other salvation-minded, antigay
demagogues' fundamental misunderstanding of lesbianism. Such
salvationists who would "cure" lesbians rigidly adhere to the
*Courtesans* myth. Bryant and other leaders of what has come to be
known as the "ex-gay" movement consider a lesbian to be saved or
cured when she abstains from sexual contact with other women. There
is no need in this salvation program to begin sexual relations with
men, but merely to become a "new creature in Christ," even if a
celibate creature.[17]

The paradox is that the celibate "new creature in Christ" may still be a lesbian. Unrecognized by the salvationists and many others is the fact that the feature distinguishing lesbians from their heterosexual sisters is their primary *emotional* commitment to other women. As Leslie, a thirty-year-old lesbian who had been married for several years, explained in an interview for this book, "Something that people don't understand is that it's not *who* you go to bed with that determines if you're straight or gay. Sex has nothing to do with it. You can be celibate and gay. Identification as gay or straight is an emotional thing—do you relate primarily emotionally to women or to men in an intimate situation? . . . That was what was missing in my marriage. Sex was okay with him. What was missing was the emotional intensity. I was never in love with him or with any other man. I didn't know what 'in love' meant until I had my first lesbian relationship."

Dr. Charlotte Wolff, in her 1971 study of 106 lesbians, found that while 60 percent had had sexual experiences with men, only 13 percent had ever formed strong emotional relationships with men outside their families. Eighty-five percent, however, formed strong emotional relationships exclusively with women. While not experiencing strong emotional feelings for men, 55 percent of Wolff's lesbians reported that they had experienced physical attractions to men.[18] The determinant of their lesbian identities was not the biological gender of their sexual partners, nor even the gender of those to whom they were physically attracted, but the gender of those non-family members with whom they formed deep emotional relationships. It is this fact that leads many lesbians to prefer the term *affectional preference* to the more commonly used phrase *sexual orientation* in describing the relationship aspects of their lifestyles.

The salvation offered to lesbians by such ill-informed crusaders, who appear to judge human identity by standards of sexual intimacy, is nothing more than a psychic con game. Along with every other aspect of the Pro-Family movement's antigay crusade, this idea of salvation is a symbolic reaction to a rapidly changing America that preservationists correctly fear threatens their most deeply held beliefs. The health of the nation, to the Pro-Family crusader, is secure only in absolute male supremacy and in its corollary, the patriarchal family— two institutions that are rapidly disintegrating.

As if to somehow compromise with reality, many Pro-Family crusade leaders seem willing to concede that some degree of homosexuality is here to stay. Admitting this, they wish only that lesbians and male homosexuals would stop making such a public fuss over civil rights. California state senator John Briggs, the crusader who lost his 1978 attempt to bar teachers who support civil rights for gay citizens from California's classrooms, repeated dozens of times, "You can be anything you want to be but if you're going to go around bragging [about] it you shouldn't teach. If you want to deviate from the norm, and heterosexuality is the norm, do it privately. It is your private right."[19]

Privacy, however, is not a right yet guaranteed to lesbians, for they have no constitutional protections from discrimination. For this reason, and on behalf of women such as those listed below, lesbians must take their case to the public:

Mary Young and Dawn De Blanc, sentenced to 30 months in a Louisiana prison for "having committed a crime against nature."[20]

Melissa, whose mother had her arrested after learning that she was living in a lesbian relationship.[21]

An unidentified woman, age 24, who was institutionalized because she was a lesbian. There, as part of her cure, she received ten treatments with Metrazol, a psychoactive chemical that induced grand mal seizures.[22]

Sarah, whose parents, seeking to cure her of her lesbianism, got a court to commit her to a mental institution.[23]

Karen, who was committed to a mental hospital by her parents to cure her lesbianism and spent two years in confinement. As she explains, "I was hospitalized in ten private places before that and I've had over forty shock treatments. I had Thorazine . . . I've been experimented on with drugs. I've been beaten. I was put in a padded cell . . . all because I was a lesbian."[24]

A Jewish woman, one among many like her, whose orthodox Jewish father read Kadish, the prayer for the dead, after she refused to renounce her love of women. Her family now treats her as dead and even refuses to speak to her when she tries to telephone them.[25]

## LESBIAN VISIBILITY

The Pro-Family drive to push lesbians back into their seventeen-century-old closets is not ill founded. Pro-Family leaders correctly sense that visibility of lesbian and male homosexual lifestyles invites examination and comparison to the patriarchal lifestyles advocated on the Pro-Family circuit and presumed desirable by many Americans. Such examination poses serious challenges to assumptions about traditional patriarchal institutions. Examination of the male homosexual lifestyle shows a surprising number of people who can pursue recreational sex, anonymous sex, and promiscuity with neither guilt nor psychological harm. Examination of lesbian lifestyles shows women without a need for nor a dependency on men, women who create warm, loving relationships and families without men. Examination of lesbian lifestyles shows a variety of viable examples of egalitarian, non-role-structured intimate relationships providing a high degree of satisfaction and opportunity for individual growth. Nowhere is the viability and joy of the egalitarian relationship more visible than in lesbian relationships.

Lesbian visibility in particular creates for Pro-Family believers an unacceptable level of confrontation with the fact that male supremacy, axiomatic to their concepts of the family and women's roles, has *no* contemporary social function. Pro-Family crusaders correctly perceive that if the male supremacist axiom is cast aside, many of its corollary values may be found wanting: monogamy, till-death-do-us-part marriage, sex exclusively for procreation, exclusive heterosexuality, macho toughness, female weakness and dependency, and countless other assumptions. While male homosexuality may make Pro-Family leaders and heterosexuals uncomfortable because it shakes their notions of what a ''real'' man is, lesbianism is perhaps the ultimate threat to things as they are because it undermines all patriarchal assumptions about contemporary male roles—save for man's momentary input into perpetuation of the species.

So Pro-Family leaders demand that lesbians return to the invisibility of the closet. Invisibility—a price exacted of all people who threaten the pleasant social conventions of the dominant majority—has for centuries forced lesbians to hide their realities not only from a society preferring a comfortable mythology to the challenges of reality but from each other as well. Within this realm—a laboratory of isolation—each woman had to determine her life's path alone and to discover for herself the alternatives to the patriarchal environment that functioned best for her. Lesbians have come from all races, all cultures, all classes, all religions, and all regions. Through more than two hundred years of American history they have been passed through the gates of a psychological Ellis Island and cloaked in invisibility. They have been labeled alien and shunted off into solitary psychic ghettos. They are America's special daughters, one in every six or ten, or three in every hundred—no one knows or counts their number. They are daughters of America, yet outcast in their own land. Long before the rest of the nation discovered its rootlessness and isolation, these special daughters had experimented with alternatives to enhance their lives in a world which for them could change from moment to moment. They are America's predecessors in the laboratory of future shock.

It is time to open the ghetto and examine what America's lesbian daughters have built there—and what they continue to build, for the job is not yet done. It is time to look at their experiments in lifestyles suited to a nonpatriarchal society, time to look at the experiments that have failed as well as those that have succeeded. In them we may find attitudes, institutions, relationships, and ways of being that can assist all of us as we encounter the death throes of the patriarchal axiom.

*Sunday's Women* is not meant to be the definitive story of America's lesbian daughters, nor is it meant to be a compendium of the alternatives they have built and continue to build. *Sunday's Women* is merely an attempt to look at lesbian lives as they are in America today with some insight into how and why they got that way and, perhaps, where they are going. It is based largely on two dozen in-depth interviews conducted in 1978 with lesbians in a variety of age groups and cultural, social, and economic situations—women with a wide range of beliefs and activities. (Their names and descriptions have been changed to protect their right to privacy and the privacy of those whom they discuss.) In addition, it draws from countless more casual talks with other lesbians. *Sunday's Women* is also the result of reading a vast collection of lesbian publications and publications about lesbians. It has also drawn heavily from two scientific studies of similar lesbian populations, one conducted in 1969–1970 by the Kinsey Institute (but not published until 1978), and another conducted in 1976 by Marilyn G. Fleener. The two studies represent the largest populations of lesbians ever surveyed by social scientists and are also valuable because the demographics of the samples are similar and because one dates from before the 1970s revival of the gay rights movement, and the second provides a glance at some of the changes in lesbian lifestyles after seven years of gay pride activism. Added to this wealth of material have been my own observations as a journalist who has reported on the lesbian and women's rights movements on and off for the past decade.

The book begins, in Part One, by taking a look at what it is like to grow up lesbian in America—the discovery of isolation, the time of self-recognition, the process of finding other lesbians, of developing relationships, and of learning to handle the termination of those relationships in humane ways. Part Two looks at the process of settling down and forging a lifestyle that is fulfilling in a hostile society. It examines the problems and challenges of living in committed relationships that are unrecognized and frowned upon by law and custom, as well as the assault the lesbian couple with children presents to patriarchal assumptions about child rearing. Part Three reports on the politicizing of lesbian liberation, both in terms of its effects on personal growth, and in relation to the options and challenges it offers to society as a whole.

# PART ONE

## Rites of Passage

From the moment of a female child's birth she enters into an intricate learning experience that will create a particular pattern from her sensations and experiences that is consonant with the heritage and tradition of her culture. In America that heritage is patriarchal and it is within this framework that her role as a properly acculturated woman will be shaped. Heterosexuality is corollary to the patriarchal heritage and she will be taught its maxims and behavior modes. Everywhere she looks she will find models for her behavior. She will, almost without exception, be raised in a heterosexually oriented family environment, attend heterosexually oriented schools, associate with peers who are being trained as she is being trained, and, if churched, she will be churched in a heterosexual religious tradition. Throughout her development she will be rewarded for acting "like a girl," and punished when she strays too far from the model set out for her. As she enters adolescence she will experiment with and begin a long and complex training in heterosexual courtship and mating practices.

If all goes well for the heterosexual child, she will enter adulthood with little more than a vague sense of dissonance between her training and what she perceives could, should, or might have been. As a more mature adult she may find all has not gone well and that her culture has sold her a shoddy bill of goods as she is left to attend to her children's upbringing with no means of earning a decent living, while her former husband goes on to explore other horizons. But as long as she is heterosexual, she will probably continue to view males as her potential mates and partners, somehow an essential part of her world view.

The woman who comes to discover that she is a lesbian has been raised in an environment indistinguishable from that of her heterosexual sister. But the discord she experiences runs much deeper than that felt by the troubled heterosexual woman. At some point in her life she realizes that the cultural training she has received is foreign to her reality, that she is someone apart from her culture, somehow alien to it. She perceives no models with which she can identify. As a consequence of the lack of alternative models available to her, she may begin to search for something more suited to her personal reality than the offerings of mainstream acculturation.

At some point she may discover that one alternative does exist that is not alien to her—the reality that has been labeled "lesbian." Once she has learned about the existence of this reality, she will begin to explore it; she will move from viewing herself as an isolated alien to the perception that she is a person who shares similarities with other women.

As her alienation from the mainstream culture grows, she will try to seek out some of her own people. If she finds that the lesbian reality fits her emotional needs, she will then try to find companionship, to explore the lesbian subculture and intimate relationships with other women. Here she enters a new world, a culture with its own courtship and mating rules, a culture vastly different from that into which she was trained to fit during her adolescence. Her situation is oddly similar to the heterosexual experience of cultural dissonance when two cultures attempt to mix their adolescent training in courtship patterns, as in this description from Britain during and after World War II:

Both American soldiers and British girls [sic] accused one another of being sexually brash. Investigation of this curious double charge brought to light an interesting . . . problem. In both cultures, courtship behavior from the first eye contact to the ultimate consumation went through approximately thirty steps, but the sequence of these steps was different. Kissing, for instance, comes relatively early in the North American pattern (occupying, let us say, step 5) and relatively late in the English pattern (at step 25, let us assume), where it is considered highly erotic behavior. So when the U.S. soldier somehow felt that the time was right for a harmless kiss, not only did the girl [sic] feel cheated out of twenty steps of what for her would have been proper behavior on his part, she also felt she had to make a quick decision: break off the relationship and run, or get ready for intercourse. If she chose the latter, the soldier was confronted with behavior that according to *his* cultural rules could only be called shameless at this early stage of the relationship.[1]

The lesbian's exploration of intimate experiences with other women is an emotionally turbulent process. It is, essentially, a second adolescence, complete with many of the symptoms common to the mainstream heterosexual adolescent period.

Such is the general process of coming out as a lesbian: emotional dissonance with her heterosexual training and its patriarchal foundation; self-identification as someone quite different from most women around her; discovery of an alternate reality that has been labeled lesbian; seeking out members of the lesbian subculture to learn if this reality fits her emotional needs; and, once having found other lesbians—or other seekers like herself—growing through a new adolescent experience of learning about courtship, differing kinds of relationships and mating styles, and breaking up with a partner. These are the lesbian's rites of passage.

The heterosexual woman's acculturation most often follows her chronological age. Heterosexual dating may begin at ten or twelve; necking at fourteen; going steady in high school; intercourse at some time between the ages of sixteen and twenty-six; and one or more marriages at some time between the ages of eighteen and thirty-eight before the heterosexual woman settles into a somewhat stable relationship lifestyle. Lesbians, by contrast, can and do begin their coming out process at almost any age. Some begin in childhood. Others don't begin until high school or college. Others do not begin until after they have been married and had children or even grandchildren. Others may begin the process and, for one reason or another, stop it, perhaps to continue it later.

No one has yet identified the reason that lesbians come out at such diverse ages. Most contemporary personality development theorists agree that a person's sexual orientation is fixed by the age of five. If this is correct, then one might presume that a lesbian would at least begin her rebellion to heterosexual acculturation at that time. For some women, however, this does not seem to be the case. When asked why she had only just come out, for example, a fifty-six-year-old grandmother responded: "I simply did not know there was any other way to live than heterosexual. I knew I was pretty miserable, but I just accepted that as part of the way things had to be."

# The Lesbian Identity

Looking back, it's clear that I've always been a lesbian. I didn't have a word for it, and somehow I knew it wasn't the way I was supposed to be, but I've always loved women, right from my first grade teacher to my high school gym instructor. While all the other girls were talking about this or that boy, all I could think about was how to get that gym teacher interested in me. It was as if boys didn't exist for me, even while I did the whole heterosexual thing—dating, the prom, the whole trip.—*Jo Ann*

I suppose I've probably always been a lesbian, but wasn't aware of it. When I was sixteen I got married to get away from home. I wasn't in love with the man. There was no romance involved, it was just a way out. I had no fantasies about marriage, love, any of that. I just *did* it. I knew that my marriage was hell, but I just assumed that was the way it was supposed to be, so I just accepted it. I didn't even hear the word *lesbian* until I was 32 and had four children. My husband was the first one to use the word with me. He said he thought I was one! I gave it some thought and decided to find out.—*Liza*

A doctor signs the birth certificate. Gender: female. It is a fact of biology that few will question. It is also a fact of caste, but few parents hope that their daughter will someday be President. It is also an assumption: female, daughter, wife, mother. Whom will she marry? Will *he* be a lawyer, a doctor, a minister? The birth certificate says female and she is presumed heterosexual. Society's heterosexual presumption is so ingrained and thorough, so overwhelming, that it is difficult to conceive of an analogy to it or even to communicate what it is like for the nonheterosexual to grow up in a cultural environment that is so monistic in this arena that alternatives are not even conceivable to its youth or to many of its adults.

Olga uses a political analogy. "It's like growing up," she says, "in the Soviet Union and thinking you can be anything but a Communist. It simply is not possible. You don't think it. You cannot think it because you cannot conceive it. Any possible alternative is non-existent. You can be a Party member or not, that is a choice, but still you are a Communist. Where would you find out you could be anything else? Certainly not at home. Certainly not in school. Certainly not in the library where you are not allowed to read the foreign press. Certainly not in the cinema. Nor from the radio. You can be a good Communist, a bad Communist, a Party member, a non-Party member, but anything else is unthinkable."

Olga, an emigré, spent many years in the United States before she learned that there was any possibility for her relationship lifestyle other than heterosexual. She explains, "Of course we did not know about lesbians in the Soviet Union either, so America is not that much different. Where would you learn in America until a year ago that there are lesbians? Your history books do not mention famous lesbians—that some were even queens, like Queen Christina of Sweden, that some were fighters in your revolution, like Deborah Samson. Your children's fairy tales are full of Prince Charmings and their women. Your afternoon television that shows everything from drugs and adultery and murder and abortion does not mention it. Even in your obituaries it is not written that 'Gertrude Stein was survived by her lover of forty years, the woman Alice B. Toklas.' Your commercial advertising tells women to buy perfumes, clothes, makeups, stockings, hair dyes—all to attract *him*. Your novels do not mention it. Even your literary classics do not mention it.

"I have even met American families with daughters who are lesbians, but their mothers never talk about it.

"Where would a young American girl even find a vocabulary to explain her feelings that she might love women? Where would she learn that anything like woman-woman love and families was possible? Where would a young American girl learn that she could be anything *but* a heterosexual?"


## GROWING UP LESBIAN

Young American girls in fact do not learn that they can be anything but heterosexual. But this does not mean that they do not, somehow, begin to try to express their divergence from heterosexual acculturation at an early age. For many lesbians, the first manifestation that they do not fit the heterosexual pattern is a rejection of the female/feminine role to which they are geared from birth. This rejection is sometimes manifested in a preference for, or identification with, the only other role visible to them—the male role.

Julie, a systems analyst in line for a vice-presidency of her company, recalled that when she was six years old, "All my relatives gave me dolls for Christmas. There were probably five or six of them. Each one had its own wardrobe of dress-up clothes and they all had shiny long hair ready for combing and primping. I only liked one of the dolls. It was one of the smaller ones. She had dark hair and wore a cowboy costume, complete with red plastic boots, blue pants, black holster, and a tiny tin six-shooter. I called her Annie, and she was the only one I ever played with. The others just stayed in the closet. Finally, my mother got mad that I wouldn't play with the feminine dolls and took all of them, including Annie, to the Salvation Army. When she asked me what I wanted for my birthday I knew better than to ask for another doll like Annie, so I asked for a pair of red cowboy boots. Instead, I got a white first-communion dress and white patent-leather shoes."

Sandy, now an attorney, remembered, "The whole time I was growing up I had the whole dual standard thing pushed down my throat. I was seeing that little boys had a hell of a lot more freedom than I had. I also saw it with my mother and my father, the role he had compared with hers. I feel to this day that my mother was the bulwark of strength in our family, even though she went to her grave never knowing how strong a woman she really was. But it was my father who had the position to be coveted. He was the one who was always in the limelight, who had all the power.

"The trip was laid on me that because I was female I was going to get married and have kids. I knew right from the time I was little I didn't want that. When I was about seven I began telling my mother I was going to grow up and live in a tent and adopt nine boys. And when the tent got dirty, we'd move.

"That was a cue that I didn't want the role that society set up for me. Society was saying that a lot of my strong points, in sports and so forth, were not looked upon as what a woman should be. It's nice to think, when you're growing up and establishing who you are, that you are living up to someone's expectations. And when you know you're not, that can be heavy. It was very painful for me. I'd been told all my life that I had to fit into a certain role and I never did fit in. I never did buy the lady, little girl syndrome. It just wasn't me."

Sandy and Julie are lesbians. Their memories of their first open rebellions against the female/feminine roles taught by their parents and reinforced by their environments are very clear to them. Many other lesbians remember similar girlhood rebellions. Many lesbians also recall girlhood desires to become boys. Explained Susan, "All I knew was that I wanted to be like my father because of what I saw as his freedom and power. So I emulated men and boys. I didn't see at the time that they are just as trapped and socialized as women are, I just thought it was better to be a boy. At the time I just figured, 'my father's got a penis, so that must be where it's at.'"

Certainly lesbians are not the only women recalling such feelings, but data assembled by British investigator Charlotte Wolff indicate that these feelings occur five times more frequently among girls who grow up to be lesbians than they do among girls who grow up to be heterosexual.[1]

This rebellion against what is seen as being female and restrictive, the wish for those elements of male identity that carry independence, is the first rite of passage into lesbian selfhood for many women.

The cultural rituals that drive women to their destiny as the lesser half of the male-supremacist equation provide one period of respite: the prepuberty tomboy years, when freedom and first class status are open to girls, at least among their peers. A substantial number of lesbians, several studies show, recall an active tomboy experience. In one study of 162 lesbians, 82 percent reported having gone through a tomboy phase.[2] While the tomboy years offer some relaxation of the demands of the heterosexualization process for most lesbians, the onset of puberty brings with it new challenges. The world again becomes the dichotomized place of girl/feminine and boy/masculine, now with an additional imperative: heterosexuality, complete with its emphasis, for girls, on attracting the boys who will become their future protectors and guarantors of social acceptability. It is at this time, when the young lesbian notices her peers' growing interest in boys, that she learns that her emotional fascination with women—teachers, movie stars, or others of her age group—signifies that she is someone different from her schoolmates. It is also apparently at this time that many of the lesbians who once wanted to be boys integrate their wish for freedom and independence with their biological gender—only 2 percent of the 162 women reported that they still wanted to be boys after puberty.[3]

The young lesbian realizes that she cannot be a boy, yet also realizes that she cannot be like her female peers and in many cases she feels a sense of intense isolation. Recalls Viv, in a memory shared by many lesbians, "When I was in high school I thought I was the only one like me. I felt like a fish out of water. I felt like a stranger and totally alone." Viv's recollection of her high school years in World War II New York parallels that of Jan, a fifteen-year-old high school student in California's farm belt. Jan is seriously questioning her affectional preference and comments, "All the rest of the girls are talking about their dates, or their boyfriends, or about what they did and how far they went in petting and which of the girls is already on the pill. I feel very out of place. I don't care about boys at all. I have crushes on a couple of women teachers but I can't talk about that. To be accepted, you have to talk about boys. So I'm kind of a loner. Sometimes I get home from school on Friday afternoons and cry because I am so alone."

The lesbian who senses that she is somehow different in her early years carries a double burden—the already troubled emotional problems accompanying adolescence for all American youth, and the fact that she cannot find a place for herself in this tortured geography of the maturation process.

## FINDING IDENTITY

When a young woman first suspects that she is fundamentally different from her peers, it isn't long before she begins to wonder if she is truly alone or if there are, perhaps, others like her. The ages when lesbians begin this search vary. For many, it begins in their adolescence, and for some it does not begin until long after they have spent years in heterosexual marriages.

Fifty-five percent of the respondents to the 1976 study of 162 lesbians prepared by Marilyn G. Fleener reported that they became aware of their lesbian identity in their early teenage years. Tending to support Fleener's finding that a substantial number of lesbians begin their quests early is a more comprehensive study reported by Alan P. Bell and Martin S. Weinberg for the Kinsey Institute for Sex Research. Of the nearly 300 lesbians eventually included in this report, slightly more than 40 percent reported their first lesbian sexual encounter before the age of nineteen.[4]

The Bell/Weinberg survey was completed about seven years before Fleener's. These seven years encompassed a time when the gay liberation movement was beginning its most massive strides, indicating that as word of the movement spreads, and lesbian visibility increases, lesbians may be spared years of living in heterosexual relationship styles that for many women are hell.

Regardless of a lesbian's age of self-discovery, she must learn what this thing is—what is it to be a lesbian. Julie, who by sixteen had landed a college scholarship, began putting together the bits and pieces of self-knowledge through reading. "It all came together slowly, almost unconsciously. I remember when I was about fourteen reading a horoscope that said some Libras tend to be lesbians. I'm a Libra, so in that funny way, it began to click for me.

"Later, I began looking up what was available about homosexuality in dictionaries, encyclopedias, psychology textbooks. This, of course, was before people began reporting on gays who weren't always psychiatric patients, so I was filled with all those terrible stories about alcoholism, poverty, mental illness, and suicide. But even with all of that, just discovering the concept that women could love and live with women exhilarated me. It was a possibility. I wasn't alone.

"But while it was a wonderful discovery, the sickness aspects of it turned me off, so I decided to be straight."

Eventually, in an effort to change her sexual orientation, Julie got married, as did, in the Bell/Weinberg study, about 20 percent of the lesbian respondents who had considered giving up homosexuality.[5] Julie's marriage ended two years later when she "realized that even though lesbians were supposed to be terrible people, I probably was one."

Bell and Weinberg found that of lesbians who had been heterosexually married, about 71 percent ended their marriages within five years.[6] A few, however, were married much longer before recognizing their lesbian identity.

Alice, a fifty-six-year-old public school administrator and grandmother who looks ten years younger than she is, has only just begun to explore her lesbian identity. She explained, "I guess I'm part of what you'd call the Depression generation. We grew up taking life very seriously. Our concerns were the day-to-day concerns of just getting by. Lesbianism, what was that? What you did was tried to find a young man with some opportunity, you married him, and you worked your damndest to make sure your kids didn't have to go through what you and your parents did.

"It was as simple as that. We moved out from Missouri to San Bernardino in 1930 and we got lucky. In a few years my father had put together a small truck farming business. When I was eighteen I married a local boy. We had a son. The war started and Roger was sent to Europe. He came back, went to school on the G.I. bill, and we started out on the way up the economic ladder. We had a second kid. A girl. It wasn't something we'd planned, but you didn't question those things, you just lived with them.

"And we endured. It wasn't any fun, but neither was anyone else's life. He began seeing other women and I stayed home with the kids out in the suburbs just like everyone else. We stayed together until the kids were pretty much on their own and we divorced. There it was. It was 1968, I was forty-seven and single. I had nothing but a car and a house. Maybe I was lucky, I don't know. I went to college and got a degree.

"About then came this gay liberation thing and I was curious. But I didn't do anything about it. A fifty-two-year-old woman just starting a career just doesn't go to some radical homosexual parade or student dance. I read some of the books that were beginning to come out—the good books. They made me wish I was eighteen and could start all over again. I began noticing more about myself. I knew I couldn't go through another marriage. Men didn't interest me, and the thought of the opportunities and joys those young women were having grew on me.

"A couple of years ago I began to subscribe to a lesbian magazine.

"At the grand age of fifty-four I finally came to the conclusion that I was a lesbian. Great. What does a lesbian public school administrator do if she's never met a lesbian? I put it in the back of my mind. I took up a lot of hobbies—shells, gardening, skiing. I became a symphony addict. I did everything except let myself think. I probably would have lived my life out like that, knowing what I was, wishing I was younger, putting it out of my mind, resigned to gardening and conchology.

"But after Anita Bryant I just got angry. I got mad at her, mad at a world that would listen to her, and mad at myself. I told myself, 'damned if anyone is going to stop me from living, exploring, loving whom I will and when I will.' I realized that I was just using age—a number—as an excuse to put limits on my life. Why? Why put limits? This is the last quarter of the twentieth century. If there's any time we need to explore, to love, to celebrate, to live, it's now. All of us. Together. Or else that's the end of the story for every living one of us—one nuclear mushroom."

For some lesbians, submission to the heterosexual model is, perhaps, life long. Commented a lesbian historian, "I'm sure that if Kinsey repeated his early studies of sexual behavior today, the reported 3 percent incidence of lesbianism would be much higher, due, primarily, to the greater number of economic options open to women aside from heterosexual marriage. I just know that lots of those supposedly happy women in the pioneer days whom history records as happily married hausfraus weren't all that straight . . . And, you just have to look at some of the historical records of wealthier women and you'll find a lot of them who owned property together, with different last names. You just can't tell me that all those women were asexual neuters—that myth went out with the middle ages." Some data hint that this observation might be correct. Wolff, who used a heterosexual control group in her research, found about 10 percent of the supposed heterosexuals reporting feelings of physical attraction exclusively to women and 10 percent experiencing strong emotional relationships exclusively to women.[7] Bell and Weinberg found about 37 percent of their lesbian sample had been married and that 41 percent of these women reported they were "not homosexual" at the time of their first marriage.[8] Both of these reports indicate that some women who today define themselves as heterosexual might, if given the opportunity, redefine this emotional component of their identities.

## HIDING IDENTITY

Marriage and other heterosexual relationships frequently offer the first hiding places for women who, like Julie, cannot accept their lesbianism. Ironically, the people from whom these women want to hide their affectional preference is most often from themselves. Frances is another such woman. "I was probably sixteen when I realized I was gay. In those days people were always saying you could cure it. And I did want to 'cure' it. Who the hell wants to grow up a sickie? Not this kid. No one had to tell me that the way to be straight was to go have sex with men. So I did. I went out of my way to find guys to go to bed with. I must have had the reputation of the easiest lay in town.

"Finally I settled into a kind of permanent relationship with a guy. I thought, 'aha, see, you're not one of "those" after all.' I don't know exactly how to explain it, but it was just one of the worst times of my life. I got into drugs to get out of it. I'm sure I would have hung in there just to keep proving to myself that I wasn't one of 'those,' but the guy split. I kind of went through an emotional breakdown, started hearing things, stuff like that.

"I got busted on drugs and they sent me to a halfway house. That was the pits, but at least I got off the drugs. When I got out I decided I'd better get my shit together and joined a women's group. I guess that was the first time I'd heard being queer was okay. It still took me a long time to accept that about myself—I come from this real straight tight-assed family, but once I did, wow! Like being reincarnated or something.

"If I had any advice for sisters it would be to give up on trying to 'cure' yourself and thinking you're straight just because you can have sex with some guy. That's not dealing with who you are. That's just hiding. That's just killing yourself."

Contrary to the popular myth that all a lesbian needs is "just one good lay" with a man, are statistics showing that most lesbians have, in fact, had one or more sexual relationships with men. Wolff found that about 55 percent of her lesbians had engaged in sexual encounters with men.[9] Fleener's report, representing a later and younger sample of lesbians, found that 80 percent had experienced heterosexual sex, many with more than one partner.[10] Bell and Weinberg, in the earlier, but larger sample, found that about 84 percent had experienced sexual encounters with men.[11]

The "good lay" theory of curing lesbianism is perhaps finally put to rest by comparing the frequency of orgasm between lesbians with men and heterosexual women with men. Bell and Weinberg report that of the lesbians who had sexual experiences with men, only 33 percent said they *never* experienced orgasm in heterosexual sex. About 60 percent responded that they experienced orgasm sometimes, and about 7 percent reported *always* experiencing orgasm in heterosexual encounters.[12] These data on lesbians' heterosexual experiences may be compared with those found in a random sampling of women performed by Susan Wall and Nancy Kaltreider and reported in the February 1977 issue of the *Journal of the American Medical Association*. While Wall and Kaltreider found that 18 percent of their sample experienced orgasm with men "almost always," 30 percent— nearly identical to Bell and Weinberg's lesbian sample, reported they had *never* or rarely experienced orgasm.

A woman's birth certificate may tell her and the rest of the world that she is a female, but it says nothing of her affectional preference— that is simply assumed. Assumed by all but lesbians themselves who, each in her own way, must make a quest for this part of their identity within a cultural framework that largely ignores its possibility. It is a quest that may find its roots early in life, or may not begin until much later. It is a quest that may involve a period of self-denial as the lesbian buys into the myth that she can be "cured" by one (or more) good lay(s), or through marriage. It is a quest that will almost certainly involve sexual experimentation with men. For an overwhelming number of lesbians, even in this era of lesbian and gay liberation movements, it is still a quest that, for want of alternative role models, will be impaired by the myths of a heterosexual and patriarchal mainstream culture.

# 2

# The Transformation from Butch to Dyke

When I was in high school I didn't even know the word *lesbian*, much less how to be one. I just knew that I wanted to be with women the way the guys were with women. I wanted to go steady, date, and have a woman to share intimate sexual feelings with. So I looked very carefully at how the boys in school got girls to date, go steady, neck, and the rest. What I saw was that boys had short hair. What I saw was that boys wore heavy shoes and boots. What I saw was that boys wore shirts and pants. And what I saw at the time was that the most desirable boys were into leather jackets and chains, and these huge silver rings that were kind of like brass knuckles—a real '40s thing. "Okay," I said, "that must be how you get girls." So that's what I did. There wasn't any such thing as a dress code in school—they didn't need one—girls just weren't allowed to wear pants of any kind. But every afternoon when I got home I ditched the skirts for some of my brother's clothes and went strutting out around town. I developed a real hatred for skirts because to me, having to wear one was saying that I was out there, available to boys. And I definitely did not want anything to do with them.

By the time I got out of high school and away from home I was the image of the real little butch: really short hair, men's pants, white dress shirts, men's shoes, a heavy-duty ring, the snazzy leather jackets, the whole bit. Most people who didn't know me just thought I was a guy and for the first few times that was pretty embarrassing to me.

I must have looked pretty funny, but it was a very serious thing with me at the time because it worked. There were other girls who were gay and I guess I was so obvious that they had an easy time finding me.—*Viv*

Women like Viv were known in the lesbian subculture as butches. To heterosexuals they were simply bull-dykes. They fall into the exact role created by Lucian to ridicule Sappho's lesbian colony in his *Dialogues of the Courtesans* written some seventeen centuries ago:

lesbians were women who were, in appearance, indistinguishable from men. Although the origins of the phrases "butch" and "dyke" are unknown in reference to lesbians, they have, for as long as most lesbians recall, meant a lesbian who plays, to one degree or another, a "masculine" role.

Since the time of Lucian of Samasota, the role of the butch has been greatly mythologized. One of the more familiar plots in pornographic movies and books centers around a lesbian, usually portrayed as something akin to a man lacking female genitalia, seducing a lonely heterosexual woman. This pornographic illusion has seeped into the popular culture where conventional mythology holds that lesbians recruit their sexual partners from the heterosexual population, just as male homosexuals supposedly seduce young boys. Similar myths abound about the day-to-day affairs of lesbians. Closely related to the sexual myth is one that results in one of the most common questions posed to lesbians who choose to open their experiences to public exposure: "Which role do you play, male or female?" Another variation goes, "Are you the butch or the femme?" It is as if these observers, themselves trapped in the same dichotomous mental state as the young butch, see no option but to place a heterosexual standard on the nonconforming couple. This mythology has perhaps been aided by fallout from popular misconceptions surrounding the much more highly visible male homosexual subculture and its apparent fascination with its even more highly visible drag queens and professional female impersonators (or "impressionists," as some prefer to be called).

The butch/femme myth has been an enduring one, periodically punctuated with just enough reality to keep it alive. But *is* it a true reflection of lesbian lifestyles or is it rather a reflection of mainstream society?

The butch/femme dichotomy was certainly untrue of Sappho's colony, a remnant of prepatriarchal social organization, as Klaich describes:

The young women of Sappho's colony were trained in music and dance and most importantly in the composition of poetry. But of almost equal importance Sappho stressed the cultivation of *charis,* grace, in both the aesthetic and physical sense. A roughhewn talented woman was all well and good, but if she lacked *charis* she was somehow incomplete.

Sappho herself is said to have been beautifully graceful. From a few coins, from a few statues, from a few vase paintings, and from a very few written descriptions of her [written after her death], we know that she . . . had long hair worn knotted at the nape of her neck. She dressed carefully in purple and gold, often with leather sandals dyed to match. As was the custom of the day, she wore kohl on her eyelids and was heavily perfumed. Flowers were very much part of her wardrobe, worn twined in her hair. She was what society calls a feminine woman.[1]

Unfortunately, these slim references to the roles of lesbians in Sappho's colony appear to be the only reports surviving of lesbian lifestyles prior to the onset of the patriarchal hegemomy and the later era when Judeo-Christian repression of sexuality itself became the dominant sociocultural force in the West. Those scraps of history available from earlier matriarchal eras are equally unhelpful. They seem only to indicate an equally rigid role distinction between genders—their primary distinction from patriarchies seeming to have been a role reversal between the genders.[2]

The historical record of lesbian lifestyles from the onset of Christian domination of Europe and the Americas is almost equally nonexistent, just as is the record of all women and women's culture. A few glimpses offered from the past may, however, be indicative of how narrowly defined the meaning of female had become. The treatment of Joan of Arc in the 1430s presents the most fascinating and perhaps best documented story of a woman who dared step beyond the confines of the socially acceptable female role during a period of history which has left us almost no documents about women.

It is widely believed that Joan of Arc was executed for witchcraft. This is, in fact, not the case. Although accused of being a sorceress, the era was not quite ready to sustain such a charge against the military leader. Charges were instead changed to heresy. Among the twelve charges of heresey brought against her, the one that eventually resulted in her death was "her wearing of men's costume." Despite the fact that many counselors pleaded with her to save her life by repenting her alleged heresies, she stuck to her beliefs until she was led to her execution. Then, as the torch was about to be lit, she "suddenly capitulated, promising to adjure her visions and obey the Church." She was spared from the flames in exchange for a life sentence in prison. When she began serving her term, however, "her English guards took away the female attire she had resumed, and substituted men's clothes . . . The ecclesiastical court, instantly informed of her change of dress, condemned her on May 28 as a relapsed heretic.'' Realizing she was now doomed, the twenty-year-old future saint retracted her original pre-execution confession and was burned at the stake on May 30, 1431.[3]

Had her trials taken place a few decades later, Joan of Arc, the nonconforming female whose chief sin seems to have been the wearing of male clothes, and who, as was the custom of her time, bunked with the female camp followers of her armies, might indeed have been successfully executed as a witch, rather than a mere relapsed heretic. For, among the activities that were by 1460 believed to be a part of witches sabbats were ''indescribable outrages [that] are perpetrated in exchanging women, by order of the presiding devil, by passing on a woman to other women.''[4] There is no historical evidence that St. Joan was a lesbian, but at the time, little evidence was needed.

Later historical records repeat the same message; if a woman wanted a life of freedom and adventure, her only chance for it was to pass as a male, as Charlotte Bunch notes in her essay about a seventeenth-century adventurer:

Every land has its tales of women who masqueraded as men in their search for a freer life. Female roles and dress were so confining that women who could not accept these bonds pretended to be men, not because they believed men to be actually superior but because this was the only individual escape they could see . . . Many of these women were lesbians and a proud part of our history. Their lives are often ignored, or if recognized, their lesbianism denied by male historians . . .

Doña Catalina de Erauso was one such woman. A legendary figure, sometimes referred to as a Robin Hood of Latin America, Catalina was born in Spain, at the height of Christendom's oppression of women. She spent most of her adult years in male terrain, as a soldier of fortune in Mexico, Peru, and Chile.[5]

This tradition was carried to the British colonies by two lesbian pirates, Anne Bonny of Charleston, North Carolina, and her British emigré partner, Mary Read. The pair led as lusty and fight-filled a life as any pirates of the early eighteenth century. Apparently having established their reputations soundly enough to keep males at their distance, they could at times be freed of their male attire and ''were inseparable, wearing fine dresses, meant, literally, for queens, [and] sometimes dressing as men.''[6]

Women's position had improved little after the colonies rebelled to become the United States and unless a woman was tied to a man by marriage there were few options for her. It is little surprise, then, to find lesbian couples posing as man and wife. Recent historical research has uncovered several such couples. These are characterized by historian Jonathan Katz in his encyclopedic *Gay American History* as "passing women." Among the most interesting of Katz's passing women was New Yorker Murray Hall. Hall, married twice, was known for a quarter of a century—until the inquest following her death—as a man, and was, according to reports in the 1901 *New York Times,* a well-known Tammany Hall politician. Reported the *Times*: "She always voted [years before women won the vote] . . . she played poker at the clubs with city and state officials and politicians who flatter themselves on their cleverness and perspicacity, drank whisky and wine and smoked the regulation 'big black cigar' with the apparent relish and gusto of the real man-about-town." Hall's gender was concealed, during her life, by both her wives and, apparently, by her doctor. She died of breast cancer, leaving her estate to her wife and adopted daughter.[7]

For the lesbian unwilling to settle into marriage with a man in the era of rigid patriarchy, the only alternative to looking and acting (and being ready to fight) like a male appears to have been extreme wealth; in such a case the wealthy female pair could easily be written off as spinsters. The historical record (such small amounts of it as have been preserved and uncovered) gives no indication that the life of butch/ femme pairing between lesbian couples was an option. Nor does the record show that the outward appearances needed for economic and physical survival were carried into their private lives. It took male writers of the late nineteenth century to reestablish the *Courtesans* myth for the twentieth century.

## COURTESANS AS SCIENTIFIC FACT

The social strictures that locked women into so-called feminine roles so rigidly that in order to be free of them they usually needed either to have substantial wealth or to disguise themselves as men, were gospel to the vast majority of nineteenth-century men who deigned to write about women in their scientific studies. (Ironically, such writers, while thinking it terribly unfemale for women to do much more than tend to their embroidery, found nothing particularly masculine about the backbreaking work hundreds of thousands of lower class women were required to perform in the sweat shops of the industrial revolution.)

Dr. Richard von Krafft-Ebing, a noted German neurologist, was among the first to study sexual behavior. His *Psychopathia Sexualis,* which went through twelve revised editions from 1887 until his death in 1902, was the Kinsey study of sexual behavior of its day. The work, intended as a medical reference, was considered a sympathetic study of sexual aberration and included hundreds of case histories. Of the 330 or so pages that are dedicated to "General Pathology" in the English translation of the twelfth edition, about four are devoted to "Congenital Sexual Inversion in Women"—lesbianism. They set the tone of thinking on the subject for the next several decades and are worth quoting here:

Careful observation among the ladies of large cities soon convinces one that homosexuality is by no means a rarity. Uranism [homosexuality] may nearly always be suspected in females wearing their hair short, or who dress in the fashion of men, or pursue the sports and pastimes of their male acquaintances; also in opera singers and actresses, who appear in male attire on the stage by preference.

So far as the clinical aspect is concerned I may be brief, for this anomaly shows the same qualifications alike in man and woman . . .

In the transition to the subsequent grade, *i.e.,* that of masculinity (analogous to effeminacy in the male) strong preference for male garments will be found . . .

When viraginity is fully developed, the woman so acting assumes definitely the masculine *rôle.*

In this grade modesty finds expression only towards the same but not the opposite sex.

In such cases the sexual anomaly often manifests itself by strongly marked characteristics of male sexuality.

The female homosexual may chiefly be found in the haunts of boys. She is the rival in their play, preferring the rocking-horse, playing at soldiers, etc., to dolls and other girlish occupations. The toilet is neglected, and rough boyish manners are affected. Love of art finds a substitute in the pursuits of the sciences. At times smoking and drinking are cultivated even with passion.

Perfumes and sweetmeats are disdained. The consciousness of being a woman and thus to be deprived of the gay college life, or to be barred out from the military career, produces painful reflections.

The masculine soul, heaving in the female bosom, finds pleasure in the pursuit of manly sports, and in manifestations of courage and bravado. There is a strong desire to imitate the male fashion in dressing the hair and in general attire, under favourable circumstances even to don male attire and impose in it . . .

Hermaphrodism represents the extreme grade of degenerative homosexuality. The woman of this type possesses of the feminine qualities only the genital organs; thought, sentiment, action, even external appearance are those of the man . . .

With due alteration of details, the situation is the same as with the man-loving man. These creatures seek, find, recognize, love one another, often live together as 'father' and 'mother' in pseudo marriage. Suspicion may always be turned towards homosexuality when one reads in the advertisement columns of the daily papers: ''Wanted, by a lady, a lady friend and companion.''[8]

Krafft-Ebing's lesson is clear: if a woman dared to break out of her proper role in society, limited to dolls and love of art and perfume, she was queer. Doubtlessly, as many heterosexual women as lesbians suffered under Krafft-Ebing's diagnosis.


## MYTH TO REALITY

It was not long until the alleged lesbian lifestyles described by Krafft-Ebing became a real part of the public lesbian subculture. Radclyffe Hall, in her 1928 autobiographical novel, *The Well of Loneliness,* was the first self-acknowledged lesbian to write about lesbianism, and her tale of lesbian life would have pleased Krafft-Ebing. Stephen Gordon, the female hero of the novel, was the archetypical butch, and her relationships with women perfectly mimicked heterosexual roles.

Decades later, responsible social scientists found the butch/femme phenomenon widespread in the lesbian subculture, so widespread, in fact, that lesbian publications such as *The Ladder* published some studies on the subject, and a substantial amount of the short fiction pieces in the publication also carried a butch/femme cast. Arno Karlen, in his 1971 *Sexuality and Homosexuality: A New View* (another ''sympathetic'' examination of homosexuality), provided a brief summary of the rituals of this subculture based on the research of several women undertaken a decade earlier:

But among lesbians, the femme, with the ''normal'' role, is not the most admired one. Her status is lower or, at best, ambiguous. We have seen that the male role has more prestige among both sexes in most or all societies, and this is true among lesbians. The aggressive, [self-] controlled and controlling dyke has highest prestige . . . The butch and femme roles correspond to those of a straight couple, and they carry through from sex behavior to social manner and dress. The butch wears fly-front trousers, men's shirts and flat shoes, her clothes conceal her breasts and buttocks, and she may bind her breasts to flatten them. Her hair is cropped short, and she wears cuff links and other male accessories. She always hold the femme's coat, opens doors for her, lights her cigarettes.[9]

Despite such myths about the butch/femme lesbian subculture, in many cases self-perpetuated, lesbians recalling this lifestyle today have vastly differing recollections not only of its scope but of its significance.

"We know older lesbians," says Rae, a forty-seven-year-old woman who began exploring her lesbian identity thirty years ago, "who were so far into the butch/femme role that the femme was always the passive partner in sex. The butch always did the love-making, getting nothing in return. These women were about ten years older than us, I guess." Rae denies that she and her partners ever played these roles.

But Viv, who began her exploration of the lesbian lifestyle as a "real little butch," about a decade before Rae, recalls the days of the post−World War II subculture with a different perspective. "There's always been butch and femme, but not so much as everyone says and not the way they talk about it. Sure, we all got dressed up in drag for the bar scene, and it was kind of a gas. I suppose Bev was my femme, but once we got home, that whole thing turned around fast. We may have played at roles, but we sure weren't into them."

Says Bev, Viv's partner of more than thirty years, "You have to look at butch and femme this way: there weren't exactly any manuals out on how to be a lesbian. You had basically three sources of information. First was what you learned from your parents. What you were looking for was a long-term marriage, so you looked at the marriages you saw—and you saw roles. Dad worked, mom cooked. That was the way a marriage was run. Then you had *The Well of Loneliness*—that was the only real book on being gay you could find at the time. Okay, after that you had the other books—the dirty novels and the studies of abnormal psychology. And then you had what you found in the bars. So what were you going to do *but* play the game? There weren't any other role models around.

"So yes, that's the way we started when we got together. It lasted about one day, the day Viv found out I couldn't cook. It didn't even last out the night. Viv found out I was more sexually aggressive. That took care of butch/femme in our home life. Besides, we were both very career-oriented and neither one of us was willing to both work and do all the housework.

"I think if you take a look at that whole butch-femme thing you'll find out two things: it was really just a way of trying to live married, and, the 'butches' who were supposed to be so 'masculine' were really more feminine than us femmes.

"There's also a lot of nonsense that butches were supposed to be better than us femmes. That might be fine for some history book, but when you look at it, I think you'll find just like in our relationship, that's another one of those stories. Maybe if you were single and butch you thought you were pretty fantastic. But honey, once you got home things evened out a *heck* of a lot!''

## WOMEN OF VALUE

The public face of the lesbian subculture began to change in the late sixties and early seventies with the entrance of a new breed of lesbian, the lesbian who had begun to discover herself through the radical social protest movements against race discrimination, against the Vietnam war, and through the revitalized women's movement and the increasingly public struggle for gay rights.

These women, immersed in the growing literature and mood of women's liberation, began to see themselves in a new light—as truly first-class citizens held down by a patriarchal system. The signs and symbols of that patriarchy became anathema to them. Female chauvinism seemed to rule the day.

Mollie, one of this so-called new left protest generation, comments on her experiences in lesbian bars slightly less than a decade ago: "We were pretty much into the women's liberation movement. I guess you could call us radicals. We had just about had it with the male-dominated left and weren't going to stand for any more male shit. So when you went to the bars, you didn't want to see it around you—all those old dykes pretending they were men, ready to punch you out if you wanted to dance with their 'girls.' We got it from the left and told *them* to shove it, we sure weren't going to take it from our own. And there were more and more of us. We came to dominate things pretty much. We were the ones who were doing it all, we figured. I remember we even 'liberated' an older bar. We just went there together and crowded the place full and when the older crowd came around we passed out some literature and just plainly made sure they didn't get in.

"Now it sounds kind of rotten. But we were just getting in touch with our rage about male stuff.

"I don't think that that one incident of 'liberating' a bar had much to do with the older crowd leaving, but whatever it was, you just began not seeing them around anymore."

Viv recalls what sent her generation packing off to different bars, and it apparently had little to do with feminist theory. "Around the beginning of the seventies all these younger types came in, the hippy types, radicals, I don't know what you'd call them. We were just basically a more conservative generation, I guess. We thought it was important to try to dress nice. We didn't use drugs. We had a way of life and those people weren't anything like we thought people should act. I guess what *really* got us was their music. That rock and roll, acid rock! It just wasn't us and we moved on. We kind of resented them too. What the hell did they know about being gay? Maybe they'd been out two or three years. Big deal. They were just an element we didn't want to associate with."

A younger and more liberal generation seemed, for a period in the midseventies, to have won the battle of the bars—that public aspect of the lesbian subculture—and the old butch/femme pairs began vanishing slowly from a scene now increasingly dominated by androgynous women. The victory of the bars, however, was not one that was taken gracefully by some women, women like Frances, who after her prolonged and unsuccessful attempt to "cure" herself through heterosexual relationships, came out onto the gay scene as a butch. "Yeah, I was a butch, a New York dyke. I was down there on Christopher Street with the drag queens when we held off the police in 1969—the Christopher Street riots—the thing that set off this whole gay liberation movement. And then those radicals try to come in and tell *me* I'm not good enough to be gay because I'm a dyke? What a joke—who did they think they owed it all to anyway?"

Indeed, in their early quest for respectability, a great impetus in the lesbian movement had been a desire to show society that they were and could be as "feminine" as anyone. It was a momentary lapse into a trap just the reverse of the early butch's search for respect by donning male drag and posing as "masculine" women.

Conflict between the camps—those who wish to see lesbians appear like "respectable" women to the outside world, and those who take a certain pride in their bravado, continues to this day. In the interim, paralleling the development of modern feminism, lesbians began questioning roles of all kinds. Among these groups, as Gina explains, "We began to realize that roles themselves were the enemy. Not any particular kind of role, but the fact that you were viewed as, or were forced to play, any role at all. The thing was to discover who *we* were, in all our dimensions, the so-called masculine and the so-called feminine. We began looking into women's history and seeing women who played strong, assertive roles. Further back in history we found Amazons. We began to see first that this whole story about what the female role is or should be was just another trip laid on us by men, but we also saw that men were also stuck into the same trip. Who's to say that this or that person must be this or that, or do this or that, or dress or act in this or that way? The person who's living the life, that's who. And it isn't any of our business to put them down for it.

"Everything was just getting too rigid, but in a new way. We wanted to break away from all that old stuff. And we did, we are, and we will continue to explore it. We've even taken back our names— they used to put men down as 'faggots,' and women down as 'dykes,' because we didn't fit society's mold. Well, to me and to a lot of other women, a dyke is a self-identified self-defining woman without limit.

"I'm a dyke and I'm damned proud of it."

Gina's sentiment reflects that of many contemporary lesbians, women who, to all outward appearances, may seem as feminine as Betty Ford, or as masculine as Frances in her tight-fitting bell-bottom jeans and black leather motorcycle jacket.


## ROLE-FREE EXPLORATION

Contemporary lesbians seemed finally to have freed themselves of not only the role shackles of the heterosexual mainstream, but the role shackles of their own subculture. Although most are not so ready as Gina to admit publicly to being "a dyke and damned proud of it," their lifestyles are increasingly opening to experimentation and change and, in Liza's words "To hell with what anyone wants to call it. Sometimes, probably because I'm about ten years older then Olga, they'll say we're playing a 'mother-daughter' role. Okay, sometimes I do feel like a mother to her. Sometimes also, I feel like a daughter. So what? Or, because she's taller and has shorter hair, they'll say she's the butch and I'm the femme. Sometimes that's true. Sometimes the reverse is true.

"I really don't care what anyone says or thinks. If I want to learn how to bake bread, or how to saw down Douglas firs with a chain saw, I'm going to do it. I am my own woman, and anyone who tries to put a label on that is living somewhere in the nineteenth century as far as I'm concerned."

Overall, available evidence suggests that butch/femme behavior may occur in some relationships between older lesbians today, and among some lesbians who, like Viv, lacked positive adult lesbian role models in their teenage years. Explained Jan about her rural high school experience, "A lot of the kids in my school are into that old butch/femme thing. And some of them get into trouble for acting too much like boys. But there just isn't much else for us to do. There aren't any lesbian-feminist groups for teenagers here; there aren't even any lesbian groups. I think older women who are into feminism should get out here and help provide some alternatives for us women in high school. It would save us a lot of trouble."

Contemporary lesbians, and about 98 percent of the Fleener sample, deny that they live butch/femme roles. Of this sample, while all but 2 percent in the thirty-one to fifty age group denied such self-identification, 33 percent reported being either predominantly passive or dominant in their sexual relations, suggesting that some role restrictions remain. Of those age twenty-six to thirty, however, the reported incidence of dominant/passive sexual behavior dropped to 19 percent, and in those between twenty-one and twenty-six, dominant/passive sexual behavior was virtually nonexistent.[10]

The evidence of the Fleener study suggests that as times are changing in mainstream society, times have changed in the lesbian subculture. Lesbians are increasingly experimenting with and experiencing both passive and aggressive sides of their personalities and are coming to a synthesis of self-identity that will no longer fit into any existing label or conception—perhaps a whole new lifestyle freed of all of the limitations of either male or female roles. This personal synthesis is being carried forward into all of their life experiences: dealing with external reality as independent, self-sustaining women, and dealing with the private realities of their intimate relations. Perhaps this is the reason that lesbian women have been found to have a negligible frigidity rate in their lesbian sexual encounters.[11]

Butch and femme are gone (replaced, perhaps with "dyke power" as Gina suggests) but so is one of the important functions these early roles played: an easy entrée into the lesbian subculture. In a rapidly changing subculture, new ways of making connections with one's sisters must also evolve.

# 3

# Making Connections

It is seven o'clock on a Friday night. A young woman is standing in front of Maude's Study in San Francisco. She hesitates, walking up to the door, telling herself she can always turn around and go back home, but knowing that she won't. When her eyes adjust to the darkness after the door closes behind her, she sees a few women seated at the bar and another couple at a cocktail table. She sits down at the opposite end of the bar from the other women and orders a gin and tonic. The woman behind the bar serves her and then moves back to the cluster of women at the other end.

It is Joan's first visit to a lesbian bar, the first time she has seen women she knows are lesbians. For her, opening the door is one of the most courageous acts of her life. She has thought about it for weeks, ever since the bar's name and address was published in a newspaper feature on homosexuality in her community.

Although Joan does not yet know it, many women have come through that door with many of her same fears: fears of being seen going in by friends, or family, or somebody from work, or somebody who might know somebody who knows her; and fears of what she will find once inside. Images rise up that are as old as the *Courtesans* mythology of sexual depravity and pseudomen, images of people "sick" and different from her, images that have hidden in the shadows of her reflections on her own sexual identity. And there is fear, also, of taking the first step through a door that might affirm what she has often tried to deny about herself: that she is a lesbian.

With such fears looming large, it is no wonder that she finds a tremendous sense of relief after her first drink. There aren't many women in the bar. It feels safe. And the women are not as she had expected. They are women she would never have thought to be gay. No she-males leer at her lithe, carefully groomed body.

As Joan orders her second drink, she relaxes a bit. She has talked to no one but the bartender and overheard nothing except banter about the weekend entertainment. Beginning to feel conspicuous, just sitting there silently, occasionally sneaking looks at the women at the end of the bar, she leaves a tip and walks out, knowing she will return at another time.

Outside the bar, she senses for the first time that there are two worlds. Her own, inside the bar,and the other one where she lives out her life.

"I had never known how alone I was outside," recalls Joan. "All the people at work, the people on the streets, the lovers in the park, my neighbors, the whole damned heterosexuality of it all shoved in your face everywhere you go. I never realized how much of my life was spent faking it, trying to ignore and be ignored by the heterosexuality. I never knew how much I was pretending to be someone I wasn't until that first night, standing on the street, after I had just left Maude's. It was like I had discovered a refuge."

Joan returned to the bar often. "I found it was a place I could learn about myself, who I really was, talking and being with people like me. I could be with women and it was as if we were able to talk the same language. I could show affection to women. It was like going home, but to a home I never had."

## REFUGE AT JOHN BARLEYCORN'S

The lesbian bar is often the first connection a woman makes with other lesbians. It is also often the first environment she experiences that is sympathetic to her and affirms her lifestyle and affectional preference. In many ways the camaraderie around the barstool and the booze are sometimes her only safe haven from a hostile world just beyond the barroom door. Here she need not be bothered by the sexual demands of men. Here she may find comfort in her times of trouble from women who have shared similar troubles. And here she finds respite from whatever degree of heterosexual role playing her nine-to-five work life requires of her.

Whiskey's profit-hunger has seldom distinguished one greenback from another, and John Barleycorn's doors have been open to lesbians for decades. Recalls Bev of her 1948 experiences, ''I remember my first coming out bit in high school. I felt so alone, like I was the only one who had this problem. All the boys and girls were dating and I was a stranger in their midst. 'Oh,' I thought, 'if I could just find somebody else like me.' I really wanted to get out of my shell. So when I was eighteen or nineteen, just getting out of school, I started going out to the bars. Of course, I was scared to death, but I told myself, 'If you're ever going to meet anybody, you're going to have to get out there in the middle of it and take your chances.'

''When I did come out and go to my first bar, it was like I got my calling. Nothing could keep me home. I had to go to all the gay places and meet some gay girl to be my mate for life. I just kept sitting around the bars until I met these two girls and became their friend. And every Friday and Saturday night I'd go out with them. Not that I was hunting, but they knew a lot of people and so I kept meeting different people.''

While the emotional impact of that first venture into a lesbian bar has been similar over the decades, the bar scene itself has changed dramatically.

Today there are more than six hundred gay bars in the United States, and about two hundred of these are exclusively lesbian. Their character varies from the shiny large disco palaces in New York City and southern California, to more drab refuges in dozens of rundown neighborhoods in smaller cities.

Bars today range from those catering to young patrons, with their fancy disco dance steps and dashing clothes, to the quiet informal drinking bar with a pool table and a jukebox where a quarter buys three country-western hits, and to the feminist-oriented places, featuring women performers and a wide range of nonalcoholic beverages. Most lesbians who live in or near a major metropolitan area are not far from at least one bar where they may drink, dance, hold hands, or just talk with other lesbians freely, with relatively little to fear. They can learn about local lesbian bars from the gay press, from local or regional feminist publications, or from directories such as the comprehensive, women-oriented *Gaia's Guide,* sold through the mail and at some feminist bookstores and listing lesbian bars and organizations in the U.S. and foreign countries. The *Guide's* fifth edition in 1978 included over three thousand listings in the U.S. and in forty foreign countries, increasing the 1976 listings by one thousand.[1]

The relative freedom a lesbian may experience in the contemporary bar scene, however, has not always existed. "Right after the war," recalled Bev, "things were different. By the time you were twenty-one you'd heard so much about these places and the raids that you were almost afraid to go into a gay bar.

"Every once in a while there would be a place raided and someone you knew would be picked up. You'd be in a certain bar and the police would come in and decide they'd take everyone in because it's a gay bar, or maybe because the owner hadn't made the payoff. And then the papers would come out with everyone's names and addresses. First of all, even if your employer decided he wanted to keep you on after your name was published, he couldn't, because everyone else knew about it too—they had read the same paper. So he'd have to fire you. If you lived in a tight neighborhood, a lot of people knew you and the people you worked for. So the publicity would not only affect your job, but everyone you knew. The papers printed not only your address, but they gave your work affiliation and so forth.

"Bars were always closing down. There never were very many open at one time and you found out about the new ones by word of mouth. Then everyone would go to see what the new place was like. The bars couldn't advertise like they do now.

"Of course there was no dancing in the bars. You were very careful not to touch or hold hands like you see the kids doing now. You were very careful about those things because you never knew when the police would come in and close the place down."

Over the years lesbian bars have been an almost universal point of entry into the lesbian subculture, the first place a woman might meet a potential lover. Depending largely on the personalities of the owners, some bars have been served as the center of extended families, where patrons take up collections for others facing an economic crisis, where a lesbian can pick up news of old friends and upcoming activities, as well as seek advice and even leads on jobs.

Although bars are not a woman's only way of making connection with the lesbian subculture, they are still extremely important for the environment of support they offer. Bell and Weinberg found that about 30 percent of their lesbian respondents went to lesbian bars at least once a week.[2] Fleener, in her later sample, found that 68 percent

46

"of the women go to gay bars often . . . seven percent go at least weekly, twenty-five percent go several times a month, and thirteen percent at least go once or twice a year." The most important reason cited by Fleener's respondents for going to gay bars was because they felt "free to be themselves." Subsidiary reasons for going to gay bars included meeting new people and finding potential sex partners.[3]

The search for potential sex partners in the lesbian bar, however, may not be an easy one, especially for the neophyte. Explains one woman, "Most men's bars are set up for that purpose—to score a sexual partner for the night. And if a guy doesn't make it at the bar, or with one of the street hustlers, there's always what I like to call 'sex palaces,' the steam baths, where the whole point of it all is to go in, find someone you probably don't even talk to, and get it on. Women's liberation may have started up a lot of talk about sexual freedom, promiscuity, and how we should have places of our own where we can just do a sexual thing, but it hasn't worked out that way.

"A couple of years ago I knew I wanted to try sex with another woman, so I went to a gay bar I had heard about. It took me about six nights to get picked up. It was just the kind of place where women came to do their thing and weren't into cruising other women. I would go to this bar every night and just sit there. No one ever said anything to me sitting at the bar, so I figured that if I would play pool people would see me because everyone always watched whoever was playing pool. I thought maybe somebody would see me and be interested in me. It didn't work. Finally, after about my fifth night of this, I thought, 'Well, I'll just make the advance.' I was turned down the first time and the second time. The third woman I asked went home with me.

"Since then I've been to other bars. A couple of them are definitely what you'd call 'cruising bars.' It's getting kind of like a male thing. You walk in and everyone gives you a real good looking-over. Once I went in to a bar in New York with two friends of mine. We hadn't even ordered our drinks before some woman came up to us and asked us if we'd like to join her and her lover for a ménage à cinq!

"But mostly, the bars are just places to have a good time and I don't think you'll find too many where you can actually find like a one-night stand or something without an awful lot of trouble."

Comments another woman, "I've *never* found a lover through a bar, and God knows, sometimes I've sure tried."

Says a third, "Most of the bars I've been in are like clubs, places where you go to be with people you already know and maybe once in a while meet some new friends if you're coming in from out of town or something. It's just a lot different from the male scene."

Although the bars are the most obvious places to meet lesbians, many women do not make their connections to the lesbian subculture through them. Eleven percent of the Fleener sample reported that they never went to gay bars.[4] Bell and Weinberg, when asking only about the preceding twelve months, found that 14 percent had not been to a lesbian bar during the period.[5] It is very probable that the actual percentage of lesbians who have never been to a lesbian bar is much higher than either the Fleener or Bell and Weinberg findings suggest. Both studies were performed in major metropolitan areas where lesbian bars are abundant. Lesbians living in more rural areas, or in areas of the Midwest and South where there are few bars, may reasonably be expected to have much less contact with lesbian bars than their urban peers.

## UNCLE SAM WANTS YOU

The military and its related services were first publicly revealed to be havens for lesbians in Radclyffe Hall's semiautobiographical novel, *The Well of Loneliness*. Here Hall described the active lesbian subculture of Britain's World War I ambulance corps. Her description and the fact that she did not condemn lesbians in her then-controversial book, resulted in its banning from England for thirty-one years under the country's obscenity statutes. As Dolores Klaich records about the book's obscenity trial, "Hall, who had said nothing throughout the sensational proceedings, kept her silence. But when the magistrate continued, accusing the author of maligning certain Englishwomen of 'standing and position' [in the ambulance corps] . . . by portraying them as 'addicted' to the 'unnatural' practices in question, she remained silent no longer. She cried out, 'I protest. I emphatically protest.'"[6]

Lesbians serving their countries in the military are not unique to England. The American armed forces have long attracted numbers of lesbians, women who serve not only from patriotism and for the occupational opportunities they feel are afforded them, but because they seek to make connections with other lesbians. Women were not allowed to serve in the U.S. military until 1902 although they filled civilian nursing and other support capacities in every war, including the Revolutionary War. Such civilian work was not enough for some women, including an estimated four hundred who served in the Union Army disguised as men.[7] Although it is impossible to determine how many of these were lesbians, Jonathan Katz, in his *Gay American History* has uncovered an intriguing story of two Union Army lesbians in the memoirs of General Philip H. Sheridan. Each had apparently joined up with the Union forces independently, both successfully passing muster as men. One, an East Tennessee woman, was a teamster in a division wagon train, and the other a soldier in a cavalry company. Their gender, and their intimacies with each other, were discovered while they were out on a foraging expedition. Said Sheridan, "These Amazons had secured a supply of 'apply-jack' by some means, got very drunk, and on the return had fallen into Stone River and been nearly drowned. After they had been fished from the water, in the process of resuscitation their sex was disclosed, though up to this time it appeared to be known only to each other . . . How the two got acquainted I never learned, and though they had joined the army independently of each other, yet an intimacy had sprung up between them long before the mishaps of the foraging expedition."

The two were given "clothing suited to their sex," and apparently booted out of the Union Army.[8]

It was certainly not the last time lesbians would join the army and certainly not the last time they would be booted out. Although reports from early in this century (when the army and navy in 1901 and 1908, respectively, formed nurse corps as noncivilian military corps) are inadequate, there is little reason to doubt that lesbians were as present then as they were in World War II and are today. Statistics, of course, are not kept, but by 1970 the military was discharging an estimated two thousand male and female homosexuals per year with less than honorable discharges and these as estimated by the American Civil Liberties Union, represented less than 2 percent of all the male homosexuals serving (no estimate was made on what percentage of lesbians this number represented).[9] Data on lesbians in the military is nowhere publicly available, but it is probable that a higher percentage of lesbians than male homosexuals serve in the armed forces simply because the military discriminated against heterosexual women until 1973 by not allowing married women to join, and by ousting those who got married while enlisted.[10]

Jane, now in her early fifties, recalls an experience typical of many young lesbians today: "I think for me, you have to realize that I joined the navy for one reason and one reason only and that was to come out [as gay]. I had been married and had learned that that was not for me. I had learned that I loved women. But in Indiana, I believed there wasn't another gay person in the whole state. Somehow I knew that if I joined the navy I would find someone else who was gay. So I joined purposely for that reason and it didn't take long for me to find other gay women. It was all very exciting for me. There were all these gay women and I was having a ball." Jane met her current lover, Rae, who served in the navy with her, about a year after her induction.

For many lesbians, life in the lesbian military underground is by no means as exciting as Jane remembers it. Military regulations require that all lesbians or people with "homosexual tendencies" (a term that even the military has not yet defined) be immediately discharged. In 1978, the navy amended its directives slightly so that discharge is not mandatory if the lesbian or woman with "homosexual tendencies" has not engaged in lesbian sex acts while in the service. Until recently, dismissal occurred almost universally under less than honorable conditions, with consequent loss of veteran's benefits as well as the negative effects of an other than honorable discharge on the lesbian's search for civilian employment. (It is now possible, under President Jimmy Carter's amnesty program, for gay people who have been discharged under other than honorable conditions, to upgrade their discharges.)[11] These facts, combined with the emotional distress and harassment surrounding an investigation are enough to ensure that most lesbians remain well hidden. Many women who enter the military hoping for an introduction to the lesbian subculture find, in fact, that their period of service is one of the least sexually active of their lives.

Yet lesbians continue to join. Those few data that have surfaced indicate that the percentage of lesbians in the armed forces is at least equal to, and probably higher than, the percentage of lesbians in the civilian world. A survey of one thousand lesbians published by the monthly *Lesbian Connection* found that slightly more than 6 percent of its respondents had seen military service.[12] Meanwhile, at the peak of female military enlistment, in 1945, only 265,006 women served, a small fraction of the adult female population.[13] Comments one navy petty officer, "If they got rid of every lesbian in our unit, we'd be down to half strength."

Military authorities, however, perhaps recognizing the degree to which they rely on lesbian recruits, have apparently come to terms with the lesbian underground, tending to ignore its existence unless it becomes, in some way, an embarrassment. Lesbian comic Pat Bond recalls such a situation in her days as a WAC in post—World War II Japan: "It was incredible . . . It was like a huge gay bar. I'd say ninety percent of the company was gay. Openly. With men's haircuts and everything. And then they had that witch hunt in Tokyo and five hundred women got sent home for dishonorable discharges . . . I finally figured out what happened. Why it happened. When we got there we discovered that there weren't any jobs for us and we soon figured out that MacArthur wanted to show us off to the Japanese women. You know, these are independent American women and this is what they're like. Can you *imagine* his surprise? He got independent women, all right. He got dykes. And of course, that was *it*. As soon as they saw what was happening they wanted us out."[14]

Generally, the military investigates only when a complaint about lesbian activity is filed. It is not uncommon, reports the petty officer, for "people to file complaints on lesbianism when someone has ripped you off, screwed you out of a promotion, or anything. Sometimes a jilted lover will complain. More often, it seems to me, it's someone who's jealous of you for one reason or another."

One source has suggested that lesbians who stay in the military tend to be women who have difficulty forming permanent relationships. As she points out, "For a lot of people the military is a tremendous cop-out in the sense that if you're gay, being in the military takes care of a lot of problems for you. No matter how many relationships you get into, Mama Army will save you and you always know that in at least two years you're going to get a transfer that will take care of any problems you're having. Mama Army just keeps copping out for you—'What can I do my dear, of course I love you, but Mama Army has had me transferred!' "

## THROUGH THE HETEROSEXUAL MAINSTREAM

The third major route of connection for lesbians is perhaps both the most difficult and the most representative of the American lesbian experience—the heterosexual mainstream. Despite what appears to be a contemporary abundance of lesbian bars, publications, organizations, and even the availability of Mama Army, all of these cannot account for even the most conservative estimates of the adult U.S. lesbian population; some two million adult women, based on the Kinsey study of female sexual behavior which, two decades ago, found 3 percent who were exclusively homosexual. The estimates of contemporary lesbian and gay organizations such as the National Gay Task Force suggest that the true U.S. lesbian population is about 10 percent of adult women, or about eight to ten million. And because the majority of these women do *not* find their partners through bars, publications, organizations, or Mama Army, they are the most difficult to learn about. They live and make connection (if they make connection at all) within the heterosexual environment: on the job, in school, through the local PTA, church functions, or volunteer groups, or through women's social functions like the local bridge club.

Norma, one of this vast group of women, described her experience of trying to find other lesbians in the heterosexual mainstream of her native South Carolinia: "I knew that I wanted to find out if I was a lesbian. I had these feelings for women all my life. I knew the thing with men wasn't working for me. But you don't just go around asking people, 'Are you a lesbian?' So I began listening to the rumors at the plant. Everyone would always point out a few of the women and crack jokes about them—'Oh, did you know she's one of *those*?' So I arranged to be transferred to a department where there were supposed to be three of 'those.'

"Nothing happened at first. No one paid any attention to me. I didn't know how to make an approach, how to get anyone interested in me. So I began flirting a little. It was a subtle thing. It had to be. I wasn't sure about any of it and I didn't want to get labeled as one of 'those.' I was getting increasingly frustrated about the whole thing. I'd been in the department more than a year and nothing happened. Absolutely nothing.

"I decided I'd better do something. So I began checking around some more and picked on one woman I liked who was supposed to be gay. I started asking her out for a couple of drinks after our shift and then later to play tennis on weekends. Finally, she agreed to come over for dinner. The big dinner! I thought I'd finally solved all my problems.

"Nothing was happening. Candlelight, soft music, wine, the whole trip and nothing happened. I had these fantasies of her courting me, making passes, and none of that happened. So I guess I got drunk and finally when we were in the kitchen doing up the dishes, I kissed her on the mouth. I don't know who was more surprised, she or I. But that broke the ice. After she got me off of her we sat out in the living room and talked.

"We became good friends after a while, even though we never did anything sexually. But she introduced me to her circle of gay friends and I finally met my first woman lover.

"The whole process took exactly two years."

Among the difficulties of making connections with the lesbian subculture through the mainstream is the self-imposed conspiracy of silence surrounding most lesbians' private lives. Despite the increasing tolerance for alternative lifestyles in some major metropolitan areas and liberal enclaves, most lesbians will not admit their affectional preference to anyone whom they do not trust implicitly. They know that too much is at risk; their position in the community, their jobs, their relations with family members, and perhaps even their heterosexual marriages. Mode of dress gives no clue to a woman's affectional preference. The fact that two single women are living together may mean nothing more than that they are pooling their economic resources to rent an apartment that neither could afford alone.

Because of these factors, lesbians in the mainstream have developed subtle means of "checking out" other women, or even men whom they suspect might be gay. Ironically, in order to check out someone in the heterosexual mainstream, the lesbian must already know something about the lesbian subculture. This decreases the opportunities for the woman striving to make her first contact with other lesbians through the mainstream.

As Grace explains, "When I was transferred to Texas I had no friends there. I pretty much assumed there wasn't much of an active gay scene in Midland, and it's a long way from there to Houston. I was really in a bind, lonely, and wanted to get in touch with gay people.

"What you do in a situation like that is to slip certain words into your casual conversations. In Midland most people still think 'gay' means happy, so you can say things like, 'Oh, we really had a gay time last night.' If someone else is gay they'll know you're probably not talking about happy. But even that doesn't mean instant recognition because you can't be sure if you're reading the signals right. And, not only don't you want to blow your own cover, but you don't want to embarrass anyone. So you might try talking about where you've been before. If both of you had been to New York, you might mention the name of a gay bar there. You'd say something like, 'Did you ever get to The Duchess?' or whatever. If they recognize the bar then you figure they must be gay and it's safer to be more honest with them, to drop hints about your female 'friends'—meaning lovers—and see how they respond. Sometimes, even if they are gay, they'll catch on to what you're trying to do, but won't know the place you've mentioned and might not exactly be sure about you, so they'll come back with the name of another place. Eventually, it clicks.

"In more liberal places you might even talk about gay rights, or Anita Bryant, but you still go through the rest of the ritual because you don't know if you're not just talking to some sympathetic liberal who might be horrified if she knew she was talking to a dyke.

"I don't think I've ever just asked anyone if they were gay. You just don't do that."

## OUT OF THE STREETS AND INTO THE SHEETS

These points of connection to the lesbian subculture and to other lesbians—the bars, the military, and the mainstream—were all that were available to lesbians prior to the nascent lesbian liberation movement of the mid-1950s. To an unmeasured extent, the lesbian and gay organizations of today are becoming a growing point of connection for the lesbian who is coming out as well as for others just seeking companionship. This is a function of lesbian and gay organizations that is largely ignored in their more politically goal-directed function of achieving civil rights gains.

It is not a phenomenon, however, that has gone unnoticed by some activist organizers commenting on the rapid turnover in their organizations' memberships. Comments one such organizer, who declines to be named, "Sometimes lesbian liberation seems like you join a group, go out into the streets for a demonstration, meet someone, get into the sheets, and leave the group."

No data are available on how many women make their first contacts with other lesbians through gay organizations. Gay groups are most often located either in large urban centers where the seemingly less threatening and more anonymous bars are also located, or in liberal university towns where such groups are often small and likely to be in a continual process of formation and reformation as their leadership moves on to other interests or, perhaps, simply grows tired of the work involved in keeping an organization together. A frequent comment made by lesbians who have been active in such college groups is that their membership tends to be primarily male. This certainly limits the lesbian's prospects of meeting other women through them.

Similarly, no data are available on how many women make their first lesbian connections through the growing number of gay caucuses within professional organizations.

Summarizes the lesbian organizer quoted above, "I think the people who join lesbian groups are people who are pretty much already 'out' and already pretty familiar with the lesbian underground. Once in a while you'll see a new face, someone who may be at a meeting just to see what lesbianism is all about, but they generally don't want to make a commitment and you don't see them again."

During the preliberation era lesbians developed a survival alternative which serves them well even today: the formation of friendship groups. They form the lesbian's extended family, and through interlocking networks between friendship groups, form the largely invisible lesbian subculture.

# 4

# A Subculture in Hiding

In all the words about coming out, about lesbian revolution, about a brave new world, it seems like we're losing touch with the best of what we had: our tribes, our lesbian nation, our partisan underground if you want to call it that.—*Frances*

The preliberation lesbian experience was primarily one of isolation, adaptation, and persecution. These were the roots of the "partisan underground" described by Frances. Two elements—isolation from one another, and adaptation to rapid change—are the supposed critical factors of future shock. They may, if society as a whole cannot cope with them, create the third element key to a partisan underground: persecution.

The lesbian subculture described by Frances, by virtue of the persecution it faced, was one of small groups of women who had come to trust each other implicitly. Though some might call them friendship cliques, they are, more realistically, extended families. Frances calls them tribes. When one or two tribeswomen would leave for new territory—because of persecution, job transfer, or hopes of greater economic opportunity—they would join or form another support group of trusted women. It was a process that continued until the contacts made by all of the individual women involved stretched, link by link, across the nation and sometimes into foreign lands. At a few points these links crossed both socioeconomic strata and race. This is what Frances calls her "lesbian nation." It was, and for the most part remains, a subculture in hiding.

Certain aspects of this subculture, particularly the trust and emotional support it provides, are reminiscent of another kind of group that flourished when communities were more stable and when moving to a different town was a major life event: the heterosexual women's community. Coexisting with the male community as a separate subculture, women formed tightly knit support groups in which they shared the familial love, lore, and wisdom of their lives. This heterosexual women's support network, now only a relic, broke down as America became a mobile society. The elements that bound this network had been time spent together, experiences shared over the years, and histories of generations of familial ties. As these disappeared, so did much of the strength of heterosexual female bonding.

The lesbian subculture has not had a history of generations of familial ties. It has also probably always tended toward greater mobility than the mainstream, in response either to persecution or to the hope of something new and better elsewhere. In many cases the time spent together by lesbians was months, not decades. Yet the warmth and support existing in the lesbian subculture in hiding was probably as strong, perhaps stronger, than that in the heterosexual female subcultures; and it developed a lore and wisdom of its own. The primary functions of the lesbian subculture in hiding have been to provide emotional support, both in a general and in a direct personal manner, to provide survival information and news, and to offer hospitality and help to migrating tribe members.

It is this subculture in hiding, much more than the bars or organizations generally described by the media, that is America's true lesbian underground. Bell and Weinberg commented on this briefly with regard to their attempt to recruit lesbians for their study. Their recruitment attempts were made in the San Francisco Bay Area, a region offering a wealth of public lesbian connections. Recruitment was done through public advertising, bars, organizations, mailing lists, in public contacts by research representatives to organizations, and through personal contacts. Of the 785 lesbians eventually located for the recruitment pool, 42 percent were found through personal contacts. In contrast, only 18 percent of the men in the recruitment pool were located this way.[1]

## ADAPTATION DURING THE McCARTHY ERA

Viv speaks of subculture's adaptation during the McCarthy era:

"Things were getting pretty tough at the time. There we were, right in Manhattan, where everything was going on, where our friends were, where all the bars were. But during those McCarthy years people stopped going to bars. With all of the newspaper headlines people began to be afraid to be seen around someone who might be questioned. You know, the press ignores it now, but they were investigating homosexuals as well. More often than not the latest news you seemed to hear from your friends was of someone who had lost her job in one way or another just on suspicion, without any investigation. Everyone was scared.

"Then there was a big exposé in *Confidential* about some new gay organization that they said was a communist front, this was in 1954. By then you weren't only afraid if you worked in almost any kind of job, you were afraid just to be gay, that you would get called in or investigated or in some other way implicated.

"So most of our group stopped going to the bars. We started more visiting at each other's homes. One of the nicest things was when, I forget what year it was, maybe 1954 or 1955, Tallulah Bankhead had her radio program, ninety minutes every Sunday afternoon. Of course, everybody thought she way gay. [No evidence suggests that she was.] We had a group of thirty or forty of us that would get together at somebody's house, just sort of pot luck and bring your own liquor and a little food. We'd all sit around together and listen to the show. And that was a lot of fun. That went on for seven or eight months, so it kept the whole big bunch of us together. We didn't see each other all week, but we'd meet together on Sunday for the show and spend the rest of the day together. Sometimes a program brings you together like that. I think that's how we survived that terrible period."

Bev added, "Among the things we'd talk about, of course, was the purge. We'd pick up tips on what to do to protect ourselves and other gay people. I was just starting work as an intake counselor at the state hospital, and it was a real problem because a lot of people who came in there, or who were brought in, were obviously gay. You knew it would go against them if you wrote that in their record, so you wrote down anything you could think of. There was a lot of talk about what we could write. You'd put in anything, 'adult adjustment problem,' or whatever you could write in. Anything but 'homosexual.'

"I'm not in that line of work anymore, but I know counselors and psychologists who are gay and still to this day won't write in anything about homosexuality into their patients' records.''

Viv comments, ''That must have been about twenty-five years ago, and we still have friends from those days. Every once in a while, one of them that moved or something, will come back onto the scene. Those kind of ties just don't ever really end.''

Viv also recalls the kind of practical assistance her group tried to offer, ''One time, I remember, one of the group did lose her job, a teacher. You would never have suspected anything about her, I mean, she didn't 'look' like a butch or anything. She was one of the nicest people around. Apparently someone had just gone with some rumor to the head of the school and that was enough to get her out. Actually, the guy who fired her gave her the chance to resign so her record wouldn't be completely ruined. But still there were blacklists and she knew she couldn't get a job in the state ever again. She was on the verge of killing herself. That job of hers meant everything to her. We spent a lot of time with her, keeping an eye out for her. Finally she decided that she'd be better off if she left the state. Naturally, she didn't have any money, so we took up a collection. We got up a few hundred dollars, which was a lot in those days, and somebody found a place where she could stay in Pennsylvania with one of someone's friends until she got back on her feet.''

This type of personal assistance continues in the subculture today. Explains one woman, ''I had just got a job offer in Washington. We had to get there in a couple of days and we were completely broke. We were so down we didn't know how we were going to make the next month's rent. So we called around and in just a couple of hours we had rounded up several hundred dollars from people, and they weren't that well off either. They really had to dig for the money, but they did. Three of them gave us the names and phone numbers of people to call when we got up there. Other people might be able to get that kind of help from their families, but ours had long ago written us off. In a way, our real family was that extended network of lesbians. We had straight friends who offered to help, but when it came right down to it, it was those lesbians who came up with the bucks.''

Recalls another woman, ''Someone had shot through our windows and broken into our house. The police came and went, saying they couldn't do much about it except take a report. We were afraid that whoever it was might come back. So we called one of our friends, and in about an hour eight people came to our place and arranged a schedule so there would always be someone staying with us. It was incredible!''

Once accepted into the extended family, the lesbian is likely to find herself with a host of friends ready to care for her in emotional as well as physical crises. Because of a history of isolation from mainstream society, lesbians have learned that when it comes down to the wire, their real support and defense comes only from that which they can muster up from among their peers. Their peers, knowing that they may need similar assistance at a later time, do double duty to help their sisters in trouble. Explains another woman, ''One of our good friends had just broken up with her lover and was getting very depressed. We were afraid she might do something drastic, like kill herself, and we knew she needed a lot of emotional support right then. A group of us got together to look out for her. We arranged between ourselves to call and visit her often and made sure she had plenty of invitations to visit all of us. We nursed her along for about six months before her depression ended.''

A practical function of the extended family is its pool of information about reliable attorneys, counselors, doctors, and other professionals, many of whom are gay themselves.

## LORE, WISDOM, AND CUSTOM

As an important survival mechanism, the extended family has its own codes of behavior. The primary taboo of the lesbian subculture in hiding is against breaking the code of silence about members' affectional preference to outsiders—any outsiders, even other gay people not integrated into the prime unit of the subculture, the extended family. The lesbian who violates this taboo is excluded from the family. If she gets a reputation for indiscretion in one family, she may find, through the network of links connecting many such families, that her reputation has spread to other groups which will also exclude her.

Sexual indiscretions are also rapidly communicated in America's lesbian underground. One woman reports that while on a job assignment in Portland she spent an intimate weekend with a woman she had just met. By the time she got back home to Philadelphia, her lover had already learned of her affair—from a woman living in Phoenix!

It is through such networks that the members of the subculture learn (sometimes inaccurately, but often with great accuracy), which public figures are gay. This type of transmission, for a minority with few role models who have made it on the national scene, is important in sustaining the subculture's self-respect. Such transmissions have generally focused on political leaders, performers, and in the military, on upper-echelon officers. In recent years, as elements of the lesbian movement have become more politically conscious, transmissions about those involved in politics have become important in the voting behavior of some lesbians.

Explains one, "We know, on factual evidence, that one very high official in our state is as queer as a three-dollar bill. So we've kept an eye out on her career. Sometimes people like that will, maybe in an effort to hide their sexual orientation, go out of their way to go against gay people and gay rights. If that happens, you can bet they never get another lesbian vote in this state again." Even at this level, however, the code of silence is not broken. Continues the woman, "Sometimes I have fantasies about blowing her cover to the press. That would get rid of one problem. But it's just something you don't do." To date, it has not been done, so strong is the taboo against revealing another woman's lesbianism until she herself is prepared to do so.

Sexual indiscretions, perhaps communicated via the Portland-Phoenix-Philadelphia route, are likely to be tolerated within a lesbian's extended family. Explains Viv, "One thing you do is try not to take sides in fights between lovers. Now, if one of the two has been really rotten and they've broken up, you might tend to exclude the woman who's done something like taken all the property, or begun to spread lies, or whatever. Generally, even after partners have broken up, both are still welcomed. You just learn, after being around awhile, that those things happen, and so you say 'too bad,' but that doesn't mean that either one of them was wrong."

Each extended family of the subculture has different characteristics. Generally, there is little class or racial mixing within a single extended family, despite the fact that one or more of its members might have contact with other families in different racial or socioeconomic groups comprising the greater subculture. Also, different groups develop different patterns of sexual relations among their members. Some groups are comprised of primarily monogamous

61

couples maintaining careful boundaries between friendship and sexual intimacy. Others, however, are somewhat promiscuous among themselves, as Rae describes: "Before we moved, we had a group of gay friends who'd been together for years. And it seemed as if every one of those women had had an affair with everyone else in that group at one time or another. You couldn't exactly call it wife-swapping, because these affairs and new relationships lasted for several years. And you wouldn't exactly call it promiscuity because in general, once a couple got together, they stayed monogamous for a while. I don't know what you'd call it and I can't explain why they stuck together. I guess there just wasn't very much sexual jealousy. In heterosexual society, sexual jealousy is a big thing. Probably it comes from the male trip of considering women property and from the woman's fears of losing the guy who's supporting her. What was important to these women, I think, was their emotional closeness. And, of course, no one had to worry about losing her income.

"It wasn't the way we chose to live, but for those women it seemed to work out pretty well, except every six months or so there'd be this whole emotional thing when someone began taking an interest in someone new. But they all hung together. They're probably still together doing just the same thing. Maybe because most of them had lived with each other at one time or another they became a tighter group, I don't know."

In general, this kind of tolerance for sexual indiscretion is fairly widespread within the subculture in hiding. Among some women, it is almost a point of personal ethics to try to maintain a friendship with a former lover. "After all," explains Jo Ann, "what is really important about a relationship isn't just that you had good sex. What's important is that you have come to love someone. It just doesn't make any sense that when your relationship ends you stop loving them."

From this vast diversity of styles among extended families or tribes, come only a few points of similarity in terms of shared wisdom. Viv summarizes, "Besides not finking on someone, about the only other things you could say as generalizations are that first relationships generally don't work out, and, whatever you do, stay away from so-called bisexual and heterosexual women. They'll leave you every time. A lot of the kids now are trying to have relationships with bisexual women who've fallen for them. I've watched it time after time. The bisexual leaves and the lesbian is left up a creek."

# A SUBCULTURE IN HIDING

## SUBCULTURE GAP

The subculture in hiding is extremely difficult to penetrate. A major criticism leveled at the extended family institutions of this subculture by some lesbian activists is their closed nature. Women in such groups are likely to have known each other for several years, and while new members are sometimes welcome, the least welcome of all are lesbians with ties to the gay rights movement. Part of the difficulty at first appears to be generational. A mainstay of today's subculture in hiding are women who have survived the McCarthy era. These women are likely to have developed careers and a reasonable amount of economic security. They are reticent to trust outsiders. Commented Viv, who consented to be interviewed only after several assurances from people she trusted in her own extended family, "I didn't want to give an interview. I still have a hard time trusting you. I've got it in the back of my mind that there's a chance that you might blow my cover, maybe not even on purpose, maybe by accident. And where does that leave me? I'd lose everything I've spent my life building. I'd be on welfare."

On further exploration, it turned out that the difficulty between women like Viv and critics of the subculture is not generational. Among Viv's network of trusted friends are women as young as twenty-five. The difficulty between the activist and the subculture in hiding, it turned out, is the activist's activism. Said Viv, "Look, Bev and I are about as closeted as you can get. So are our friends. That's a kind of security for us. When you do hear from these radical lesbians, they're always trying to get you to come out. I've lived my life in the closet and I'm going to stay there. And I certainly don't want to be around anyone who's going to start telling me to come out. I simply am afraid of them. I don't trust them."

On the other side of the subculture gap are lesbian activists trying to organize for civil rights. Commented one, "Look, we need those women. They have the money. They have the experience. And there they are, sitting comfortably in their safe little closets as if the movement didn't exist at all. Sometimes I think they're our worst enemies."

## AN EMERGING SYNERGY?

Said Viv, "You know what finally convinced me to do this interview?

Anita Bryant. I thought McCarthy was dead. But Anita Bryant and the referendum they had in California showed me that it could all start over again. I thought about it a lot. Yes, I'm closeted and will remain that way. But if you get a McCarthy in there, even a closet won't help you. If they want you, they're going to get you. If you really think about it, they could probably find every one of us just by looking through some computer tapes—credit references, car registration, whatever. So maybe this is just my small way of fighting back.''

Added Bev, ''This gay rights stuff wasn't much of anything to us. We managed before it. We never had any hassle over the last twenty years. It just didn't seem necessary to make an issue out of it when you thought there wasn't any problem. But now, maybe it's time to do something.''

The potential for a creative and valuable synergy between the subculture in hiding and the public lesbian subculture has been developing over the past two decades as women have emerged from their closets to struggle for civil rights. Some of these women, generally viewed as less radical than most gay activists, have, over more than two decades, built contacts and eventually bonds of trust with members of the subculture in hiding. The foundation laid by these early lesbian activists—women like San Francisco's Phyllis Lyon and Del Martin, and Philadelphia's Barbara Gittings and Kay Tobin—has set a precedent showing that it can be safe for closeted lesbians of the hidden subculture to retain their anonymity, yet still contribute to the movement for social change.

As a result, while there is still no merger between the two subcultures, they more and more frequently cooperate, making the experience and expertise of the subculture in hiding available when called upon.

And called upon they were when the 1977–1978 antigay backlash of Anita Bryant, California state senator John Briggs, and others provoked a fear so threatening that many of the subculture in hiding were forced to remember the repression of the McCarthy era, and rather than see its persecutions re-emerge, helped gay rights activities as best they could.

As the lesbian subcultures enter the 1980s, it appears that both the public one and the one in hiding are at least accessible to each other through trusted intermediaries. One of the greatest ironies of such accessibility, and of a future when lesbians may not need to face the degree of isolation that created the subculture in hiding, is that the subculture itself may disappear. As the lesbian is increasingly accepted by mainstream society, her need for such a tight trust-bound network of support may diminish. She may then face the world of future shock without the survival mechanism that might make her uniquely adaptable to it.

# 5

# Relationship Experiments

I spent years living as if life were some kind of thing you had to get through, a job that had a few high points and lots of low points, but something you did nevertheless. It was living, I guess, but there didn't seem to be a whole lot of meaning to it. I was just putting in my time.

I'd had a couple of sexual experiences with girls in college, but those weren't supposed to be "real." Neither of us wanted to admit there was anything more to it than a kind of game.

Finally, many years later, when I accepted that I was a lesbian and began to go out and get in touch with others of my kind, I met Ruth. We fell immediately, passionately, and ecstatically in love. It was as if, all those years before, I'd been starving for something and didn't even know it. And now I grabbed for it, rolled in it, sucked it in ravenously, devouring an essence of life I never even knew existed before—*Sally, describing her first lesbian love affair at the age of fifty-two*

There's a renaissance today in the lesbian community. It's marvelous, it's like Paris all over again. And yet there's an unsettlingness, especially with a lot of younger lesbians. It is "politically correct," they say, to have multiple relationships, relationships without commitment—a kind of promiscuity. In that way you're not supposed to be oppressing other women. That kind of "I don't want to share any commitment" relationship works for who it works for. It is not workable for me. It's like I'm a closet commitment person. I have to whisper about it. When you tell people these days you want some kind of commitment, it's as if you are a jailer and want to box somebody in. I don't know why commitment isn't popular. Except that there are so many women available today. it's like a market place and when you don't want to be together with one person anymore, there's plenty more out there.—*Susan, commenting on San Francisco's public lesbian subculture*

The lesbian has journeyed through several rites of passage. She has developed a consciousness of her identity and explored some of its ramifications in her life. She may have tried any number of ways to deny this fact of her identity. Finally, though, she has sought out and found other lesbians, either through the public subculture, the mainstream, or the fringes of the subculture in hiding. She has yet another rite of passage—her first lesbian love affair. Until she has experienced this she may never be quite certain of herself or of her identity. The sexual, passionate, in-love experience with another woman is a final emotional step in solidifying her self-identity.

Anyone's first love affair is seldom forgotten. The lesbian's first love affair, however, whether formed overnight or developed over several months, perhaps has even more significance than the first affair of her heterosexual sister. Here the lesbian finds herself in a way that shows her the ultimate rightness of what she has believed or suspected about her affectional preference. Sally, quoted above, has had several long-term loving relationships with men, but her first lesbian love affair was an explosion of self-realization for her.

The first, reciprocated in-love relationship experienced by a lesbian is important to her in a number of ways seemingly unrelated to the relationship's intimacy. Comments from lesbians about their first affairs are as varied as these:

"I felt like I'd finally come into my own. Finally I was a whole person, as if, at twenty-eight, I'd finally grown up and learned what life was all about."

"It's kind of like 'Amazing Grace': before, I was lost, now I'm found."

"A world of aliveness opened up in me I'd never known was there before."

And, from yet another woman, "I'd always thought there was something missing in my life. I wasn't sexually naive or anything. I'd had sexual affairs with both men and women, but that was it. They left me with the feeling that probably I preferred women and the knowledge that I was a sexual being. But then, bang, I fell in love with a woman. From then on I *knew* where life was at for me!"

A lesbian's first affairs seem more involved with her process of self-definition than do the affairs of her heterosexual peers. Bell and Weinberg, asking about changes their lesbian respondents experienced as a result of their first lesbian affairs, found that among their category "other changes," the largest number (16.7 percent) responded that they had become more committed to their homosexuality.[1] (Who would imagine 17 percent of a heterosexual female sample reporting that their first affairs with men made them more committed to heterosexuality?)


## INTENSITY, PRESSURE

A lesbian's first love affair, aside from having a unique significance, often carries with it a set of pressures that do not confront heterosexual lovers. The lesbian, often still hiding her identity from the outside world, finds in her love relationship one of the few places where she has ever been truly able to express, and perhaps even explore, her total reality.

Generally, she spends at least eight hours a day in her work environment, in a place where she may fear rejection by her peers and perhaps even loss of her job if she expresses that most fundamental element of her human essence—the nature of her love. She may also endure the same phenomenon in other hours of her life: at the grocery store where Saturday shoppers have their children in tow; at the laundromat where most appear to be washing clothes belonging to two different genders; on the subway with its intense heterosexual pressures on women; and during such social intercourse as she has with friends, acquaintances, and family.

A lot of her life energy may, by necessity, be channeled into covering up, lying, hiding. When she arrives home to be with her lover, (most lesbians chose to live together during their first affair),[2] her entire reservoir of life experience, until then hidden, is released into that one intimate space where she may finally be completely herself.

Explains one woman, "I was in love for the first time. It was spring. It was a beautiful time. All I could think about was getting out of work to be with my lover. But could I say as much in the secretarial pool where everyone else was chasing the young male ad execs? No. I bought flowers for my lover on my lunch hour and would explain to the women that they were for my mother, for my grandmother, or for some friend in the hospital. I could have invented a male lover, but then they would just ask more questions and I'd have to do more lying. The flowers were always for someone, but never for my lover.

"Then I would go home, and there she was. It was as if a whole day of deadness and phoniness had to be made up for that night and on weekends. At home was my life. The rest was just an uncomfortable, often painful routine."

When nothing in the outside world has offered anything so intensely life-enhancing as the ardency of the first love relationship, the relationship itself carries a heavy burden—not only its own sustenance, but the sustenance of the partners' self-identities. A woman's first lesbian love affair may take on the critical quality of a life-or-death situation. As a result, many normally inconsequential events are given great meaning in the relationship. Explains Julie of her first lesbian love affair, "Our love was an all or nothing thing for me. Anything that threatened it, even the smallest thing, became a life-or-death issue, something I had to fight as if I were fighting for life itself. If Mimi woke up grouchy, I wondered what was wrong, asked myself if our relationship was somehow going bad. If our sex wasn't always perfect I would immediately begin to wonder how long our relationship would last. I was always reading stupid little signs for anything that might mean the relationship was going to end."

Adding to the pressure of the first affair, and perhaps unrealized by the lesbian at the time, is the fact that she may have plunged headlong into a relationship totally unsuited for her. Those questions that might enter a heterosexual woman's mind before she moves in with her first lover—or certainly her parents' minds if she is still under their influence—are not generally asked by the lesbian racing seventy miles per hour into the first in-love experience of her life. The heterosexual woman, through her future-husband-referent adolescent training, may have learned to seek answers to questions such as these: Will we be compatible? Are our values similar? Will this relationship interfere with my own future life plans? Will it get in the way of my experiences with other potential mates? Is it just an emotional or sexual fling, or is it really serious and does it have what it takes to last? These are not important questions for the lesbian who has not been acculturated through the heterosexual lessons of adolescence. Spouse-referent training geared to a male spouse had no applicability to her situation. So she may, and often does, race into her first experience of ardent, all-encompassing love without such heterosexual notions as waiting, experimenting, proceeding with caution.

Comments by lesbians about their first love affairs are typical:

"We spent the night together talking and the next night we spent in bed. By the end of the morning we knew we were in love and began planning who was going to move in with whom."

"We had a beer, she asked me to her house, we made love. Suddenly, I knew she was the woman I always wanted and I was passionately in love with her. Two weeks later we were living together."

"I knew I was attracted to her. The feeling seemed mutual. We spent a week together and knew that we wanted to spend the rest of our lives together."

Such swift selection during a lesbian's first love affair should not be ascribed to what may at first seem obvious: "Sure," commented one male cynic to this writer, "they hit the sack and that was it. Sexual deprivation will do it every time." Most lesbians have had a great many more sexual partners, both male and female, than they have had love affairs, as both the Fleener and the Bell and Weinberg studies confirm. Explains Julie, "My God, I was *in love* for the first time in my life. All that was important was that single fact. We were in love. Hell, I didn't think about all those things like 'Is she right for me?', all of that. It just never entered my mind."

Also putting pressure on the lesbian's first love affair is the fact that society offers no support for it. The heterosexual woman can explain to her workmates that she is having a madly passionate affair with some man and receive a certain amount of social approval. She may become engaged, engendering even more approval. She may marry, gaining the approval not only of her church, if she is religious, but of the state as well. She may even live with a man without benefit of marriage and find, in many circles, a high degree of approval. For the lesbian there is none of this unless she is fortunate enough to have found nurturing contacts within the extended family network of America's lesbian underground.

Such first lesbian relationships, which are built on little more than the opportunity of sharing with another person the joys of being in love—yet without guidelines, role models, or social approval—and which tend to involve a large part of the lesbian's self-identity, generally don't last long.

Reports one woman about some of the things that crippled her first love relationship with another woman: "Everything was supposed to come from our relationship. We didn't see friends, we didn't see our families. We clung together as if we were on some kind of sinking life raft. I began to drown. The demands of the relationship were more than I could bear."

First affairs between lesbians tend to last between one and three years. A very small number of them extend for decades.[3]


## ON THE ROAD TO DISSOLUTION

The lesbian's own lack of experience in forming intimate partnerships and stable relationships leads her too often to the adolescent presumption that "in love" means love forever. Says one woman, "What a big surprise that was. I bought into the whole Madison Avenue romantic trip. You're in love, all your problems will vanish, and you'll live happily every after. What a crock *that* turned out to be."

Isolation from other lesbians in America's lesbian underground may have aided the development of this romantic notion of love; in their first relationships few lesbians have access to a practical experience of what to expect in the ebbs and flows of an intimate lesbian relationship. The division between the public subculture and the more experienced one in hiding can thus bar a woman from the practical knowledge she might need to manage a long-term relationship.

Says Donna, with contacts only in the public subculture, "I asked a few friends what to do when things began to get rough in our relationship. They just sympathized a lot and agreed with me that if the passion wasn't there any more, then that was it. I didn't think about it at the time, but none of the women I talked to had ever had relationships that had lasted much longer than mine and Cheryl's—not exactly the most qualified people to go to for advice!

"I guess if we had been straight we would have gone to our parents, to a minister, or to some kind of marriage counseling or something to talk over our problems before deciding it was over. But we instinctively knew better than to go to any straight agency and there weren't any gay ones around." (Most metropolitan areas now have, if not full-fledged gay counseling services, referral services to gay counselors in both public agencies and private practice. These counselors report a land-office business working with couples in relationship crises and with women whose relationships have just ended.)

Sandy and her partner were more fortunate: "When we first got together we had a couple of good friends who'd been together for eleven years. Eleven years seemed like forever to us. We became very close to them and they sort of adopted us and held our hands when things got going rough in our relationship. It was good just seeing that another couple could fight, argue, be bored once in a while, go through asexual times, sometimes feel no passion for each other at all, and still enjoy their lives together, knowing that their relationship had and always would have its ups and downs. They helped us a lot. But when we talked to our other friends, it seemed like we were the only ones who knew anybody who'd been together for more than two years."

The lack of long-term relationship role models affects the lesbian's experience in her early relationships. She sails into them blindly and then flounders. It is not that long-term relationships don't exist, but long-term couples seem most often to be a part of that subculture in hiding, a difficult one for the neoadolescent lesbian to enter.

All of these factors-the intensity of relationships, the lack of mainstream supports for them, the unrealistic expectations of the neoadolescent, and the lack of role-models—combine to ensure that the ending of the lesbian's first relationship not only comes sooner than it might have in other circumstances, but that it is an emotionally stormy one.


## A NEW MYTHOLOGY?

Perhaps also contributing to the early demise of many lesbian relationships is a new scientific mythology created by a bias in many researchers' studies of the duration of lesbian relationships. These would have us believe that the vast majority of lesbian relationships last no longer than five years. It is interesting to examine the possible biases that are contributing to this conclusion.

One Los Angeles lesbian counselor has suggested that no lesbian becomes mature until she is thirty-five years old. Her suggestion is not a specious one. Lesbians do, of necessity, proceed through a neoadolescent period lasting several years. This is no surprise; the heterosexual youth spends about a decade in her adolescent acculturation into the mainstream. The lesbian, however, must acculturate herself both as an alien in a straight society, and as a member of an extended, but minority tribe. Researchers to date have done lesbians a great disfavor by not taking this factor into account in their studies.

This bias is most glaringly reflected when data are presented regarding relationship duration. There appear to be two distinct elements in this bias. The first of these is that when lesbian populations are questioned about their relationships, all relationships are lumped into one category—those that are part of her neoadolescence as well as those following her acculturation as a lesbian. This type of questioning is comparable to asking a heterosexual population about the duration of their relationships including everything from junior high and high school sexual experiments to college flings and, finally, marriages.It would be little surprise if a heterosexual population, faced with this type of questioning, would generate data supporting the thesis that the average heterosexual relationship lasts only three to five years and is therefore unstable. The second element of bias in studies of lesbian relationships is the apparent failure of researchers to realize that lesbian relationships, like heterosexual ones, can last twenty, forty, fifty years—even a lifetime. This failure is illustrated in questions on relationship length that give a vague outside choice of "five years or longer."

The results of such surveys, needless to say, tend to indicate that lesbians have series of relationships averaging three to five years throughout their lives. Such biases and the results they produce lead many people, including lesbians themselves as well as their parents, to the conclusion that "lesbian relationships are unstable."

If survey responses are viewed from a different perspective, one that acknowledges that the lesbian must spend a period of neoadolescence before finding herself—a period that may extend a decade or so from the first time she recognizes herself as gay—the facts provide a different picture, one that substantiates the observations of informed lesbians on their subculture.

The Fleener report of relationship duration, like the Bell and Weinberg report, tends to support the mainstream thesis. As Bell and Weinberg blandly put it: "For a little more than one-tenth of the respondents, the current affair was of more than five years' duration."[4] However, when Fleener's survey responses were analyzed closely, correlated with age, and examined with a consideration for the number of years between the date the subject responded to the questionnaire and the date of her *first* (neoadolescent) lesbian relationship, the picture is remarkably different.

Fleener's questionnaire gave only one option to the long-term relationship experience: "five or more years." Even this, on examination of the original survey responses in view of the considerations described above, is enough to indicate a trend, especially among those over thirty:

Of lesbians age twenty-one to twenty-five, 14 percent responded that their longest relationship had exceeded five years.

Of lesbians age twenty-six to thirty, 10 percent responded that their longest relationship had exceeded five years.

Of lesbians age thirty-one to thirty-five, 26 percent responded that their longest relationships had exceeded five years.

Of those age thirty-six to forty, the percent of women with relationships in excess of five years rose to 66 percent.

Of those age forty-one to fifty (excluding one who had just had her first lesbian experience within the past year), 80 percent reported relationships in excess of five years.

Additionally, some of the respondents, apparently angered at the "five years of more" limitation, made a point of commenting that their current relationships had lasted thirteen to fifteen years.

There, of course, might be many explanations for the above trend aside from the neoadolescence postulated here. It would, however, be incalculably valuable if future researchers were not only to explore this thesis, but if those who drew up questionnaires for such research surveys allowed for relationship durations beyond "five or more" years. It would be a sad commentary on the status of contemporary research if future studies of lesbian relationships were to end in the creation of the kind of mythology about lesbianism authored by Lucian of Samosata so many centuries ago—a mythology that may eventually be incorporated, as was Samosata's, into the lesbian's self-perception.


## DISSOLUTION

If there are inadequate facts about the duration of lesbian relationships and few role models available for managing a lesbian relationship, there are even fewer for the dissolution of lesbian relationships. All that separates a lesbian from the end of her relationship is the front door. Bound by no marriage certificate, governed by no laws, she may just close the door behind her, never to return. This, however, is not the way most relationships seem to end.

Few first relationships are ended by mutual decision, an observation that Bell and Weinberg's findings substantiate. In 82 percent of the cases studied, the relationship was ended by one of the partners. The most frequently cited reason for the breakup was a "romantic involvement with someone else." Viv, a woman who's been around long enough to watch many relationships come and go, comments, "The problem was there before any so-called 'romantic involvement.' You really don't go around looking for [other involvements] unless you started out with the wrong person, or there's a problem between the two of you that should have been worked out long, long before there was any reason for any looking around." Viv's experience also explains the second most frequently cited reason for the ending of the first relationship—that it was "unsatisfying," a selection chosen by 24 percent. The feeling that the relationship was "too weak," was cited by 11 percent of the respondents as the reason for termination.[5]

After such high expectations at the beginning of a first lesbian relationship, one partner, especially the one who has found a new "romantic involvement," may feel a great deal of guilt over the ending of the affair. In any case, both she and her former lover are trapped in the same underground. Lesbian institutions are few and friendship circles tend to overlap. The lesbian seeking companionship is likely, sooner or later, to run into a former partner. Also, when ending a relationship, she may fear losing her ties to that part of the underground that her former partner had made available to her.

These circumstances tend to combine to ensure that among many lesbian partners, some agreement is eventually reached that includes retention of friendship bonds between the two.

Explains one woman, "I was the one who initiated the breakup. There was no one really to blame but me; I just fell in love with another woman and wanted to be with her continually. There was absolutely nothing wrong with the relationship I was ending except that it lacked passion. Jeanette continually asked me what had gone wrong, why I was leaving. I didn't have any answer. I felt tremendously guilt-ridden. When I finally had enough guts to leave, I left virtually everything I owned with her. I was much too down on myself to hassle who was going to get the frying pan and who was going to get the rocking chair. I just let Jeanette have it all.

"After I left, we continued to see each other. She kept demanding to see me, playing on my guilt. But I wanted to reassure her of my caring for her, wanted to make sure we at least kept a friendship out of the experience. It took about a year, lunch or dinner once a week, and her finding another lover of her own, before the emotionality of the parting got out of the way of our relationship. Now we are very good friends."

Joni, whose former lover had abandoned her for a new romance after twelve years together, comments, "I know she ran shit all over me during our twelve years together. But hell, I still cared for her. When she called up after we split up and wanted help, I gave it to her, I tried to help her."

The phenomenon of pulling good friendships out of old love affairs is so frequent in the lesbian subculture that it has drawn much comment. No observer of this phenomenon could have been more amazed than Aimee, a woman whose primary relationship experiences prior to meeting Joni had been heterosexual. Commented Aimee, "I just couldn't understand this. The old lover, who treated her like a piece of shit, calls, and Joni goes running. It was as if I had just been married and was telling my husband that I had to go help out an old boyfriend, or he had to go be with his ex-wife, even though they didn't have kids. I was absolutely shocked by it!"

## ALTERNATE ENDINGS

The continued friendship between two ex-lovers may come to involve the new partner in a kind of emotional threesome. In an intriguing variation on the attempt to maintain friendship between women who have decided to part ways, some lesbians attempt to bring the new romantic involvement into their partnered relationship in an intimate threesome.

Explains Kay, "We'd been living together for three years and I became interested in another woman. I felt guilty. At different times my partner would threaten suicide or swear that she would seduce my new lover. It was quite brutal on all of us until the three of us got together and talked about it and decided to work things out as humanely as we possibly knew how. We decided to live together.

"We did, the three of us, for about six months, trying to work it out. It was a very emotionally draining time. We spent hours each day talking. They became marathon sessions. We slept together—which finally ended any sexual jealousy if there ever really was any—and found out that my old lover wasn't as turned on as she thought to my new partner. But that didn't end the emotional hassles. Finally after about six months of this, we'd all had it. We were all totally emotionally drained and decided to go our separate ways. My new lover and I stayed together and the old lover decided to move on.

"I wouldn't necessarily recommend this as a parting ritual, but the three of us all remain good friends. And I value friends very highly. They are hard to find."

As yet unresearched, this kind of threesome—intimate liaisons preliminary to the ending of one coupled relationship to begin a new one, appear to be more frequent than many would suspect. A careful scrutiny of the Fleener survey data seems to indicate that, for lesbians under forty, slightly less than 8 percent of lesbian relationships end via the threesome route.[6]


## FORCED DISSOLUTION

Not all lesbian relationships end through a real decision by either party. Many are simply forced apart by outsiders. Such intrusions account for the 6 percent of Bell and Weinberg's respondents who cited "forced apart by others" as the reason for the end of their first affair.[7] Such forced endings, often brought about by a parent or other authority figure (such as a military authority which might discharge one of the lesbian partners without ever learning of the other), are probably the most devastating ones for the lesbian. It is in such breakups that we see the heinous failure of the law to provide some degree of protection for lesbian couples.

Recalls Liza of her first lesbian relationship, "We'd been together a very rough eight years. Her family was continually harping at her to leave me. They finally succeeded. They got to her head with that Catholic religion and bribed her off with the offer of a new house. We had a house. We had put it in her name for tax advantages since she had the higher income. But we shared the mortgage expense equally. We had both come to consider it to be *our* house.

"But apparently as the package deal, I and my four kids—who by then had come to love her—had to go. Just leave the house we'd both invested so many years, hours, and dollars in. It was in her name. There was nothing in the end I could do but leave." Since leaving, Liza has never heard from, nor about, her former lover.

Pat Bond recalls the effects of forced separations during her post V-J Day military experience. "They sent 500 women home from Tokyo, the whole company. One woman, 20 years old by God, killed herself. They had said to her, 'We're going to give you a dishonorable discharge if you don't give us the names of 10 of your friends . . . She'd had an affair with her roommate and she was interested in a guy—she just didn't know where she was. We were all persecuted for whatever our sexuality was at that age. Who knows: maybe some of us came home and were never gay again. When you're trapped in a situation like that, at that age, where does your sexuality go? . . . Most of the women I know that were in the Army, in that era or 10 years later, got dishonorables. Any number of them never had an orgasm until they were in their 40's. It's really threatening to your sexuality to be terrified at that age. To be told that what you are is evil, rotten, no good, is terrifying."[8]

Even under the best of circumstances, though, not all lesbian relationship terminations will result in friendship. As in heterosexual relationships, more than a few end brutally—as the Bell and Weinberg data on suicide attempts and blackmail attempts indicate.[9]

Whichever way the lesbian's first relationship ends, she has completed her rights of passage and has matured through a neoadolescent experience. She is a bit more prepared for what the future may bring, and, perhaps, a bit more cautious in her selection of partners and in her expectations. She may even determine that the style of her first relationship was inappropriate for her and go on to experiment with new relationship styles.

## ALTERNATE RELATIONSHIP STYLES

It is not uncommon, especially in the larger cities, for the lesbian who has just concluded an intense relationship to enter either a period of celibacy or a period of promiscuity, rather than immediately jumping into another committed relationship. Both, perhaps, stem from the fear of entering a new relationship. Fourteen percent of the Bell and Weinberg sample reported experiencing fear of beginning a new relationship as a result of the termination of their first affair.[10]

Explains one woman, determined to have a period of celibacy, "The end of that relationship just wiped me out. I just don't want to get involved again for awhile. I really discovered that I needed space to get to where I was at. The whole thing left me with a lot of questions about who I was and what I would want or need or be able to give to a relationship. I'm finding that through celibacy I'm able to stay more in tune with myself, just really get in touch with some of the answers to those questions."

Another woman comments on her experience, "That relationship burned me out. For several months I just couldn't face another woman, I had put so much of myself into that relationship. But then, I guess, you forget some of that pain and go on with your life. One thing I desperately wanted at that time was to be with other women. But I didn't want to make any promises or get involved seriously. I just wanted pleasure and enjoyment. I finally figured I deserved it so I went out and found women—just for that moment, or night, or few days of intimacy and warmth. Just for our mutual pleasure. No ties, no bonds, no promises. I don't know if I'm going to get more involved than that at this point, but that's where I'm at now—out on the town to have fun."

And, even though lifelong marriages are less and less common in the heterosexual mainstream, a large number of lesbians continue to pursue the long-term relationship ideal, many seeking it soon after the dissolution of their first relationship. Despite this pursuit, the goal seems elusive for many lesbians who move from one short-term monogamous relationship to another, through two, three, or more in a kind of serial monogamy.

Although some lesbians, like many heterosexuals, frown on serial monogamy, others, in increasing numbers, are learning to value it as a viable lifestyle which offers its own special compensations.

One homosexual institution that has accepted the reality of serial monogamy is the Universal Fellowship of Metropolitan Community Churches (commonly referred to as MCC). In its Holy Union services, originally created as an alternative to the marriage blessings that heterosexually oriented churches bestow on couples, the vows of faithfulness are exchanged to endure "as long as love shall last."

"And why not?" asks one lesbian who recently completed such a Holy Union. "The unique thing about a relationship is shared love. Why force people to stay together if that is no longer there?"

The ritualization of relationships contracted for "as long as love shall last" removes one burden from the lesbian relationship—the assumption, taken from the heterosexual mainstream, that love relationships, no matter how ill-conceived or ill-matched the partners, must be kept together until one or the other of the partners dies. It also accepts the reality that, for many couples, love perhaps does not last as long as life. Consequently, as at least one partner of such a Holy Union observes, "You don't have to be continually looking at everything as a threat to your relationship. You have more time and energy to spend enjoying the love you share, to explore its good points instead of always worrying about what's wrong with it. And if it ends, for one reason or another, you don't have to blame yourself and be full of guilt about breaking some 'till-death-do-us-part' promise."

Serial monogamy seems to suit some lesbians quite well. Comments one woman, now forty-nine years old, "Much of my life energy goes into my work. It always has. My identity comes from my being and the way I express it in my work, not through some other person's love. But who wants to live without love, without the passions and joys of love? And who wants to live through the hell of continually trying to 'keep our relationship together' when obviouly it's not going anywhere?

"I've had about ten love affairs. Some lasted a few months, some lasted a few years. I've enjoyed and treasured all of them.

"They were monogamous simply because when you're in love you aren't looking around for other sexual partners. So, I guess you could call it serial monogamy. Whatever you call it, it adds a lot of vitality to my life and work."

Other women learn that the presumption "in love, therefore we must live together" is not realistic for them. Many live singly, as do slightly more than a quarter of the Bell and Weinberg sample of women with partners.[11]

Explains one such single, but coupled, woman, "About the only criticism I can find is that it costs more. The best parts of living separately are that you have a greater chance to maintain and develop your own individuality. And you have time alone. I personally need a lot of time alone, time when I am not being distracted by another person's presence. It is a kind of time of spiritual rest for me.

"Then, of course, by living singly, you avoid all the hassles and compromises on things that might seem stupid but are really an engrained part of your life, almost part of your identity—how you furnish and keep up your house, when to water the violets, that kind of thing.

"Both of us appreciate the privacy we have, yet we enjoy each other and spend time together as often as we can."

The lesbian who has survived her rights of passage has a vast horizon of relationship styles open to her. She has passed through a neoadolescence and is more able to determine which style is best for her, and when. Her expectations, once so inflated, are now more realistic. She knows what's in store for her. She may know some of the pitfalls to avoid. She has met and dealt with other lesbians on many levels, from public arenas to the most intimate spaces. She has become a part of the lesbian subculture. But most important, she knows herself and her own emotional capacities far better than she did before she entered her first relationship.

The neoadolescent lesbian has matured.

# PART TWO

## The Lesbian Couple in a Heterosexual World

While many lesbians have lifestyles based on celibacy, singleness, serial monogamy, or, more recently, communality, most tend to pursue the ideal of a long-term, committed, and usually monogamous relationship. About one quarter of Bell and Weinberg's lesbians reported that a permanent living arrangement with a lesbian partner was "the most important thing in life." About one-third rated it as "very important." Only about 14 percent rated such permanency with partners as "not important at all." The remainder commented either that such relationships were "nice, but not important," or "somewhat important."[1]

The pursuit of a long-term coupled relationship is not an easy one for the lesbian. Many things stand in her way, most notably the assumptions, laws, customs, demands, and rituals predominant in a heterosexual society. It is against these that the lesbian couple must struggle in its quest for stability.

Frequently, the couple's first response to the overwhelming pressures from the heterosexual mainstream is to maintain the privacy of the relationship, forging as much stability as is possible "in the closet." This situation, however, brings pressures to the relationship that can cripple the very stability the lesbian couple seeks. Breaking free of the closet can be an equally precarious proposition for the committed couple; many relationships have foundered when one of the partners has taken a brave first step (or has been forced, by outsiders), out of the closet, much to the horror of the other, who still clings to the closet situation out of fear of the unknown. In contrast, to

83

those couples who survive it, breaking free from the closet is one of the most exhilarating and growth-producing events of their lives, both for the couples and for the individuals.

Closeted or not, the lesbian couple must somehow manage the demands made upon them by their respective families. Most parents have never anticipated their daughter bringing home a new "daughter-in-law" for them to meet, and lesbians are well aware of this. To the committed couple, the problem of parents and families can be another nightmare that threatens the stability of their relationship; if an accommodation can be made, however, being considered a part of a biological family unit may enhance the lesbian relationship.

Lesbian couples who have children face some of the most difficult situations. When an ex-husband or other interested party tries to separate the lesbian family, the full force of the patriarchal hetero-sexual presumption about how children should be raised and what constitutes a family is thrust upon the biological mother, her lesbian partner, and their children, revealing its seemingly innate savagery. By contrast, life in a lesbian family untroubled by challenges from outsiders is not that much different from life in a heterosexual family, and successfully raises questions about the types of child rearing and family life best for American children.

Heterosexual law is biased not only against the lesbian family, but against the lesbian couple itself and can pose serious problems for the long-term couple. Heterosexual law, however, has its loopholes, and lesbians—much like corporations—have found them, developing not only some protection for themselves, but new concepts of relationship practice that may go far toward ensuring the stability that not only lesbians, but heterosexuals also, seek. In some ways the most difficult, and in others, the most simple aspect of the lesbian couple's search for stability is the freedom available to both partners to develop their relationship in any manner they choose. Having been rejected by the heterosexual mainstream, they reject in turn many of its presumptions about committed relationships in every area from sex to housekeeping.

It is here we find the results of the lesbian couple's successful struggle for stability against the patriarchal heterosexual imperative—in its egalitarian and role-free relationships, a model many Americans seek, but few are privileged to find.

# 6

# The Closeted Couple

When I was at the University of Kansas my mother discovered one of my letters or something and concluded that I was having an affair with my "best friend." She went to the university dean and I was called in for warning number one and last: if I was seen with Anne again, I would be kicked out of school. So would she.

That didn't stop us, naturally. We were in love. But it made us go to great lengths to keep people from learning that we were still seeing each other. If, for example, we were driving in the car together and one of us saw someone we thought we recognized, whoever was the passenger would hide down on the floorboard until the driver gave the all clear.

Once I was sure I nearly killed her. Some woman had come to my dorm room. Anne was there of course, so I told her to hide in the closet while I got rid of this other woman. Well, this woman had decided that this was the night she was going to pour out all her problems to me. She was crying, hysterical, and it didn't seem as if she would ever stop. At that point I was afraid to kick her out because I thought that would be too obvious, that she'd suspect something.

So Anne stayed in the closet while I listened to this tale of woe for about six hours before the woman finally left. I was just lucky Anne didn't suffocate in that damned closet—*Anne's lover*

The story told by Anne's lover, though true, is also a metaphor of the experience of lesbian couples in the closet. Closets are the places we hide the things we don't want other people to see when they come to visit. What lesbians are trying to hide from view is their love of other women. But in addition to merely hiding this element of their lives from visitors, lesbians themselves are visitors in a heterosexual world and the closet is a permanent part of their public mufti.

## AS SOCIETY DEMANDS

The closeted lesbian is doing what society wants her to do: remain invisible, blend in, cause no strains in a patriarchal framework that supports a dying socioeconomic system. She abides by society's rules from sheer terror, a terror that is partly rational, partly irrational. In most places, with the exception of a handful of cities, it is legal to discriminate against lesbians, whether single or coupled. Discrimination in employment is legal, discrimination in housing is legal, discrimination in public services and accommodations is legal. Discrimination in all areas of economic and social life is absolutely legal and the lesbian has little protection against it because the courts, to date, hold that her basic human rights are moral, and not legal, issues. This conflict will eventually have to be resolved either in the U.S. Congress or the Supreme Court. To date, Congress has been immobile, with no more than 10 percent of its members willing to cosponsor gay civil rights legislation, and with a majority willing to vote against gay rights. The Supreme Court has also been intransigent, shying away from hearing gay-related cases brought before it. Such lower-court decisions are often based on the argument that the issue of homosexuality is a moral one and therefore within the discretion of the laws of individual states.

In addition to the technical legality of such discrimination, many states have enacted laws that clearly allow discrimination to occur. Were the laws of the states thoroughly enforced, lesbians and male homosexuals in nearly forty states would be in prison for violating laws against ''unnatural'' sex acts (as would be a lot of heterosexual men and women).

Were the laws regarding the licensing of trades and professions enforced—laws that require that candidates for licensing be of good moral character—American lesbians would be unable to work in most professions and most public trust jobs. Were a lesbian to be open about her relationships she could not serve her country in the armed forces. Neither could she be (at least as of 1973, apparently the last time a compilation of such morality laws was made): a limburger cheese maker in Wisconsin, an astrologer in Georgia, a cemetery salesman in Mississippi and Kentucky, a cotton classer in Alabama, a building contractor in Minnesota, an exterminator in Florida, a lightning rod salesman in Massachusetts and New Jersey, nor a fortune teller in

South Dakota, Minnesota, or Oregon.[1]

Nor do such laws preclude the possibility that new discriminatory laws will be passed. Oklahoma, in a kind of tribute to Anita Bryant, passed legislation banning homosexuals from the teaching profession. And in California, similar legislation was introduced by state senator John Briggs who tried, by referendum, not only to ban gay teachers, but to ban anyone who spoke in favour of gay rights.

Such laws are seldom enforced. Lesbians assure that they are not remaining in the closet.

## HOW LARGE A CLOSET?

Most American lesbians live in the closet to one degree or another. Bell and Weinberg's statistics on closetedness are revealing. They are representative of the open segment of the lesbian underground in the San Francisco Bay Area, where there is more tolerance of lesbians and male homosexuals than in most parts of the country. These findings could easily be doubled or tripled to reflect other, less tolerant, parts of the country.

The researchers found: 49 percent of the lesbian sample had apparently not discussed their affectional preference with their mothers; 62 percent had not discussed it with their fathers; 45 percent had not discussed it with a *single* coworker; and 16 percent had not discussed it with a *single* heterosexual friend.[2]

The fear that one's affectional preference might affect one's job is not an illusion. Fourteen percent of Bell and Weinberg's lesbians said that their homosexuality had a negative effect on their careers; 5 percent of the total sample reported that they had lost or almost lost their jobs on account of it. Twenty-one percent of the total sample, meanwhile, reported having been threatened with exposure for money, other material benefit, or favor.[3]

Statistics are only partially revealing, however.

Society tells the lesbian that she may have a job, rent an apartment, use the subway or the library and other public facilities, be treated like any other female, if she keeps her so-called private life private. "We don't care," antigay advocates claim, "what they do in their bedrooms. We just don't want them to flaunt it."

But what is it that makes a private life public?

In one small Oregon town a high school girl who had dropped by her popular teacher's home for a surprise visit, noticed that there was only one bedroom in the house and that the teacher lived with another woman. The girl told her mother. The lesbian's private life became public knowledge. After a school board hearing the teacher was fired from her job, never to regain it, despite court tests that went all the way to the appeals court level.

Another woman was in an auto wreck in a small Alabama town. The police, looking through her wallet for identification, found a photo of her lover, signed on the back with a scribbled note of romantic tenderness. This woman not only lost her job as the town's librarian, she was run out of the county.

A mother happened on a love poem in her daughter's dresser. The poem, obviously written to another woman, was enough evidence for the mother to drag her daughter to a psychiatrist who recommended institutionalization and aversion therapy.

A neighbor-child, peeking through a window, saw two women in an embrace and told his mother. The women were evicted from their apartment with no legal recourse.

A curious mail carrier noticed that a woman on his route, in fact the head of a local public hospital, received a lesbian newsletter. It was not long before the gossip spread and the woman was drummed out of her job.

The question for the lesbian couple seeking to maintain its privacy—and also for those who would have the couple do so—is, to what extremes must the couple go in this effort?

Information leading to suspicion of a woman's affectional preference is certainly available to anyone who wants it badly enough. Is a certain lesbian among the 350,000 names of homosexuals kept by the CIA? Is she mentioned among the FBI's Cointelpro files for perhaps subscribing to a lesbian publication as a school research project? Is she a registered voter living in the same household as another female registered voter with a different last name? Such voter lists can, and have been, compared—as one closeted gay couple in Philadelphia found out when they received a mail solicitation for a homosexual magazine in 1977. Do two females with different last names have registered motor vehicles at the same address? Such lists can also be generated. Has a woman contributed to a gay person's election campaign and had to register her name, address, and occupation? In such a case she may receive volumes of unsolicited prohomosexual mail that may turn out to be embarrassing for her.

## MAINTAINING A FAÇADE

The incidents above are rare, but real; real enough to incite fear among some lesbians; real enough to ensure that most lesbians will probably continue their lives in the closet. But there is no single closet. Degrees of terror and psychic self-imprisonment vary. There are, however, some common threads among many closet lesbians' experiences. The first of these is that they mention their female lovers to as few people as possible. The second is that they try to conceal their relationships from fellow employees and bosses by a number of ruses. Explains one woman, "I got by for years with made-up boyfriends. I had to have something to tell the women I worked with. Finally, after they kept pressing to meet this fabulous guy, I invented a fiancé in the war in Vietnam to keep them off my back. On the day I split up with my lover I couldn't hide my heartbreak from my coworkers. I told them my fiancé had been killed in the war. That got me by for about a year. Then I quit and moved on to another job."

Explains another woman, "Sometimes it is just easier to give in to peer pressure at work. Finally, I began dating one of the men from work. Once or twice a week we would go out together. It was a good façade for the women at the office and especially for my boss who had his own eyes on me anyway, but it caused hell for my relationship. The guy would come over to our place to pick me up. My lover posed as my roommate and smilingly sent me off. Then she cried until I got home. Then we fought. But we could see no other way to get by."

Few women are willing to discuss their experiences of closet life. It is a traumatic one and often recalled only with great pain. One couple, however, was willing to discuss its life in a kind of ultra closet in which they hid for over a decade. So great was their degree of hiding that they went, as many lesbians in hiding do, to a kind of extreme far beyond what is called for to pass as a pair of heterosexual roommates. Heterosexual women are allowed a degree of affection and closeness in public that these women were afraid to take. They are both career school teachers, now teaching public school in what many consider to be a very liberal East Coast school district.

Explains Louise: "We were extremely careful to keep our secret hidden. You could never know what tiny thing would reveal you and ruin your career. Wherever we lived, we always made sure we had two bedrooms. When we had visitors, we made a run through the house to make sure there were no compromising things left out and to make sure that both bedrooms looked like they were in use. In one house we lived in, we even installed a timer for the lights in the unused bedroom so our neighbors, should they look, would see that two bedrooms appeared to be in use.

"We never did the shopping together. We always did our laundry separately. We rarely left the house together, all because we were afraid some neighbor might notice something strange about us.

"On holidays we each went off to our own families. They didn't know about us. I don't think we ever have spent a single holiday together.

"In school, and this was the worst part of it, we taught what we were told to teach. We dared not stand up for our own people. When homosexuality came up—this is when it was supposed to be a severe illness—we taught that it was a severe illness. Once in a while the other teachers would crack some joke or another about someone they thought was a lesbian. And I remember laughing at these jokes with them, even though it tore at my heart.

"Once, and this is something I will never be able to forgive myself for, one of the teachers in my school was being too obvious as a lesbian. Everyone knew about her, she was that obvious. And I really convinced myself that I was doing the rest of us a favor (I knew there were other lesbians on the staff) by filing a report on her with the principal. She was fired. I wish I could find her now, just to apologize to her.

"When we were in company together, which we made as rare an occurrence as possible, we always were careful to act cool to each other, as if we didn't really even like each other. We were always afraid we would give ourselves away by a glance that was too friendly, too intimate. We never talked to anyone about each other, not even about the most casual things. In public we made it seem as if we didn't even have a roommate, which came as a surprise to the few people who did visit us. At school we made up stories about the guys we were dating. If we'd had a fight the night before, when we got to school and the other teachers asked us what was wrong, we told some story about fighting with our boyfriends, or breaking up, or just anything to satisfy their curiosity without giving each other's secret away.

"We became very accomplished liars. Every day we lived we lived in fear and we lived a lie. It became a way of life for us. It even got so that we didn't notice it so much after the first couple of years, except during one crisis or another.

"I can never forgive myself for that time when Judy had to go to the hospital for a gall bladder operation. I worried about her tremendously, yet we were both afraid for me to come to the hospital to visit her, afraid I would show too much concern, that she would show too much affection, afraid that someone would notice. So she went through the surgery with no one. I visited her once—to check her out of the hospital and drive her home.

"It became a habit. We lived in two worlds. The straight world and our own, when we were home alone, the shades pulled down, and certain that no one could see us.

"Over the years I think it wore on us. All of our human feelings were loaded into those few hours when we could be ourselves. The rest we repressed. I think even some of the feelings for each other got repressed too."

When a couple is closeted, there is very little outlet for the rage and frustration of lives they know to be half-truths or lies. These emotions take their toll, either on the individual psyche or on the nearest available target—the lover.

Louise started drinking every afternoon as soon as she got home from school. The drinking got heavier and heavier, and eventually she became violent when drunk. Judy stopped wanting to be with her and moved into the second bedroom.

"The lie we lived during the day finally came home with us in the afternoon," Judy said. "There was no intimacy left between us."

In 1975, after a decade of this life together, two gay male acquaintances asked the couple if they were gay. "We said yes," Judy explained. "It was the first time in our lives we had ever told anyone. It was the first time we even used the word *lesbian* in reference to ourselves."

91

They began their long journey out of the closet, and Louise out of her drinking problem. Today, by most people's standards, they are still closeted, but they have at least come out to each other and a few gay friends. They are planning, next year, to spend their first Christmas together.

## OTHER TOLLS

Unknown thousands of lesbians are living out their lives in confines very similar to Louise's and Judy's. Others have made different adaptations, each at a different cost.

Some women are unwilling or unable to invest so heavily in lies, yet still accept the fact that they must live with a degree of closetedness. A few of these have simply decided to live separately, visiting each other nightly, but giving the public appearance of being single women.

A few have undertaken marriages of convenience with gay men, feeling that the abbreviation "Mrs." is sufficient to cover anyone's suspicions about their lives.

Others have simply lowered their economic and career expectations in order to live less closeted lives. Says one such woman, "I work in a factory. No one there gives a damn what I am, who I am, or who I'm seeing. I could just as well be another machine." This woman has a master's degree in linguistics. Additionally, she is fluent in eight languages including two Chinese dialects. She continues, "I could probably get a job fairly easily, at least as a translator. I could live in a nicer section of town. I could buy a lot more consumer items, a nicer car, all of that. But I gave it a lot of thought. I thought about the kind of life I would be living, a life in the closet. A life of continual fear. I decided not to do it. Here at the factory I can be pretty open. I even got my lover a job on the same shift.

"We don't go out of our way to tell anyone, but we don't have much to hide either. Who cares about a factory worker? So they fire us. We can get another job.

"Anyway," she concluded in the gallows humor common to many lesbians, "the way things are going I think factory workers are making more money these days than linguists."

In some situations the toll is a life without love. Explains a woman holding a high appointive post in the federal government, "I live alone. I never go to any of the gay bars—I don't want to be seen. They just think I'm a career-driven bitch and that's how I get by. I have no relationships. I have no lovers. I have no real friends. That's the price of the job and the price of my career if I want to continue in it. Who knows, maybe I am a career-driven bitch?"

Like Louise and Judy, many female couples with intimate partnerships do not use the word *lesbian* in reference to themselves. These are truly women in hiding—hiding not only from a homophobic society, but from each other as well. Similarly, it would appear that there are perhaps an even greater number of lesbian couples who retreat further into hiding from themselves. Among these are women who live together as couples, have formed primary emotional relationships with their partners, are committed to their relationships, and are even affectionate with each other, but who pay one of the closet's maximum tolls—not only do they not use the word *lesbian* to describe their relationship, they also abstain from sexual relations with each other. It was, not surprisingly, impossible to locate any such women for an interview for a book about lesbian life today, but the revelations of two interview subjects do bear on this issue.

One woman describes several years she spent in a convent before she realized she was a lesbian and decided to leave: "I think that subconsciously I decided to become a nun because I wanted to be with women. I didn't know I was a lesbian then, but I had these very strong feelings for women and none for men.

"Catholics, of course, are down on sexuality of any kind, except to make babies, but I think the older women running the place were on to women like me. I'll never forget the almost continual warnings we got about getting too close to any particular woman. They called them 'special friendships.' We weren't supposed to have any 'special friendships.' Of course they didn't *ever* use the word *lesbian,* but you got their meaning.

"There were a lot of 'special friendships.' A lot of women felt guilty about them and stopped them. Not me. My first 'special friendship' developed into a full-blown, but secret, sexual affair. I guess that's when I 'came out' as a lesbian. I explained it all to the mother superior and I left the convent."

Another woman describes an interaction she had in 1977 with her older cousin and the woman she lived with: "I had always wondered abut my cousin. She had lived with the same woman for at least thirty years, they met somewhere on the job, at some hospital where they were nurses. Eventually, they retired together to Florida. I went down there to help fight Anita Bryant and naturally, I asked if I could stay with them. They agreed.

"I was pretty timid about mentioning the subject, but after I saw how they lived—one bedroom, sharing everything, the whole deal, I just asked them, 'Haven't you ever been afraid that someone might figure out you are lesbians with all of this publicity about Anita Bryant?' They were totally aghast. I thought for a minute they were going to throw me out, sleeping bag and all, that instant. But I guess they calmed down and thought they had to show some tolerance for a person they suddenly realized must be totally nuts. I'll never forget their answer. 'How could anyone think that? We're not *lesbians*. We've *never* done anything *sexual* together.'

"I tried to explain to them that sex didn't necessarily have anything to do with it—that I wasn't having sex with anyone either but that I *was* a lesbian. It was as if we were speaking two languages, and finally I exhausted their tolerance and they very kindly asked if there wasn't someplace else I could stay.

"When I got back home I was still puzzled about them. I talked a bit to my mother, who knew them a lot better than I did, and all I could pick up was that before they met each other they were apparently very sexy ladies and that after they met they totally lost interest in anyone else, stopped dating, and the whole thing. I still don't understand. In my book they're as gay as I am. Everything I saw about them when I stayed with them showed that they loved and cared for each other very deeply. It's almost as if they didn't know that women could *do* anything sexual together. Or maybe they just repressssed it all. I don't know."

Some lesbians have so much much invested in the cover they have built for themselves that when it is threatened, they can no longer live with themselves. Recalls the friend of one such woman, "One day they found her in the garage. She killed herself with carbon monoxide. A group of us tried to find out why. She didn't leave any note or sign. Eventually we heard that someone had threatened to expose her at work. I guess she just couldn't take it."

Self-fulfillment, economic opportunity, relationship stability, sexuality, and even life itself are daily tolls the closet takes of lesbian couples. Yet many closeted women have become institutionalized, like long-term prison inmates, and would not leave the apparent protection of their psychic prisons even if given the opportunity. It is impossible to communicate to closeted women the freedom they would feel were they to overcome their fear, justified though such fear may be in a homophobic society. It also seems impossible to communicate to the heterosexual who has never had to hide her love, what life in the closet is like and how crippling it can be.

## FROM THE OTHER SIDE

Rachel and Jane, who met in the navy twenty years ago and who remained closeted for seventeen of those years, explain some of their observations of closet life from the other side of the closet door, the open side: "When I was closeted I was putting all my eggs into two baskets, my job and my relationship with Rae. This made me super-dependent on our relationship," Jane said. "It was almost a smothering kind of thing, feeling almost panicky if I should lose the relationship because so much of my identity was tied up in it. So I tried to bind Rae closer to me and yet could never be satisfied that it was close enough.

"As I came out I began to learn that I can get my needs met in a lot of different places, that there didn't have to be just that tiny world, at home with Rae.

"I also began to develop a great deal more confidence in myself. In terms of my just being myself, and my ability to get my needs met outside—that has been a big thing. Now I have these friends that I am open and warm with, and that has a good influence on my relationship with Rae. It removed a lot of pressure from it."

"I can't separate out my own individual growth from where I am in the relationship," said Rae. "I totally came out, told everyone I knew at work, my friends, everyone. I feel that it made a big difference when I came out, not just in terms of my own growth, but in terms of our relationship. I don't think I realized until then the amount of energy that is involved just in keeping that part of yourself hidden. It's hard to explain, but coming out made such a big difference it took me a few months to even realize how much freedom it gave both me and Jane.''

''When I came out,'' said Jane, ''I realized a whole sense of myself, a whole value in myself that doesn't stop anywhere. You can't consider yourself valuable and put down being a homosexual and think that doesn't affect your relationship.''

''If you deny your relationship, like I did when I was still playing the closet scene,'' Rae said, ''that in effect is putting your relationship down. To deny to people that this relationship is an important part of my life, of me, is to somehow say that there is something wrong with it, that there is something wrong with me, and that there's something wrong with my partner.''

# 7

# Breaking Free

If closets are terrifying places, so is the process of breaking out of them. No one can say when the coming out process begins or how it begins. In some cases it begins involuntarily: a woman receives a blackmail threat and instead of capitulating, explains to her boss. Someone asks her if she is a lesbian, and instead of saying no, she says yes.

Often, however, the coming out process begins simply because the façade of heterosexuality requires too much energy to maintain. One couple forgets to check the house before visitors arrive. Another couple forgets to remove the lesbian literature from the bookshelves before the family comes to visit. The painful and draining ruse of phony boyfriends is dropped for whatever will follow.

Sometimes a wall is broken down when a lesbian couple decides to find a lesbian bar just to see what it's like. Another wall may come down in a consciousness-raising or group therapy session.

Each lesbian as an individual and as part of a couple has her own threshold of tolerance for the expediencies and fears of closet life which she can comfortably sustain emotionally. If the climate of the lesbian's professional activity is liberalizing, she finds she can relax a bit. If she is able to find self-employment, she may similarly find a greater degree of freedom to express herself without constraint.

The liberalized climate that followed the first two decades of the gay rights movement and the recent decade's resurgence of the women's movement has made it a bit safer everywhere for closet doors to be opened a crack. A lonely couple today may feel more free to call a gay organization or religious group to find counseling, companionship, perhaps even friends. A lesbian may, with relative safety, direct her political energies into the struggle for equal rights for women without too much criticism if she still feels the need for a degree of closet-edness. Each of these is a momentous step away from terror and intimidation.

Rage, too, may be the impetus for a lesbian to open up and fling aside her psychic chains. Explained one woman, "There was going to be a hearing at our school to determine if one of the physcial education teachers should be fired. There had been rumors around that she lived with another woman and talk that maybe she shouldn't have such close contact with girls. I was sitting on the board that would make this decision. I don't know what came over me. Some man next to me said something like, 'We don't need any of *her* kind on the faculty,' and I exploded. I told the bastard, 'Well, move over, buddy, you're sitting next to one.' It was the shock of his life. That was also the end of any discussion of firing anyone."

Most frequently, it seems, lesbian couples first break down the barriers by coming out to the friends they most trust. Here, there is less threat of unwanted exposure, rejection, and economic loss. In some cases, as in this couple's, they found that their friends, a male couple, were also gay: "We'd decided to see what would happen if we let our secret out. We knew these two guys who always hung around together and who we did a lot of stuff with. We had even double-dated with them on those occasions when we needed male partners for parties. We didn't know much about their personal relationship, just that they might be closer than 'just good buddies.' One day when they were over at our place and we'd all had a few drinks, we just asked them, 'Are you two gay?' They said yes. We said, 'So are we!' It was amazing that we had gone so long without ever broaching the subject. We had a big celebration that night and shared a lot of our feelings about our fears and compared notes on gay life together. It was wonderful. Through them we met other gay guys and finally some gay women. Before that it had always seemed like it was them—the straights—against us. Now we saw that 'us' was just more than the two of us. We began to get socially involved with a whole clan of gay friends. It was an exhilarating time for us."

At other times the lesbian may begin the first steps out of her closet as the result of coworkers' or friends' solicitations for help on some gay-related project. Recalls a university professor, "I was approached one day by a colleague who asked if I wanted to join a group at the school who would act as advisors to a student gay rights organization. He didn't say anything about whether or not I was gay or if he was gay. He simply solicited my help. I couldn't say no, remembering what hell my own college life had been without any gay rights, much less gay organizations, so I said yes. This was the beginning for me, of contact with a support group of colleagues, many of whom were gay. It broke down some of the barriers of isolation I was feeling. It was my first step out." Recalls another woman, "I couldn't believe it. One day I got this phone call out of the blue asking if I would help campaign against Senator Briggs's antigay initiative. They got my name from the list of registered Democrats, I guess, and they didn't have any idea whether I was straight or not. It scared me for a minute—I'm pretty closety—but I just *had* to say yes. So I went down and volunteered. There were both straight and gay people so I felt pretty comfortable. After a while I got to know some of the other gays and finally told them that I was gay too, and so they plugged me into a whole support network I would never have known about it if wasn't for that."

## STRESS ON THE COUPLE

Typically, the woman in the ultra-closet will not form a relationship with a woman living a less closeted life. Her fear of confrontation with the other's openness, and her own terror, are too great to allow contact with openly identified lesbians. She seeks a woman, like herself, who is trained in the rules of self-imposed secrecy. Unfortunately, it is she who is least likely to find a relationship partner, for wherever she looks, she will be placing herself at risk.

This pattern of partner selection reflects a division in the lesbian subculture itself. Organizations and institutions such as bars, private clubs, and civil rights groups tend to differentiate themselves: closeted people in one place; open, more activist people in another. The division is a process of self-selection rather than ritual or rule. Closeted and noncloseted do not feel comfortable with each other.

The problems of coming out are generally shared by both members of a lesbian couple, even though there might be differences in their degree of fear of exposure or differences in their practical reasons for remaining closeted. These differences may cause one to begin moving out of the boundaries of her closet while her partner remains in, clinging to its apparent security. This can cause tension in the relationship. Both partners feel frustrated: one because she feels threatened by exposure as the result of the other's openness; the other because she is unable to share her new-found freedom with her partner.

As Florence explained, "When Rita began to come out to her friends at work, I was frightened. What if some of my friends saw me with her? It was fine for her, she was in a more liberal profession than mine. I had to work with all these engineers. I just couldn't see them relating too well to working with a dyke.

"As she continued to come out, eventually going around to professional groups to give talks on homosexuality, I was proud of her. I really wanted to tell my fellow workers what she was doing, but of course that would have blown it for me. Meanwhile, I was still afraid to be seen with her."

Said Rita, "Coming out is like getting religion. It's just something you've got to share with everyone, especially with your lover. All these wonderful things were happening to me—I was establishing good friendships on my own, I was feeling more self-esteem, I was becoming an autonomous person in my own right. I wanted these things to begin happening for Flo, too. But she was just afraid, terrified of it all.

"She had a tremendous amount invested in her career—about one more year to retirement—and she was petrified at the thought of losing that. She didn't want me to bring my friends home when she was there, and I could kind of understand that, but it hurt.

"Eventually I suggested that we both go to a lesbian therapist I had heard of who had a good reputation among my friends. But she was too afraid to do even that. Rules about confidentiality or no, she was afraid word might get out.

"Things just got worse for us after that. We began to grow further and further apart as I began to enjoy my new life free of the old closet hassles I used to put up with.

"In the end, we broke up. That security of her career, her retirement, was too important for her to lose. And the pressures from me, I guess, got to be too great. It seemed to me like she needed her closet, that she was a closet junkie, and here I was trying to get her off it. It just didn't work."

## COMING OUT TOGETHER

Those couples who have worked on the coming out process together, perhaps because of greater commitment to their relationships, or perhaps because they had realized the psychic damage of the closet/prison before they became institutionalized to it, report periods of tremendous growth. Reflecting on her closet relationship and the process of opening up from it a bit with her lover, one woman recalls, "After we began to come out with our friends and a few people at work as a couple and individually, I began to see what being closeted had done to us. It had made us totally dependent on each other for every kind of emotional gratification. It was a kind of slavery. *All* we had was each other. So neither of us could make a move that didn't seem to threaten the relationship.

"We're still not out in a political sense. We don't wear signs or march in parades, or anything like that, but we have, at least, a good circle of friends who know about and support our relationship. Also, we've lost some of that fear about our jobs. The first things I began to notice on the job was that the homosexuality issue didn't really seem to be a big deal to anyone. What it was is they either want to deal with you in terms of who you are, or they just want to deal with their projections of you. So there were some people who were very uncomfortable having their projections shattered when we came out with them, and there were other people for whom it totally took a wall away—the people who were eager to relate to who we *really* are. And, everywhere you work there are gay people, so coming out a little bit put us in touch with some gay people on the job and we can kind of share things with them, even if it's just a friendly smile or nod in the hallway."

Breaking free of the closet is not an overnight process. Rae and Jane spent seventeen years on their way out of the closet. Here they describe in greater detail what the process was like for them:

"We spent a year and a half in the navy together in Hawaii and that was a lot of fun," Rae explained. "But there was a lot of tenseness, tenseness from just knowing we were in the navy. I think we were a little scared at first because I felt like we needed to be careful in terms of being found out. I didn't feel all that good about myself then as a gay person or about my sexual life, so I had these terrible fantasies that if they found out about Jane and me, there would be this big court-martial. And that fantasy wasn't so far off, especially at that time. There was always such pressure of exposure. I always felt that somebody was kind of looking in a keyhole at us. I couldn't wait until our enlistments were up and we could get out of there.''

"After we left Hawaii," said Jane, "we decided to go to Boston to go back to school. We had met a couple of navy nurses there who were gay and we became a very close foursome. Both Rae and I were pretty naive about homosexuality. It was the days of the CLOSET and it didn't really even occur to me that other gay people existed outside of the military. We were very much in the closet and so we were happy to find two other gay women. And so the four of us did lots of things together. We had a lot of fun and we began to get attracted to these two women and have affairs with them.'' Eventually these affairs almost caused Rae and Jane to break up. After they finished college, they left Boston for Washington to take up their careers.

"We thought we would try the suburban kind of life," Jane said. "I think we were lulled into thinking, 'Well, God, we've had this crisis and weathered it and all our problems are solved.'

"We selected this really middle-class neighborhood and a house with a swimming pool and three bedrooms, just the most middle-class—and closety—place we could think of. We were into thinking all our problems were over and now we could get on with life and live just like the rest of the world supposedly lives. Everybody has a house and three bedrooms and a garage and a dog and a station wagon and we had it all, the epitome of happiness, the American dream. We hated it.''

"We were terribly unhappy," said Rae. "It was one of the most miserable times of my life. We were pretty much dependent on each other and I think we missed the gay people we had known in Boston. I had a lot of professional hassles going on as well as the personal stuff. I was young, I was scared about my job and I didn't feel very confident about myself.

"Jane and I had never lived like that, the suburban thing, that whole way of life, glassed in. It was a period in our life when we grew distant. I think part of what was going on with us then was being closeted. We were both closed. I was closed about myself, not sharing who I was with people and therefore I felt stopped in my own growth. And then I decided to begin to try to come out.''

"I had this terrible job where I was miserable all the time," Jane added. "I remember Rae telling me that she had told someone she worked with she was gay. I suddenly felt the world was going to come down on us, that someone would find out about me.

"Then I went to work one day and there it was, my first threatening letter: 'I'm going to turn you in because you're a queer.' So immediately I quit my job. All I remember now about it was that it was really scary and that I decided to join Rae's therapy group. It turned out to be a tremendous thing for me. We were in an all-gay group and it was a very warm kind of thing.

"I began to get that self-confidence and then I began to come out. In terms of my own self-esteem and my ability to get my needs met outside of our relationship, that was a big thing. Now I have these friends that I am open and warm with, and that has a good influence in our relationship. Now Rae can go off and do her thing and that's fine and I love it, and I help her to whatever extent I can. And I do my thing. It's not this nice little black and white world where here's Rae and here's work and they don't meet.

"I think for me, coming out of the closet constantly reinforces my self-value. That, in turn, reinforces the value of our relationship."

"I feel that our relationship is more autonomous now," said Rae. "I see it as much more of a partnership. There is a stronger commitment to each other's growth. That mutual support has partly come about in the last couple of years as we have shared the coming out process. I think maybe that's been the main difference in our relationship in the last year or so.

"Since we've opened up and begun coming out of the closet mentality, I think we've been able to be more intimate with each other too. I used to be afraid of being intimate; things felt so good when we were really close and I was scared of losing that because I was so dependent on the relationship. So I used to find ways of pulling back.

"I feel like now I allow myself to be more close because I don't have those kinds of fears I had, that degree of almost exclusive dependency on our relationship, those kind of closety fears we had before."

Not only can the coming out process enhance the lesbian relationship, but the partners can often help each other through it. Explains one woman, "Both of us were pretty much out when we got together. We had only one thing left to face and that was our parents. And for us, that was a *real* heavy trip, heavier than any of the rest of the coming out deal. We decided to talk to our parents, one set at a time. I became the guinea pig because my parents were supposed to be more liberal. It was still really hard, and the emotional support I got from my lover during that time was very important. I don't think I would have made it without that support. Anyway, we got through that and had learned some things about how to handle parents, so then we went on to tackle my lover's parents who are from the South and are pretty fundamentalist, conservative oriented. I think my going first gave her some of the strength she needed to come out to her family, and certainly the emotional support from me was really strong. If they rejected her— even though in the end they didn't—at least I would be there behind her 100 percent. It wasn't a thing she had to do alone, and I think that really helps."

## IS "OUT" BETTER?

Those couples who have been through the coming out process together, broken the bonds of the fears that limited their lives, would doubtlessly agree that out has been better for them. Some do so with almost religious fervor, proselytizing for "coming out of the closet."

Bell and Weinberg found that those who were out tended to have a higher occupational level than those who were not. The women who were the furthest out of their closets (who had high degrees of what Bell and Weinberg call "extra-familial overtness") also had high ratings on their level of sex activity, the variety of their sexual repertoire (they used a greater variety of sexual techniques in their lovemaking), and the number of sexual partners during the last year. They also tended to be in a coupled, or committed partnership. Their greatest worry, among the factors correlated by the researchers, was about "making conversation," a worry greater than those about their own sexual performance.[1]

It would appear, from the Bell and Weinberg correlations, that being out tends not only to reduce fears of exposure, but is strongly related to a woman's level of sexual activity, and to the lack of problems she experiences in her sexual activities.

But breaking out of the closet is a tremendous risk, a risk many women are unwilling or unable to take. However, as one woman explained, "You don't have to be OUT-out to be out, or to get off on the high of being out. Coming out isn't the big overwhelming mountain it's made out to be. What it is is a series of very small steps. You just take them one at a time, as you are ready. If you're really paranoid about being discovered, or have a lot to lose, that doesn't mean you can't be out. Send a money order to some gay organization. Sign a phony name on the money order and don't give a return address if you want. Or send cash. *That* is a step out.

"Every step is just one move along a path that never stops. Even women who are really OUT, women who've been written up in newspapers and been on TV, women who think everyone must know they're gay still have to come out—every so often someone will ask and they'll have to come out all over again.

"No one should look at coming out as a whole package. We're always in the process of coming out in some way, even if it's just to ourselves. It's growth. It's a process. And it's healthy: even if it's a phony name on a money order that can't be traced, it's an affirmation of yourself and your relationship. And with all the shit coming down from society, we all need every bit of affirmation we can get."

# 8

# Parents and "In-Laws"

Of all the outsiders from whom the lesbian wants acceptance, approval, and understanding, her parents matter most. Since her birth they have symbolized godlike authority, and approval from them can help overcome the pain that accompanies rejection by other authority figures. Parents are also seen by their lesbian daughters as ties to something still in the "other" world, ties to genealogical roots from which no amount of social disapproval can sever them. It is as if the lesbian refuses to be totally alien, wanting to belong somewhere in the mainstream scheme of things as daughter, granddaughter, sister— family member. Her major hopes of belonging seem anchored in her family.

Consequently, and contrary to myth, a large number of lesbians— 82 percent of the Fleener sample—maintain regular contact with their biological families.[1] This figure appears to vary little with age or social circumstance.[2]

Openness about affectional preference, however, is not quite a family matter to most of America's lesbian daughters. When parents inquire about boyfriends, dates, possible marriages, the lesbian is faced with the knowledge that she is probably presumed to be heterosexual. Most often she does little to change this presumption, for that would require an emotional and painful confrontation which, she fears, might end in ostracism from her family.

Explains a young college student, "When my parents ask, as they always do, about boyfriends and when I'm getting married, I just tell them I'm not even thinking about it until I get my degree. I've been going with the same woman now for four years and my family accepts her as a good friend. I don't want to blow the scene by going into all the gory details."

There is good reason for the lesbian to feel rejection from her family. In 1977 and 1978, for example, large majorities of voters in several cities voted against lesbian and male homosexual rights to equal opportunity in employment, housing, and public accommodations. Comments one Minnesota woman, "My God, if four out of five people in liberal St. Paul voted against my right to have a job or rent an apartment, what do you think my parents' reaction would be in Apple Valley?"

The fears that such civil rights setbacks inspire, however, are catch−22 situations. A Public Research Associates poll conducted in 1978 to test voter attitudes about lesbian and male homosexual teachers in California found that among those who personally knew one or more gay people, attitudes toward gays were more liberal.[3] To attain civil rights protections then, it would appear that lesbians must come out, at least to family members—especially in towns like Apple Valley, where the risks seem to outnumber the benefits. About half of the 980 registered voters surveyed by Public Research Associates said that they would accept their child if they learned that the child was gay. Slightly more than one third of the 980, however, indicated they would want the child to see a psychiatrist.[4] (About 14 percent of those lesbians who had sought psychological help in the Bell and Weinberg study said they were "forced or ordered to go").[5] The degree of acceptance of the pollsters' hypothetical gay children dropped alarmingly among conservative voters with high school or less education living outside urban areas. Among this group, largely Protestant, nearly all parents would want a gay daughter or son to seek psychiatric help. Nearly all of those also believed that all homosexual sex should be made illegal.[6]

## COMING OUT TO PARENTS

A substantial minority of American lesbians (about 42 percent of the Fleener sample) do brave the possibility of rejection to make their parents aware that they are gay.[7] Most of these, after agonizing hours of soul-searching, tell both parents. Most agree that telling their parents about their love for women is one of the most difficult experiences of their lives.

Explains Susan, "After I'd decided to tell my mother it took me about six weeks to get up the nerve to actually do it. I was petrified of what her reaction would be. You can hear all you want of the stories that if they love you they'll accept you, but those stories are always someone else's family. Mine wanted me to marry a nice doctor and have grandkids.

"I didn't want to continue hiding such an important and fulfilling part of my life from them. Somehow the thought of them rejecting not just me, but that part of me that had given me the most happiness in my life, made it even harder. I had dreams about my mother telling me to get out of the house; I actually woke up from a nightmare as she was going to get dad to kick me out with a shotgun."

Susan, like many lesbians, had a surprise in store for her when she finally took her mother out to lunch and told her she had something serious to discuss. Her mother sensed, somehow, not to ask if she had just eloped, knowing that some other news was on its way. "Mom, I'm a lesbian. I know that . . ." and then Susan's mother interrupted, as so many seem to, with "Well, I'm glad you finally told me. I'd thought that you might be for a long while now."

Although remaining calm in front of her daughter, Susan's mother spent many months trying to deal with the reality of the now confirmed fact that her daughter was a lesbian. For many parents, coping with the realization that their daughter is gay can be nearly as traumatic as it is for their daughter to tell them. Some concerned parents, recognizing the pain involved in this process, have formed support groups for parents of gay people.[8]

Not all families react as acceptingly as Susan's. A few succumb to the thought that it is their daughter's lover who had "converted" her to the gay life and try to separate the pair. Recalls one woman of the family pressures that finally ended her relationship, "My lover's family was rigidly Baptist. They were also rich. As soon as they found out what was going on they began bribing her to leave me. First they tried the guilt trip, the religious trip. Then they bought her out. All of their pressure finally worked: she kicked me out." Six percent of Bell and Weinberg's lesbians reported that other people had forced their first affairs to end.[9]

Such attempts to separate partners appear to be especially vicious when the couple is young. Said Bonnie, "I had my first lesbian affair at nineteen. That lasted almost three years. Pat and I were roommates in college and that's how we got together. We ended up fucking in a couple of months and we both felt very guilty about it because we both thought it was wrong, bad, sinful, sick. After a couple of months of this I overdosed very badly and had to spend a week in the hospital. My family had figured out what was going on and suggested that perhaps I should come home. So I went home and they gave me the lecture about not allowing myself to be 'led astray' by Pat. They threatened that if I saw Pat again, they would have me committed to a mental hospital to be 'cured.'"

Recalls another woman of her high school experience, "I was in love with another girl in high school. She looked quite butch. Eventually my mother figured things out; I don't think I actually told her anything. But she assumed it was Debbie who was leading me astray. She called the dean of women at my high school. The dean of women called the school nurse. The school nurse then called me in for an inquisition about how Debbie had 'seduced' me. I denied everything. After all, we hadn't even kissed each other. But I guess it wasn't quite good enough. The nurse ended up calling the mothers of all the other girls in school—there were only about a hundred of us—to warn them about Debbie's 'threat' to their daughters. When Debbie got back to school the next day everyone knew. They began taunting her. A couple of boys roughed her up pretty badly. She left school the next day, just three weeks before graduation."

Some parents, usually those from extreme fundamentalist religious backgrounds, do, in fact, ostracize their lesbian daughters. Commented one respondent to the Fleener survey, "My mother said she'd rather see me dead than be a lesbian. She told me never to try to talk to her or any of the family again."[10]

Most families, however, seem to abide by a contract of silence. Some women in the Fleener survey reported that they had lived with the same woman for from five to thirteen years and yet did not think their parents knew they were gay. In most cases, those lesbians with partners who thought their parents didn't know, also reported that their parents accepted their partners as "members of the family."[11]

Yet most of these parents, if asked, would probably deny that they know any lesbian personally. Both daughter and parent join in a partnership of silence and invisibility, accommodating to it as best they can.

## ACCOMMODATING IN-LAWS

The couple involved in a stable relationship tends to feel like a married couple and, often, seeks validation of their relationship from at least one of their sets of "in-laws." In cases where one woman's family would not accept a lesbian "daughter-in-law," as 18 percent of Fleener's coupled respondents reported, the other woman's family might. Nearly 60 percent of Fleener's adult lesbians reported being closeted to their *own* parents, yet nearly three quarters of the lesbians with partners reported that either one or both of their families knew about their affectional preference, and presumably, about the intimate nature of their relationship.[12]

The lesbian couple, then, usually finds that one of the partner's families is more accepting, and intrafamily relationships are adopted accordingly. Says Sandy, "Both our families know about us; we made sure of that, but my mother is a real bitch about it. She just goes out of her way to make things very uncomfortable for my lover when we visit her. So finally I confronted her with it and told her that since my lover's family accepts me completely as a family member, she'd better shape up or I was going to be spending holidays and everything else with my lover's family. My parents aren't very family-oriented and even that ultimatum didn't change their attitude. It bothered me for a while and I stopped visiting my parents, kind of wrote them out of my life, but now I've been adopted into my lover's family who care about me and like me a lot, and it's just wonderful."

Such family acceptance as does exist for lesbian couples, is never quite the same as family-oriented heterosexual relationships. Most women report that their parents have never met their lover's parents. The daughter-in-law may be accepted, but seldom are the other in-laws. In recent years, commitment ceremonies such as the Holy Union offered by the Metropolitan Community Church and other gay-oriented religious groups have tended, at least initially, to bridge this gap. Generally, women participating in such ceremonies tend to invite their families, and often, the families come. There, at least, they get to see each other across the aisle.

Even completely open couples that are fully accepted by both sets of parents can have a difficult time with in-laws, problems shared perhaps by unmarried heterosexual couples. Holidays are a particularly trying time for these couples. One or the other family insists on their daughter's presence. Even so, the open daughters-in-law manage the demands of their parents. Says Susan, "We just take turns. One year it's her family, the other year it's mine. No one gives us any hassle. But of course it took a lot of explaining before our parents saw it our way. Sometimes I think they may be a little resentful, but they go out of their way to be nice."

Another open couple arranges holidays this way, "Her mom is into huge Thanksgiving things. The whole family comes, from about three states. There must be at least forty of them. My family's into Christmas. So we spend Thanksgiving with her family and Christmas with mine."

Many open lesbians resent the fact that even though they are, in their opinion, married to their lovers, their families still expect them to come "home" for the holidays, rather than visit in *their* home. One couple tried to remedy this situation by hosting a Thanksgiving for both their families at their own home. "We were just angry that they didn't recognize *us* as a couple as we thought they would if we were straight. So we tried getting them together at our place for Thanksgiving. God it was terrible," they recall. "None of them had ever met. They were all very polite, like proper icicles. It was as if they were hiding some sort of secret from each other. It seemed to us as if they were eyeing each other, like two feuding clans, each secretly blaming the other family for having the daughter who 'corrupted' their own."

Comments Viv, who's well into her thirty-first year with Bev, "Sure, both our families know. And we were into that holiday thing for ever and ever. Finally we realized, 'Isn't it kind of dumb, at our ages, to still be going home to our parents' for the holidays?' Now we celebrate our own holidays and if any of them want to join us, that's fine. The rest of the year we just visit them all once in a while and that seems to keep both them and us pretty happy."

About one quarter of the Fleener respondents who were in relationships remained closeted to both families.[13] In cases such as these, where neither parent officially knows that their daughter is involved in an intimate and perhaps permanent relationship with her female "friend" or "roommate," the daughters are treated as single. They are expected to report, alone, to traditional family gatherings, including weddings, funerals, and, of course, holiday functions. The Christmas season is an especially trying time for lesbian couples who are still closeted with both sets of parents and may precipitate relationship crises. Explained one woman who has lived in a closeted relationship for seven years, "It was Christmas. Both of us were expected to go back 'home' to our 'families' for the holidays. We are as married as any of our family. We are in love. We live together. We intend building our lives together. Yet every time the family called, that was the end of our home life. It was as if *we* weren't a family. Holidays like Christmas had always been very important to me and I want to be with my family, and *my* family is with my lover. It's like saying, once or twice a year—Thanksgiving is the other one—'Well, you really aren't my family. This house really isn't our home. I have to go *home* now.'

"Until last year we never had our own Christmas together. The year before we had made one final try at sharing Christmas and keeping at least some family members happy. My lover called up and asked her mother it if was okay to bring a friend. Her mother said fine. But once we got there, although everyone tried to be very nice to the 'guest,' I was afraid to even look at my lover. After all, I was just supposed to be the friend with nowhere else to go, not a part of the family."

In response to the alienation many lesbians feel during the holidays, their extended families within the subculture may go out of their way to make provision for them. Comments one woman, "I remember too well what it was like to be alone during Christmas, knowing that my parents wouldn't accept me and that my lover of the time had to go 'home' for the holidays. Now, much as my current lover and I might like to share that day alone, we always see to it that those people we're aware of who have nowhere to go get invited to share our home with us. We have a tree we decorate. Usually we'll cook up a big turkey and everyone knows they're free to come by and share the specialness of the holidays with us."

Problems that show the difference between family attitudes toward open couples and closeted couples usually do not surface until a time of crisis. It is then that the open couple finds that the energy expended in nurturing their families into acceptance of their relationship was worth it; it is then that the closeted couple suffers.

Explains Abby, a member of a closeted couple, "My lover was in a car wreck. The doctor said she was critical. I was worried out of my mind. I knew I had to call her family; I knew she would have wanted them to know. So I did. And they arrived. All of them. And from the moment they got on the scene I ceased to exist. I had no say about anything. They even made sure I couldn't visit my lover in the hospital."

By contrast, one member of an open couple recalls the support she received from her lover's relatives in a similar emergency, "They couldn't have been more helpful. They kept encouraging me, trying to see that I didn't get too depressed or worried. I don't think I would have survived it without the love from her family."

Deaths, for the closeted couple, are even more harrowing. "Ella died. We had been together twenty-one years and neither of our families knew about our relationship. There was no one I could go to for comfort. No one asked me if I needed help.

"When Ella's family got there they took over everything. They didn't even give me a chair at the burial.

"They arranged for a reception at Ella's and my home without even asking me. And then the bickering began about who would get what. I was too grief-stricken to stop them.

"One of them, I don't know which one, even took Ella's and my family album when they left. What in God's name could it have meant to them?"

# 9

# Lesbian Families

Anita Bryant shouldn't be preaching against gays. My mother is a lesbian. Me, my younger brother and two older sisters have been living with her and her friend Ruthie since I was three. Ruthie is just like a second mother to us and has always helped all of us and mom in everything. We never had any trouble in our family like Anita Bryant talks about. There is a lot of love in our family. We all go to church and sometimes I pray that Anita Bryant could have some of the love we have in our family.—*Letter from a twelve-year-old girl*

Of all the assaults the lesbian presence makes on the patriarchal family presumption, perhaps none is so challenging as that of the lesbian mother and her children living in a lesbian household. While lesbianism challenges our social axioms in the macrocosm, the challenges of lesbian families are often fought out in the microcosm, in a very personal and direct way between husband-father and wife-mother in battles over the custody of children.

A story recounted in *Mom's Apple Pie*, the newsletter of the Lesbian Mother's National Defense Fund, is illustrative. Two women in rural Washington—women who had never before heard of lesbianism—discovered they were in love and decided they wanted to build their lives together on their own farm. Their husbands, when told of their affection, slapped divorce proceedings and custody suits on them. On the day of the custody hearing, the women's house was burned to the ground. During the prolonged custody battle, the women had their cattle and horses stolen, their gas tanks filled with sugar, their cars' tires slashed, and the brake lines severed.

Explained Geraldine Cole of the Defense Fund, "The husbands tend to have a lot of anger when they find out their [wives are] . . . gay." Even in those rare cases when a court awards custody of the children to the lesbian mother, such anger is not always restrained. Ex-husbands have been reported to have removed their children by force to other states and to have continued harassment of the mothers for years. In one such case, according to the Defense Fund, the father was a known child molester.[1]

Courts determining the custody fates of children are, by law, arbiters of what they determine to be the child's "best interest." Key to traditional American thinking about child development is the concept that a father or other male role model is essential to the healthy psychological development of children. (Somehow this concept is lost in the case of the welfare mother who must prove there is *no* father or male role model present in order to receive payments under programs designed to assist needy children.) Nothing so clearly demonstrates the fallacy of this American axiom as the thousands of children being raised in lesbian homes, who are, as researchers are now learning, as psychologically well balanced and as frequently heterosexual as their heterosexually raised peers.

One such researcher, Dr. Richard Greene, professor of psychiatry at the State University of New York, reported in 1978 that his study of twenty-one children reared by lesbian mothers found that the children showed no remarkable differences from the heterosexually raised control group. He reported that the children, aged five to fourteen, are "developing normally," and commented that his findings raised "new and provocative" questions about our assumptions of a child's need for so-called appropriate gender role models.[2]

Greene's research findings are among those now being used by lesbian mothers in their attempts to retain custody of their children in dozens of court battles. Almost universally, however, courts cling adamantly to the theoretical notion that the mother's affectional preference for women and the lack of a male role model in the family will somehow a priori be harmful to the child. Judges of this persuasion often award custody of the lesbian's children to anyone except the mother, no matter how competent the mother is proved to be as a parent, or how incompetent the father.

A California appellate court ruling which gave custody of a lesbian mother's children to their grandparents in Washington state is indicative of much judicial thinking. "In exercising a choice between homosexual and heterosexual households for the purposes of child custody," the judges opined, "the court could conclude that permanent residence in a homosexual household would be detrimental to the children and contrary to their best interests.''

The court elaborated, ''This factor [lesbianism] is not merely fortuitous or casual, but rather it dominates and forms the basis for the household into which the children would be brought if custody were awarded . . . [The mother] does not merely say she is a homosexual. She also lives with another woman with whom she has engaged in homosexual conduct, and she intends to bring up her daughters in that environment . . . The fact that in certain respects enforcement of [sodomy laws] may be inappropriate and may be approaching desuetude . . . does not argue that society accepts homosexuality as a pattern to which children should be exposed . . . or as an example that should be put before them for emulation.''[3]

As ordered by the court, the children were sent to live with their grandparents. They soon managed to run away to return to live with their mother in southern California.

Some judges are far less eloquent in their expressions of social attitudes. One Ohio judge, denying a mother custody of her children, said ''Orgasm means more to them [lesbians] than children or anything else.''[4]

Such has been the pattern of custody rulings, a pattern that is slowly changing.

Court-fought custody battles are only the beginning of the story of children raised in lesbian families, however. The Lesbian Mothers National Defense Fund, which discourages lesbian mothers from court fights if they can be in any way avoided, reports that of some two hundred cases referred to it, one-third have been resolved in favor of the lesbian mother through negotiation with the lesbian's ex-husband. Such negotiations, comments one lesbian mother, may mean, ''You get the kids, but you don't get any child support or alimony. In other words, like my ex-husband said to me, 'Okay, you want 'em that bad, you got 'em, but you ain't gonna get a damned thing more!'''

## LATE SELF-DISCOVERY

A sizable minority of lesbians have been married and, as Bell and Weinberg report, nearly half of these were not aware of their lesbianism before marriage. These researchers found that 37 percent of their sample had been married at least once.[5] Wolff found that 23 percent of her British sample had been married.[6] The actual percentage of lesbians who have been married may, as some observers suggest, be substantially higher. Both the studies' samples were drawn from urban areas where lesbian organizations and bars were known and available. The samples obviously included only those women both accessible to researchers and willing to respond to interviews, excluding a vast and silent group of women such as these described by Geraldine Cole: "We got people writing us from Kansas, Iowa, Georgia, and Louisiana. Some have never even heard of the concept of homosexuality, and they then find they are in love with another woman."[7]

Of those women accessible to researchers, a substantial minority report living in lesbian households with children. Fifteen percent of the Bell and Weinberg sample were mothers, 15 percent of Wolff's sample were mothers. Seventeen percent of Fleener's sample reported living in lesbian households that included children, and of 1,008 responses to a survey of *Lesbian Connection* readers, 16 percent reported living in lesbian households with children.[8]

Not all lesbian mothers, according to Fleener's respondents, had problems retaining custody of their children. Only one of the eleven mothers who reported that their children did not live with them said that the reason for this was that a court or former husband would not allow it. Although Fleener did not ask why the other ten mothers were not living with their children, such authorities as Cole suggest that many women are too afraid to endure a custody battle, and they give in to their husbands' demands without a fight.[9] Eight mothers reported to Fleener that their children lived with them but that they did not receive child-support payments from former husbands.

For the lesbian mother who does put up a fight for her children, win or lose, there is ample anguish. Says Cole of these women, "A lot of women freak out when they have all that anger thrown at them. They grew up in the same world we did, believing all those nice, romantic things about relationships. When they find this monster [their ex-husband] trying to viciously and deliberately hurt them, they freak out."[10] The Defense Fund offers referrals to sympathetic therapists for such women.

Even if a custody battle is won the lesbian mother may continue to live in fear that her husband will return, drag the story of her lesbian relationship into court, and demand custody (as he is allowed to do if he can prove the children live in circumstances that have changed from the time when custody was awarded), or that disapproving family members on either side, or even nosey neighbors may interfere with her custody. It is a fear that seemingly has no end. Explains one woman, "Their father ran out on us. I never know when he'll be back, when he'll decide to go to court and grab custody. I never know when some neighbor is going to complain to child welfare authorities, or some teacher is going to complain and some state or county official appear on the scene and take the kids away. It is like living every day with the fear of a death sentence hanging over you."

As a consequence of such fears, some lesbian mothers suggest that they overcompensate in their efforts to be good mothers and provide the best environments possible for their children. "As a lesbian mother," says one woman, "you know that your relationship, custody of your children, everything important to you is in continual jeopardy. So you work harder trying to do what is right, to be a good mother. I think we paid more attention than most people to our kids' welfare because the custody thing was always on our minds. My lover and I made sure my kids had everything in the way of love, support, and opportunity we could give them."

At the other end of the spectrum for the lesbian mother is guilt, which may be felt long past her children's maturity, guilt because she could not earn "enough" money, could never afford all that she felt she might otherwise have given her children. It is a common consumer-society nightmare, doubly emphasized for the lesbian mother, as a woman whose four children are all in their twenties explains, "Somehow I was always feeling guilty. Not guilty about being gay, but guilty because I could never afford everything that everyone says a middle-class kid is supposed to have. I could barely earn enough money to feed us all, let alone pay for college educations. All those things that we could never have. That whole American dream. Well, I just was never able to catch up with that dream, and so I carried around a lot of guilt for many years until I realized I had bought 'it'—a whole mythology about life that had nothing to do with the *important* things about raising kids—the love and guidance you gave them. When I got *that* into my head, I finally stopped feeling guilty, as if I had somehow failed as a parent. I knew better. I could see it in my kids who are all fine, loving adults.''

Other difficulties the lesbian mother faces are her own fears that her affectional preference may somehow harm her children. She wonders if and how to tell them about her affectional preference, how much to show, and how much to keep secret. She also wonders how her children's peers will react if word gets around that their mother is a lesbian. All of these questions bring the mother into direct confrontation with the recognition of her love of women. ''It hit me, bang. There was no way I could get around it,'' said one mother, ''I was a *lesbian*. And I had to deal with that pretty fast. I didn't have years to think it out or ponder about it. It was there. I couldn't run from it, hide from it, or pretend it didn't exist.''

Many lesbians apparently avoid some of these conflicts. Bell and Weinberg report that about 30 percent of the lesbians' children over the age of twelve neither knew nor suspected their mother's lesbianism. While about 46 percent of the Bell and Weinberg mothers said that their children over twelve had guessed their sexual orientation, fewer than 30 percent were told by their mothers.[11]

Those who counsel lesbians, like Los Angeles therapist Betty Berzon, do recommend that their clients discuss their affectional preference with their children for a variety of reasons beneficial to both the children and the mother herself—but primarily so that the children get their first exposure to the subject from someone who feels good and positive about it in a nonthreatening environment.[12]

### THE CHILDREN

Children themselves appear to be much more adaptable than either the courts or many lesbian mothers might imagine. Of the mothers who reported to Bell and Weinberg that their children knew or suspected their lesbianism, 65 percent said that this knowledge brought no visible reaction from their children. An additional 6 percent said their children reacted to the knowledge with indifference. Only 9 percent reported a negative reaction such as ''shock'' or ''horror.''[13] Although the Bell and Weinberg report does not indicate it, it is likely that those children reacting with "shock" or "horror" were those who were told of their mother's affectional preference by outside and possibly hostile sources such as husbands suing for custody.

Recalls one woman, "There was no way of getting around going to court, so I decided I should at least try to explain as best I could about lesbianism to the two older kids—thirteen and fifteen. That was more easy than I expected. But I wasn't exactly sure what to say, or how to say it, to my eight-year-old son. Well, his father took care of that for me and what I had on my hands when he got back from the weekend was a young little boy who was very hostile to me. He clammed up on me entirely. Finally, I got out of him what was wrong. 'You're a *queer*!' he blurted out to me. 'I don't want to be around *queers*!' I don't think he even knew what the word really meant, just that it was something very bad.''

Children also seem to be very accepting of their mothers' lovers. Of those responding to the Fleener survey who said that their children lived in the same household with both mother and lover, only one mother reported that the lover was not accepted, "and there is open hostility.'' The remainder of the mothers responded that their children accepted their lovers "completely.'' The situation was similar for those lovers who reported living with mothers and children. Only one reported that the mother's child accepted her only "sometimes.'' The rest said that the mother's child or children "seem to accept me completely.''[14]

"I've been living with my lover and her two kids for twelve years now, and we've never had any trouble,'' one lesbian recalls. "They really accepted me in a way I never dreamed would be possible after the initial three months or so when they were working out a jealousy thing. I think what finally proved it to me conclusively was when her older son brought his fiancée home and introduced her to both of us—apparently he'd done some explaining to her because she very discreetly let us know that *both* of us were part of her new family. Then, when the wedding invitations came, we were both invited. I guess somewhere I'd always worried about the kids accepting me, but that invitation finally convinced me. I just cried, I was so happy.''

Children do not easily articulate their feelings about their lesbian families to adult interviewers. They do, however, communicate much about their family lives by their actions. Visiting a lesbian household is much like visiting any home with children. There is abundant noise and confusion. Younger sisters tattle on older ones. The oldest brother says goodbye to his mother and her lover, telling them he's going to pick up his girlfriend for a date. He is reminded to be back home by midnight. An older sister has been on the phone too long. Her mother tells her to get off and get back to her homework: "Are you ready for that science test tomorrow? Your grades better be up this term!" A neighbor girl comes over: "Can Shirley come out and play?" The lover responds: "No, she's grounded." The middle brother asks if he can go camping over the weekend with his friends: "You'd better talk that over with your mother, and I think you'd better figure out what you're going to do about cleaning up the yard this weekend." Middle brother to mother: "She said I could go camping if you said I could" Mother to middle brother: "Don't play that con with me. Let's talk about it together."

And so on, through the daily lives of families.

## PROBLEMS

The only people who seem to interfere with the children's acceptance of their lesbian families are hostile authority figures. These cause difficulty not only for the parent and her lover, but for the children as well.

Explains one mother, "All my kids are interested in is what other kids are doing and the same thing seems to hold true for their friends. They don't spend a lot of time talking about their parents except in terms of what parents will and won't allow, unless someone makes a bigger issue of it. And that usually seems to come down from other adults. Our neighborhood is pretty mixed, it's not exactly what you'd call middle class, mostly it's working class—about all we can afford. At first I felt guilty because there we were, without any child support, having to move into a poorer neighborhood. But then I got into the fact that it's good that the kids are exposed to a variety of people, different races, and ethnic backgrounds. They've also been exposed to some of the prejudices.

"Last year, our neighbor from across the street told her daughter that she couldn't play with mine because we're lesbians. That was a big upset because the girl was my daughter's best friend. There simply wasn't much I could do about it except explain to my own daughter that some people are just very prejudiced. The way it worked out in the end was that I think they still play together where the other girl's mother won't see them and what happened wasn't that my girl blamed me for it at all. Kids are pretty smart about those kinds of things. I think what's happening though is that the woman across the street has a daughter who's really mad at her and it could turn into a whole big problem for them. I tried talking to the other mother, but she wouldn't even open the door for me. I feel pretty sorry for what they're going to go through.

"Naturally, it went around school that the girl's mother was a real pig. It never came back on my own girl. Kids don't really care about what their parents *do,* so much as what they do to *them.* So I turn out Mrs. Clean and I sit here wondering if that kind of prejudice isn't hurting me more than my daughter."

"Church," explains another mother, "can be a real hassle. It really got bad when gay rights got to be an issue around here. They were preaching against homosexuality. I talked to our minister about it and he was immovable and I'd be damned if I'd let my kids go to that kind of church, so we just stopped going and *I* do the Sunday school lessons. But I know, after hearing that one sermon, that my kids are now aware that Jesus didn't like queers, no matter how I explained it to them. At their age though, it's a matter of loyalty. In our case, the family won and the church lost. I think if some of those ministers knew how many people they are turning away from religion, they'd have to do some real soul-searching of their own. They've got to know that they're losing the kids, and they're going to have to do something about it besides just sit up there and tell people how awful their parents are."

Another mother comments, "We didn't have any problems until the kids began to get older, like in junior high and high school. Then, I think, they begin to question a lot of things they're taught. And one of the things my kids were taught in a class on sex education was that homosexuals were sick. They had to face a kind of schizophrenia: at home they knew that lesbians were people like any other people, but at school they got the other. It was a problem they had to wrestle with—what do they believe, their own eyes or the teacher?

"I guess they've had to grow up in a kind of schizophrenic world—homophobic in everything they hear and see on the outside, but [with] direct personal evidence that what they see out there isn't true.

"Dealing with that was sure an education for me. First I had to get over my own programming about homosexuality, then I had to figure out a way of communicating to them about it in a positive way. I finally dealt with it by doing a lot of late-night reading—both of their textbooks and of some other books in a whole variety of areas, especially history. I was able to teach them to question all those supposed authorities and make their own decisions based on their own evidence.

"The lesson that finally worked, I guess, was when I began talking with them about what they were being taught about American history. Their textbooks were just full of distortions and outright lies. They were in World War II and were all up in arms about the German concentration camps. The books they were studying didn't tell them about our own camps, the Japanese internment camps. So I made them read about them.

"It was a growing experience for all of us. They learned not to just blindly take for granted everything some authority figure told them, and I learned about history. In the end, maybe they will decide that homosexuality *is* some kind of terrible thing. But at least it will be based on their own thinking and experience, not what some teacher said in high school."

It is not only children who may have difficulties arising from the fact that they live in a lesbian household—the lesbian couple may also have problems because of the children, perhaps similar to those any step-parents might have. The Fleener survey found, however, that children came between the couple in only 15 percent of the households with children.[15] Such situations may arise when the partner is unused to being around children, as one woman explains, "My brothers and sisters were all a lot older than I was, so I was raised as an only child. I've never been around kids. In this relationship my lover has five kids and I get to the place where I just can't take another day of them and need to get away. The kids don't listen to me. I can tell them to do something and they'll completely ignore me. Then I'll go out and get their mother and she'll come out and then they'll do whatever it was I had told them to do.

"I have this fantasy that on the kids' eighteenth birthdays I'm going to get each one a set of luggage and a one-way ticket to wherever they want. Then my lover and I can begin to enjoy our life together."

It would have been seven years before all five children were eighteen, even if the fantasy could have solved this woman's problems. The woman finally gave up and moved out after six months. She and her lover still see each other, but they are no longer a lesbian household.

## LESBIAN FAMILIES BY CHOICE

Not all children in lesbian households are the products of heterosexual marriages. Of the mothers in the Fleener sample, 15 percent had adopted children and an additional 15 percent had children with a male partner whom they did not marry. These options are being more frequently chosen by lesbians who want children, as a sizable minority do. If gay people were allowed to adopt children, Fleener's respondents were asked, "Would you like to?" Thirty-four percent answered yes.[16]

Although in most parts of the country it is practically impossible for an unmarried person (be she or he straight or gay) or a lesbian couple to adopt children, a few local jurisdictions have, in view of the number of unwanted children continually being shuffled through foster homes and other institutions, seen the wisdom of expanding their adoption policies to include both single people and lesbian couples who are otherwise qualified to provide good homes.

Where adoption is not an option, increasing numbers of lesbians appear to be seeking males to consent to be biological fathers. One such couple has planned to have a child this way for two years and they have bought a home near a good school in a nice child-oriented neighborhood. Their major problem has been that the woman wanting to be the biological mother has not yet been able to get pregnant. This, they presume, is because she does not have sex regularly with men, but infrequently, for the sole purpose of becoming pregnant by a male who will have no future interest in his offspring. Many lesbians desiring to have their own children, however, prefer to find a male partner they know and like, often a gay male, and the two agree to share parental responsibilities. Such liaisons as these, whether with male friends or strange men, appear to remove from the would-be mother the threat of having custody of her child removed by legal action brought by the child's father.

Those couples desiring to add children to their lesbian homes appear to divide into two camps: women who want to have their own children, and women who do not care so much about the biological process. Says one woman who wants her own child, "I want to go through and experience pregnancy. That is a part of my womanness I want to have." But after the question of biology versus adoption is resolved, lesbians settle into serious thought about adding one or more children to their families, as this couple explains:

"First," said Beth, "we tried to think of all the negative things. How would the kid get along with a couple of lesbians as parents, would she or he 'adjust' and grow up without psychological problems; just what kinds of problems might the kid face because his parents were different from other children's parents, that kind of thing.

"Then, we really looked at our own motivations. We were really hard on ourselves. Both of us like kids a lot, but we wondered if there wasn't some hidden agenda behind all this talk of adopting children. Agendas like, 'Oh, it'll make us seem more straight, more acceptable,' or, 'It'll get my parents off my back who keep demanding grandchildren to show off.' We were really tough on each other about that and what it finally came down to was that there weren't any hidden agendas. It was just that both of us had always wanted to be parents.

"After taking care of all the negatives, we began to look at the positive things. We're both pretty stable career-wise and certainly can afford to have one or more children. We both are committed to a stable relationship—it's been going six years already, so we don't have to worry too much about splitting up a family. We've both been around children a lot so we know what we'd be getting into. And finally, we thought we had a lot to offer a kid—a loving, supportive environment; a philosophy of tolerance; and a reasonable chance of being able to offer a really balanced sense of ethics and responsibility, and certainly a good, well-rounded education.

"We are open with both of our families, so children would have not only us, but our families as well.

"The positive factors really outweighed the negative ones. Then we decided to let the matter rest and see how we felt about it in a year. We felt even more positively then.

"Then we dealt with the practical matters. Birth or adoption? Neither of us had any big thing about creating little clones of ourselves, and neither of us were into the idea of a nine-month pregnancy, labor pains, hospitals and all of that. We decided adoption was the way to go. And, we weren't really looking for a baby. We weren't looking for someone who was white like us. I guess when it got down to it, we thought we could not only offer a lot, but would really like to help some of the kids that no one else wants because they're 'too old,' or they've been in trouble with the law, or they're not white.

"Maybe it is old-fashioned, but we were into giving some of what we were lucky enough to have, as well as enjoying watching and helping kids grow up. Once we were really convinced of that, it was just a practical matter of finding a way to legally adopt. Because of our social standing, our financial position, and the help of a good lawyer, we didn't have a lot of trouble legally adopting our children. We have four kids. All of them were orphans—two from Vietnam and two from Mexico. It has been one of the most rewarding experiences of our lives."

Beth and her lover were fortunate because their wealth and social standing eased the adoption process for them. Few lesbian couples have that lucky combination. Some lesbians have begun to talk about, and seek, artificial insemination as a means of having children and avoiding hassles over the child's custody. Once such practices are discovered and publicized by sensation-seeking newspapers, as happened in London in 1977, a public furor arises, however.[17] The furor is not over the fact that the lesbian has become pregnant, but that, heaven forbid—she will be a lesbian mother! A grave sin to those who hold the patriarchal family tradition in higher esteem than the fact that children who are wanted are generally brought up in loving and caring homes.

It is clear that a large number of American children are unwanted by their biological mothers or fathers. Within the near future, courts and law-making bodies will have to decide whether it is best to keep such children moving about from foster home to foster home, from one institution to another and perhaps eventually into juvenile halls, or to abandon the outdated notion that every child needs two heterosexual people as role models in order to be wanted and to be loved.

Many lesbians are ready to bring such children into their households.

# 10

# Living with the Law

The one legal institution that most obviously symbolizes America's patriarchal family presumption is that of marriage. Lesbians, supposedly because they do not procreate, cannot legally marry. (The law, of course, overlooks heterosexual couples who cannot procreate.) Because the lesbian couple cannot marry, the partners not only are unrecognized as an entity, but they also lose many of the legal protections afforded heterosexual marrieds concerning mutual responsibilities, financial rights, and means of separation should the relationship end. Because theirs is not a legal marriage, the partners of a lesbian couple are also not able to become each other's closest kin. The lesbian couple cannot do much to change the presumptions of the law without taking political action. But lesbians *are* finding ways of working through the law, its inconsistencies, and occasionally its loopholes, to help rectify some of the most outrageous damage its heterosexist presumptions can do to their relationships.

Partners in a lesbian couple have all of the legal remedies open to any single person, many of which, if used correctly, can guarantee them some of the protections offered through marriage. Unfortunately, many lesbians, just like their unmarried but living-together heterosexual counterparts, don't take advantage of these remedies until they reach some crisis point. Few lesbian couples have wills, for example. Yet all states allow any person to bequeath his or her property to anyone she or he wishes. If the lesbian dies without a will, her partner will be completely ignored as the state takes over disposition of her property according to its own laws—all of which disinherit the surviving partner of a lesbian couple.

## WILLS

The lesbian's complaint about wills is similar to that of living-together straights, "It takes the romance out of the relationship," as one woman explained. Or, as another said, "It's not time to think about dying." Married heterosexuals also often neglect wills, but the fact of their marriage will at least guarantee that the surviving spouse will get some, if not most or all, of the property.

Unlike living-together straights, however, the lesbian's will, should she leave one, will probably run into greater difficulty in court should her surviving family try to challenge it.

Shirley and her partner, although they don't own much more than the mortgaged house they live in and one old, but paid for, Volkswagon, bit the bullet and faced the possibility that one of them might die. "We both have families," Shirley explained, "who, while they are nice enough to us now that we're alive, would come in and grab everything down to the retreaded spare tire if they could, once one of us died. We've seen them do it to other relatives, and we know they'd do it to us because we're gay and fairly easy prey. So about the first thing we did was go to a feminist attorney and get ironclad wills."

Their attorney, familiar with the wiles of property-hungry relatives, gave them two pieces of advice no lesbian couple should ignore. Said Shirley, "She explained to us that a common way families like ours try to break gay people's wills is to prove that the surviving partner used 'undue influence' to force their dead relative into willing away her property in what seems, to the family—and sometimes to judges—such an irrational manner. The other route would be to prove that the person signing the will wasn't of 'sound mind,' another area where the lesbian might have some prejudice running against her in court.

"So, we were told first to make sure and name each and every one of the relatives whether we were leaving them anything *or* whether we were disinheriting them, just to show we hadn't slipped a cog and forgotten someone. Then, we were told to redraw our wills every couple of years as additional evidence, should it be needed, that the dead partner really intended dividing her estate as it says in the will. That way, the family will have less chance of proving that their poor dead daughter wasn't of 'sound mind' when she drew up the thing and disinherited poor old Aunt Matilda and left her mother only the hubcaps as a remembrance."

The advice given Shirley is that given by many feminist attorneys familiar with the special problems of the lesbian couple.

## A PROTECTING PAPER WEB

Other legal options that may legally protect a lesbian couple from a marauding family were explored by Margo and her lover Lilly. They became, in a business sense, partners. Virtually every element of their joint lives is regulated by a mutually negotiated relationship contract into which the couple entered after research on the differences in legal status between married and unmarried couples. Their approach is one that is attracting substantial interest among unmarried heterosexual couples as well as gay couples.

Their legal partnership was triggered by a medical emergency. Explained Margo, "I had to go to the hospital for breast surgery. We had heard about problems other gay couples had experienced in this situation in terms of the hospital preventing them from seeing one another, not allowing them to make critical decisions about one another's treatment, or whatever. I had visions of something going wrong and needing a blood transfusion or whatever and them having to call my mother some two thousand miles away for permission. No way would I have that happen. If anyone has to make decisions for me when I can't, I want that person to be Lilly.

"That presented our lawyer with a totally new problem. He suggested that we draw up powers of attorney for each other giving each other the right to take care of any business matters that might come up while the other wasn't available. We did that, and then about a week before I went into surgery we went to the hospital and discussed things with them. We didn't mention a word about sexual orientation or anything. I just pointed to Lilly and said, 'Whatever may have to be done, I want her to do it. Here's a copy of the power of attorney.' I guess that had we been straight we could have just posed as husband and wife and not had to go through that, but the hospital people just nodded and said 'Yes, yes, that's perfectly okay.' It probably helped that we had an official-looking document to wave in their faces.

"There weren't any problems with the surgery, so we didn't see if it would have actually worked, but there have been quite a few times when the powers of attorney have been useful for business-type things. The great thing about them is that you can make them for a limited amount of time if you're worried that your partner would try to misuse the power. Anyway, even if you do want them permanently, it's a good idea to renew them every so often because someone might take a look at the date and if they saw it was ten years old, they might not honor it.

"When we move to a different state, we have our wills checked out by an attorney because laws on inheritance vary from state to state. Now we've learned to check out the powers of attorney as well.

"When we moved to California, for example, we went to a feminist attorney who had some experience with unmarried couples, both gay and straight. Her feeling was that the powers of attorney weren't sufficient protection for us against our families if one of us became incapacitated as the result of an accident or something. We could just imagine one of us in a car wreck and the mother coming in to take over everything.

"The lawyer suggested that we nominate each other as each other's conservators. This, as our lawyer explained it, makes up for a real gap in the powers of attorney. Powers of attorney, she explained, are valid only so long as people think that the person who has given it is actually competent to make decisions like that and is free to revoke it. Naturally, if you're in a coma, you're not legally in a position to either make or revoke a power of attorney, so parents or other relatives could come in and then that piece of paper would be meaningless. Again, it's the same question: who do you want making decisions like that for you? In the case of a married couple it's a question that never comes up because the spouse is the nearest kin.

"The way the conservatorships work, should we ever have to use them, is that if the emergency comes up, I would, let's say, go to a judge with Lilly's nomination of me as her conservator. I'd probably have to show that she was incompetent to handle her own affairs which wouldn't be difficult if she were in a serious accident or something. You also have to show that you *are* competent to handle the other person's affairs in their best interests. In our part of the country judges just tend, if you have already nominated someone, to approve whomever you've chosen. It's a complicated business and laws and practices change from place to place and time to time, but a lot more lawyers are looking into this as a way of giving nonmarried couples some freedom from intrusion by unwelcome and perhaps hostile relatives.

"There's a remarkable trap in this though. Once the supposedly incompetent person is back on her feet, she has to prove her competency to the court. This might not be too difficult for a simple medical problem, but an emotional or mental problem might be an entirely different thing. It's not like a power of attorney that you can revoke any time you please, the court has to revoke the conservatorship.

"The other catch is that conservatorships give a lot more power away than a simple power of attorney that is mainly for business transactions. Your conservator, once appointed by the court, can do virtually anything she wants to you. All of your basic human and civil rights have been transferred to the conservator. That's a really heavy situation and you've really got to trust someone to give them that kind of power over your life.

"But once a conservator is appointed, the family and everyone else is pretty much left out in the cold. Again, it's a matter of whom you trust."

## PROPERTY: DISPUTES AND REMEDIES

Just as wills, powers of attorney, and other legal protections are most often forgotten in the bloom of new love until some crisis reminds the lesbian couple of their vulnerability, questions of property ownership are also usually left to be resolved until someone wants out of the relationship. Property disputes, here as in heterosexual divorces, can and frequently do cause undue agony for the separating couple. Often, if the parting is an especially vicious one, there is little one woman can do when she finds her former lover running off with everything they purchased and invested in together, perhaps leaving nothing but the bills which may be in her name.

Most attorneys now recommend that the couple planning a long-term relationship decide early how they will divide whatever property they acquire should one or both of them eventually want to end the relationship. Many attorneys argue that it is simplest to keep each woman's property separate, save, perhaps, for a household account to take care of utilities, rent, and groceries. In such a system, an inventory listing the property that each has brought into the relationship is signed by both partners. As new property of any substance is acquired, simple agreements about who owns it and how it will be divided later should also be signed. Such agreements about property are legally valid and enforceable. Usually, however, as with most contracts, there is little need to enforce them. In general, the mere fact of having made an agreement that both partners can remember (because it is in writing) is sufficient to take the edge off separation-of-property pains.[1]

## KICKING OUT THE STATE

Further along on the legal frontiers are those lesbian couples like Margo and Lilly seeking, as an alternative to marriage, legally binding business contracts covering all aspects of their relationships, from formation to separation. These contracts are valuable for several reasons.

The first and primary benefit is that they may be tailored to meet a couple's needs. Another benefit is that because such agreements are business contracts, and are made between two people, there is no third party (the state) hidden anywhere to cause trouble later on. An additional benefit is that because they are business contracts and contract law is uniform in all states, what is agreed to in one state doesn't change if the couple moves to another state, as marriage rights often do.

When Margo and Lilly proposed this to their attorney a few years ago, she was at a loss. Few models of such contracts were then available, and their attorney advised them to draft one of their own and she would look it over. Recalls Lilly, "We first did a careful study of marriage laws to learn exactly what married couples do and do not get. It convinced us of one thing—if marriage ever became legal for gay people, it would be the *last* thing we would ever do although a lot of our friends wish they could get married. [One third of the Fleener sample said they would marry if lesbian marriages were allowed.][2]

"Wealthy people get around some of the worst problems of marriage by negotiating prenuptial agreements. These are business contracts whcre one person, Jackie Kennedy, for example, agrees to marry someone, Aristotle, under certain conditions—for a fee. This way, Aristotle gets his marriage, and upon divorce or separation, Jackie isn't left out in the cold. These agreements are legitimate business contracts. Jackie is offering what is called in legal jargon a 'consideration'—marrying Aristotle—in exchange for some consideration—money—from him.

"The interesting thing about the business contract is that it is made between two people with no government interference as the third party like you have in marriage where you're actually marrying not only your spouse, but the state as well. It's always fascinated us that the business contract is held in such high esteem by law. People can do anything they want between themselves with their property as long as it isn't a crime, and the state respects that. But God forbid you should decide to live with someone or have sex with someone who happens to be another woman.

"We began looking into the business contract as a kind of model to build a relationship contract around just to see if it was possible to express some of the protections you get in marriage in business terms in such a way that the contract would be legal.

"Some people do it on a piecemeal basis. They write specific contracts just to take care of their property, but this isn't tied to anything human, like living together, and we didn't want just a property agreement.

"It was an intriguing problem that took us about a year to work out. One of the more interesting challenges of making a relationship contract that would hold up in court, we found, is that you cannot contract to do anything illegal. Therefore, you cannot contract for sexual relations. In the first place, taking money or anything else for sex is prostitution which is illegal in most states—unless you're married and you exchange support for sex. And in the second place, gay sex is illegal in most states. So writing anything about sex in a business contract that would be valid in all states is probably impossible.

"It's okay, though, to contract for companionship. An elderly dowager, for example, might contract with another woman to accompany her on a trip to Europe or to live with her in her declining years. Well, if you're not breaking any labor laws about minimum wages or whatever, that is a perfectly legal business contract. If the dowager refuses to pay, the companion can take her to court and collect. So we decided to model our agreement around that kind of contract, the companionship contract.

"The other area of business contracts we found useful was the part where you make provisions for what to do if one or the other of the parties wants to get out of, or can't keep, the agreement. This parallels divorce and is probably one of the most useful elements of our contract.

"In order to get out of our contract, you've got to give the other party written notice and explain your reasons. We pegged that at sixty days' notice in our agreement. This kind of provides us with a cooling-off period. The written notice provision has been interesting because it's very easy to slam the door and decide you're going to leave, but when you actually have to sit down and construct, in writing, a notice of intent to terminate a business agreement, it puts the whole thing in a different perspective and really cools you off fast. That single provision, we think, has helped us to keep our relationship together on more than one occasion.

"Our contract also says we can mutually agree to terminate or renegotiate it without much problem, but if there is some dispute, then we have to go to an aribtrator to negotiate our difference. That's the business terminology. In terms of a relationship, it means marriage counseling—couples' counseling with someone who is mutually acceptable.

"There are, of course, agreements about the property aspects of our relationship and our economic relationship to each other. If one of us loses her job, or whatever, the other is obligated to support her. And, to an extent, if the arbitration didn't succeed in getting us back together or in renegotiating a new agreement, then there are some provisions that help whichever of us is less financially well-off with money until she's back on her feet—alimony.

"It took us forever, but we included all the possibilities we could think of and that almost no one ever does think of until it's too late."

Although Margo and Lilly's contract is a lifetime contract, they have stipulated that they can renegotiate its terms any time they like. This gives them flexibility in changing circumstances. They point out, also, that contracts like theirs can be signed for just a year or a few years, giving women even more flexibility. They just happened to prefer a lifetime agreement.

"When we took the contract to our attorney to look over," added Margo, "she added a provision we had forgotten—something married couples are stuck with but we aren't. Then she suggested that we separate so she could run it through the courts to see if a court would actually uphold it because so few contracts of its kind have been tested in court. We decided not to become her first test case, so we still don't know what a court would actually do with it."

The answer to what would have happened to Margo and Lilly's contract in court may have come in 1978 when a California judge ordered a lesbian "husband" to pay her "wife" $100 a month temporary support. Superior Court Judge Byron F. Lindsley's order was an interpretation of an earlier state supreme court ruling in a suit brought by Michelle Triola against actor Lee Marvin. In that landmark opinion, the high court held that putative spouses holding themselves out as husband and wife may sue for community property rights if they can prove that an implied contract existed between them.

The ruling in the lesbian case, thought to be the first of its kind in the nation, came as the result of a suit filed by Sherry D. Richardson who claimed that she quit her job as a cosmetologist in New York to live with Denease Conley in San Diego. Richardson, who said the pair had been "married" at a Metropolitan Community Church service, asserted that they had come to both oral and written agreements that Conley would support her and that they would divide any community property during their "marriage." The relationship ended after one month, and Richardson filed suit in civil court against Conley for community property, breach of contract, and $6,400 in damages for "reasonable value for services rendered." The $100 monthly support payments ordered by the judge were to continue until the case came to court for trial. Judge Lindsley told a *Los Angeles Times* reporter that both Conley and Richardson had agreed to the monthly support and he could find no legal reason to block it. "The fact that they were of the same sex," the judge added, "is of no legal consequence."[3]

## EXTRALEGAL BENEFITS

What makes Lilly and Margo's contract work for them, they say, "isn't so much that it could be enforced in court if it came down to it, but the process that we went through to negotiate it. We had to consider every possible situation we might run into in the future and decide what agreements we wanted to make. For example, what if one of us wants to move and the other doesn't; what do we do if one of us has an outside affair; what do we do if—dozens of questions. It really made us sit down and talk about what we really wanted and expected from each other.''

''Paperwork and legal things seem to intimidate most of our friends,'' said Margo. ''Few of them even have wills. So when we first tell them about our contract they look at us as if we're nuts. But after we explain it all, we find there's really a lot of interest in it because so many people have heard so many stories of the kinds of problems gay couples can get into with their families when a death or emergency comes up. Also, there's a lot of interest in it because some people want to get legally tied for romantic reasons and can't get married. They have some sort of romantic fascination for an agreement that will bind them into some kind of partnership. Actually, it's not romantic at all. It's a practical necessity.''

''It has helped us a great deal,'' added Lilly. ''It forced us to really look at our needs and capacities and make agreements about them. And 99 percent of contracts that are written, unlike marriages, don't end up in court at all. It's as if there's some sort of moral compulsion for people to keep contracts that they have had to carefully negotiate. Marriages, like most lesbian love affairs, aren't really negotiated at all. Maybe that's why so many of them don't last.''

# Role-Free Living

The patriarchal axiom of American society dictates that among heterosexual couples certain roles and tasks be delegated by gender. These, in many states, still remain codified in law. Wives are expected to provide the family's nurturing and to service their husbands' sexual desires. A husband is expected to provide the bulk of the family's income and to be, as family "head," the unit's final arbiter. As the patriarchal family system implodes, many of these roles are breaking down and many heterosexual couples are experimenting with alternatives to them.

The lesbian, however, was never included in this system, and so she starts with a clean slate upon which to create the rules and roles of her relationships. Few lesbians presume they must play any role or fit any stereotype taken from their heterosexual counterparts. Nor does any lesbian presume she must trade her independence for economic security. Most lesbians are used to making it on their own and neither expect nor demand special privileges from their partners. Nor do they expect to give any.

A lesbian's lifestyle, while outlawed in most regions, can become a stage on which she may experiment with freedom. With the shackles of heterosexual presumption removed, she is free to play out any role she chooses, to create roles that perhaps do not yet exist, and to find the lifestyle that fits her needs best. The choice is hers to make. Some women, unaware, unaccustomed, or unhappy with their freedom choose to adapt the heterosexual role models they see around them to fit their needs. Others, while appreciating their freedom, would be happier with a few more relationship guidelines, some paths to follow along freedom's trail. Many lesbians welcome their freedom exuberantly, dancing on their outlaw stage through many experiments in egalitarian living.

But even on her outlaw stage, freedom is not total. Society has provided many of the props, the background, and the scenery for her play. Despite the fact that these are only images, they are real enough. However a lesbian couple may decide to play out their relationship, the symbols from a patriarchal environment may intrude upon them at any moment. Chief among these symbols are those that carry social value: so-called feminine chores that are considered second-class; income, where more appears to symbolize better; and sex, often as much of a power symbol as a physical act. It is the intrusion of these artifacts of patriarchal society that most frequently causes strain in new lesbian relationships as the partners find their particular patterns of interaction creating neither dependence nor independence, but mutually sustaining interdependence.

## HOUSEHOLD CHORES

Fortunately for many lesbians who have not really learned the lessons of heterosexual family life quite so well as their heterosexual sisters, there are no standards that they feel compelled to follow in their household affairs. A woman's partner does not expect her to keep house like her mother did, nor does she expect to do so. This does not mean that the two women do not have different standards of tidiness to which they have adapted, however; nor does it mean that one may not have a preference for certain household chores: one may be a gourmet cook and the other an expert at fixing plumbing. Or one may be both cook and plumber and her partner useless indoors. But it is often the "tidiness" issue that seems the most difficult for the lesbian couple to resolve, again because society's scenery has created the image that certain chores are second-class.

Recalls Olga, "We fought and fought over keeping the house clean. Liza was a slob. I read and reread my feminist books and gave Liza all the arguments I had about how housework should be equally shared. I told her I did not want to play 'wife' to her 'husband.' I must admit, that argument seemed to work. It worked for exactly one week, that is all. So again I began doing all the cleaning and I resented it more and more. Liza, I told myself, just thought of me as a very convenient person to have around, a 'wife.' And I did not come to America, discover my lesbianism and fall in love with Liza to be anyone's wife or servant."

This couple's housework hassles continued for about a year. Liza explains how they finally resolved them. "I asked Olga why she was doing so much cleaning. Why she *insisted* on mopping the kitchen floor every morning. Why she had a fetish about putting the dishes away before we went to bed. I asked her who she was doing it all for. She said, 'For you.' I said, 'Not for me. Obviously I couldn't care less about a perfectly kept house.' That, I think was Realization One for Olga—that if she was doing it for me she was deluding herself.

"That didn't stop her though. She admitted, 'Okay, I'm doing it for me,' but she still resented doing it.

"So we went into phase two: 'Isn't there something you'd rather be doing?' I really gave her a low blow, I guess. 'You mean you'd rather be doing the dishes than making love with me?' That, I think, sank in."

Explains Olga, "I got the point. It took awhile, but I began to look at my housework habits. A lot of it was foolish. Some of it I was really doing because I liked to see things certain ways, but most of it was just a habit I had picked up. It was just something I did, not something I chose.

"I stopped playing Mrs. American Clean. Yes, the house is a bit less tidy, but I have grown used to it. Now I have more time to do the things I *want* to do, not the things that some book on being a woman says I *must* do."

Other couples resolve the conflict differently. Says Grace of one of her relationships, "We just divided our apartment into two areas—hers and mine. She could keep hers any way she liked. I just learned to ignore it. If we had company, she cleaned up her area and helped with the rest of the place. I never understood how anyone could live with such clutter, but she seemed to function quite well. It never ceased to amaze me."

Explains another woman, "We just came to an accommodation. We both agreed that we both hated housework. So we analyzed it. There were things that were essential: dishes, garbage, fixing leaky washers, whatever. It turned out that of the necessary chores each of us preferred one or the other with the exception of vacuuming, which we both hated. So now we each do the chores we prefer and we take turns with the vacuum cleaner.

"In making up our list we redefined housework to suit our needs. A lot of things that other people might think important, like waxing the floors once a week, we just let go until one of us decides she wants to do it or until it really becomes a need, rather than a fixation. You'd be surprised how much of what we used to consider 'housework' simply does not exist for us."

Bell and Weinberg found that about 92 percent of their lesbian couples did not share all household tasks equally, but an even larger group—about 94 percent—denied that they did either all the "masculine" or "feminine" chores.

Housecleaning appeared to be the most frequently shared task, 61 percent saying they shared it equally with their partners. Second in line of tasks most often shared equally was shopping: 55 percent reported equal division of labor at the grocery store. Household repairs, apparently, tend to fall either to the most mechanically adept or the most interested women. Only 39 percent reported sharing the job of repairs equally. Cooking appears to fall to the one who enjoys it most—35 percent of Bell and Weinberg's lesbian couples reported sharing the cooking equally.[1]

## MONEY

While the allocation of household chores seems to be a remnant of patriarchal indoctrination that brings strain to lesbian couples, money, apparently, does not. It might be argued that because lesbians are women they have not been acculturated to value it so highly as men may have been. However, Bell and Weinberg's data on the money affairs of their gay couples were nearly the same for both men and women. In most lesbian households, both partners have incomes (78 percent of Bell and Weinberg's couples) but seldom are the two incomes equal. The number of women reporting incomes equal to their partner's was only 14 percent. When asked if income disparity had any effect on their relationships, only about 6 percent reported it had a negative effect.[2]

Those couples reporting that their income disparity had a negative effect on their relationship may have had an experience similar to Kathy and Toni's, where the disparity was so great it was bound to cause some problem. Kathy, a stockbroker, earned in excess of $40,000 a year. Toni, a free-lance writer, averaged only about $8,000. Recalled Kathy, "When we started our relationship I did not want to make Toni feel like she was dependent on me. So we sat down and made out a budget for household necessities and we each contributed half. This soon became a major problem. Because of the fact that she didn't earn nearly as much as I, I had to lower my standard of living to accommodate a budget that she could afford. This didn't work out at all and continually caused us problems."

Added Toni, "When we started out, I didn't want her to get off on a trip of her feeling like she 'had to support' me. No one has supported me since I was sixteen."

Eventually, the couple negotiated a settlement that seemed to satisfy both. Explained Kathy, "We finally looked at money and its relative importance in our lives. Money didn't actually mean that much. What was important was our time and we felt that our time was equally valuable. What we got paid for our time was something that had very litle to do with anything about or within ourselves—what we got paid for our time was all based on decisions we had little input into and seemed fairly irrational anyway.

"So we finally agreed to contribute to household expenses according to our income. If I earned four times as much as she, then I contributed four times as much to the household account. This gave us a lot more freedom and we began to live in a lifestyle that I was more comfortable with. Naturally, if our income relationship changes, then the percent contribution will also change. After all, she could strike it rich one of these days, or the stock market might fold tomorrow."

Many lesbians appear to have similar attitudes about money; earning capacity and income disparity is not a major influence affecting relationships. It is almost as if the lesbian has rejected the idea that money is equivalent to status or personal value along with other lessons of patriarchal culture. Explains one woman, "Money never had much meaning for me except in the sense that there was never quite enough of it. In our relationship the fact that one of us earned more or less didn't mean much either. What was important was whether we had enough to do the things we wanted to do. I've been unemployed and my lover's supported me, and I helped her while she went back to school. No matter who earns what, it goes to help us get and do the things we want, so who cares that much about where it comes from?''

Said another woman, ''Good financial management between un-married couples can also provide tax savings. It's simple—the one who earns the most and is taxed at the highest rate, pays all the bills. Then she gets all the deductions for interest or whatever. If one of us is employed and the other isn't then that gives extra exemptions. My father was a CPA and he always said the laws are there for your protection. I took the lesson to heart and we use every one we can.''

For some lesbians, however, a separate income is a very important sign of their independence, one which they are unwilling to give up. Explains one woman, ''One of the things I've always been proud of was my ability to get by on my own. I guess it's a big part of my self-identity and I guess I'm just not ready to give that up in our relationship yet.'' About 30 percent of the Bell and Weinberg sample said that they kept their incomes separate from their partner's.[3]

About 14 percent of Bell and Weinberg's lesbian couples said they kept some of their incomes separate and combined some with their partner's, apparently in one variation or another of the household account management system described by Kathy and Toni.[4]

Nearly half of lesbian couples (47 percent of the Bell and Weinberg sample who were involved in coupled relationships) combined all of their incomes, but not necessarily out of commitment to egalitar-ianism.[5] As one woman explained, ''We went through everything. For the first year we kept our money in separate accounts and put some into a joint kitty for food, rent, and utilities. That got to be a drag each month, figuring out who should put in how much for what, so then we tried the separate household account routine. Each of us just put 50 percent of our money into it and we bought all the household stuff we needed out of it. That was sort of silly too, because most of the things we bought we bought together and by mutual decision. So the joint household account eventually became our single joint account and now we just deposit our checks directly into it. That way, instead of having to keep track of three separate accounts, we only have to worry about one. It saves us a lot of rubber checks.''

The woman's lover added, "We kind of like it that way. To us it symbolizes that we're really together, that we really trust each other, that we're really a couple and not just a pair of roommates living together from day to day."

## SEX

One interesting and significant difference between lesbian and heterosexual relationships is the role that sex plays in them. Sex, even though lesbian couples often enjoy a full sex life, is not viewed as a dominant factor in most lesbian relationships. While 30 percent of Fleener's lesbian couples said that sex was "very important," 57 percent ranked it as only "fairly important" in their relationships. The remainder said sex was either not very important or not important at all.[6] Fleener's data tend to be confirmed by Bell and Weinberg's findings that of the "other things" their lesbian respondents were getting out of their current affairs, sexual satisfaction ranked a low third, with only about 20 percent of the respondents checking it off. Ranking second was "Peace, happiness," and first was "Love, warmth, friendship." (Again, interestingly, data for coupled gay males and females were not very different.)[7]

Perhaps, as one woman explained, "That's because sex doesn't come first in a lesbian relationship; it grows out of how you feel about someone. Heterosexuals have a real power thing going about sex. You keep hearing about the 'war of the sexes'; well, I think that, for straights, is played out under the sheets. Maybe for heterosexuals, sex is where it's at, while for lesbians sex is *part* of where it's at."

The most important part of lesbians' relationships with other women, Fleener found, was emotional commitment. Half the Fleener sample reported that this was the most important component of their relationships. An additional 45 percent said that friendship was the most important part of their relationships with women. Only 5 percent rated physical closeness or sexual satisfaction as most important.[8]

The axiom of lesbian relationships is equality and it is carried into their sex lives. Neither partner is expected to be, nor expects to be, the exclusive "provider" of the other's sexual satisfaction. The majority of the women responding to the Fleener questionnaire, 82 percent, said that in their relationships mutual sexual satisfaction was more important than either self-satisfaction, or satisfaction for the partner.[9]

The lesbian couple's sexual relationship, while different from heterosexuals' in many aspects, shares some important similarities. Unfortunately, little information is available about the sexual problems of lesbian relationships, perhaps because few wish to upset the self-flattering myth that all lesbian sex is always great. Some problem areas became apparent in the interviews for this book, however.

After the first flares of sexual passion have cooled, lesbian couples report three major kinds of adjustment difficulties. The first of these is common to all couples—differing levels of sexual drive which may vary, not only between partners, but during different periods of their lives together as well. The second is also common to many coupled relationships of either affectional preference: the use of sex as a not-so-secret weapon, either withholding sexual attentions or demanding them at inappropriate times as a form of punishment for some presumed misdeed. The third adjustment, and perhaps more frequent in lesbian relationships than in heterosexual ones, centers on the couple's struggle to maintain their independence as individuals in their relationship.

Dixie and Tracy were only a few months into their relationship when they ran headlong into the dependent versus independent problem. Says Dixie, "The first four months we were very close and didn't see anybody; actually, we spent as much time as possible in bed together. Now we're getting to the point where we're breaking out, inviting people to come down and spend time with us, wanting to be with other people, either independently or together. Tracy used to say she didn't like being so close, us being so dependent on each other; and that's the hardest thing we've had to deal with; keeping our independence, our individuality."

Tracy comments, "I just wanted her to let me go, let me loose. That's the way I've always been. I am independent. I'm into the kind of thing where you do your thing, I'll do mine, and we'll do some things together. She sort of latched on to me so I began to feel like I was living for her. My life was her life."

This conflict was most dramatically manifested in the sexual arena. Explains Dixie, "For example, I would be sexually frustrated a lot. This was my first lesbian relationship and it's as if I've been building up all that sexual need for all these years. But there were times when Tracy didn't seem to want any part of me, and naturally, the first thing

I thought about was rejection, a hard thing for anyone to deal with.

"But she was just trying to get the point across to me that she just wasn't in a sexual place at that time that I was. She was saying to me, 'Take care of it the best way you know how. Masturbate, go out and fuck somebody else, just deal with it, but don't blame me for your frustrations.' I'd feel so frustrated that I'd just want to kill somebody. I couldn't get what she was saying.

"I finally did get it. I got that just because I live with her and she's my lover, that doesn't mean she automatically services me every time I get horny."

Most lesbians appear to maintain some degree of sexual autonomy through masturbation. According to the Fleener survey, of those women with partners, only 20 percent never masturbated. Twenty-two percent reported they did masturbate, but seldom; 12 percent said occasionally; 24 percent said sometimes; and 22 percent reported they masturbated often.[10] Masturbation as an alternate way of resolving sexual dependency conflicts is apparently threatening to neither partner in the lesbian relationship.

Recalls one woman, "I went through a time when I was just one hundred percent committed to a project I was working on. All of my energies were directed toward it, including my sexual energies. This caused some problem for my lover who knew I wasn't rejecting her—we'd been together too long for that—but still had sexual needs and desires. I suggested she masturbate. She was raised in a very puritanical family and apparently really caught hell the first time she ever tried it, when she was five or something, and so she had a hard time around that. The first thing I guess she wondered was whether or not that wouldn't somehow threaten me. 'Well, of course not,' I told her. My God, that notion seemed absurd to me. It must have been something she picked up from her earlier straight marriage. The whole process of learning to pleasure herself was very foreign to her, especially in anything that seemed to involve *sex*. She's been working with that for a while, and although she's still reluctant to masturbate, at least she's learned that it's okay, that pleasuring yourself is like taking care of yourself, being good to yourself. But that early antisexual training was a real problem to overcome."

Some coupled lesbians, including women who have been in relationships for a decade or more, find the need to assert their autonomy through sexual relationships with other women. Explains one woman, "We'd been together for thirteen years and I was beginning to wonder if I was still attractive. I can't exactly explain it. Anyway, I went out and had a couple of affairs. Big deal. I proved my point, I was still attractive, still able to get it on with someone besides my lover. I felt rather foolish about the whole thing."

Another woman explained, "Our sexual relationship has always been very sedate. In the beginning that was okay because I didn't know any differently. But when I turned forty I went through a thing of 'God, what have I missed. My life is going by, pretty soon I'll be too old to do anything.' Of course I know now that you can go on until you croak, but I didn't know it then. All I knew was that our sex life wasn't really satisfying and I began to get curious. I wanted to be able to express myself sexually, but I was frustrated. I knew I loved my partner, I knew I enjoyed sex with her, but I wondered what it would be like to make love with other women.

"We began socializing in the gay bars and then I realized, 'My God, there are other women out there,'and I wondered if I'd like sex with them.

"The first few experiences I had, although they weren't physically all that hot, were exciting to me because I got a whole new sense of awareness about myself! The first thing that happened was that I became more enthralled with the fact that I was a woman-loving woman. And I knew I wanted to explore that, to revel in it. I wanted to get that out of my system and I knew that if I didn't, it would be in my mind for the rest of my life, 'Why didn't I take that opportunity when it was there?'"

After about a year of experimentation, this woman and her partner agreed that they would be happier living separately. Both enjoy their new autonomy, although both also consider themselves just as much a committed couple as they ever did during their previous twelve years together.

Living separately while in a committed relationship is a lifestyle that appeals to a significant minority of lesbians. Twenty-six percent of those of the Fleener sample who had partners lived alone.[11]

Said one woman about her decision to live alone, "I love June deeply; we are as committed a couple as there could be. In fact, we are monogamous. But we each value our freedom and our independence. We found that by living separately we both had a lot more freedom and space. It saves us a lot of time as well. When we are together now, which is almost every night, we are being there together, not hassling over some detail of our daily lives or something like why the electricity bill was so high. We've found that the more autonomous we are, the more we enjoy each other, the more we have to share with each other, the more we each grow—both together and as individuals—the deeper our relationship becomes."

Freedom. Space. Growth. These are what a lesbian seeks. The passage from independent woman, through the limits of dependency that can accompany any emotionally committed relationship, to the maturity of autonomous interdependence and mutual support can sometimes be a long one for the lesbian couple. It represents the maturation of their relationship, and few lesbians who have experienced it would choose to live any other way.

Concludes Jane, "Last Valentine's Day we had our twentieth anniversary. A few years ago I felt that if anything happened to our relationship or to Rae that my whole world would be lost. But we have helped each other work through so many of the things that stood in the way of our development that now I no longer feel that way. I could live, and I could live *well*."

The lesbian has been given her own stage upon which to create her life and her relationships, to dance as she sees fit, troubled only by the props and scenery remnant of the last show, the patriarchal extravaganza. One woman, who recognized her lesbianism when she was forty-eight years old, summarizes, "I have never met a single heterosexual woman who went through even a day wondering why she was straight. It was a question I spent months with—why am I gay? What *is* gay? What does being a lesbian mean? My first answers were that it meant I was an outcast from society, condemned as a human being, and violating a law every time I expressed my love and sexuality. I realized I fit none of the rules the mainstream had set up, that no matter what I did, I would *never* fit any of the rules.

"It was like being born again. I found myself at a new beginning where since none of the rules fit, I could challenge *all* of the rules and assumptions; I was free to create myself, nothing need stop me, and no assumption should get in the way of that exploration and creation. As I began to create myself, I felt more and more like an outsider, looking in at a world that others had created. I began to see its sickness. I began to see its misplaced values: material things over spiritual things, status and power over love and human relationships.

"I began to see the possibility of a life without limits, a place where I was free to challenge everything I chose, and free to try to change those things I wanted.

"I cannot express it. It was joy, it was freedom, it was power. It was an epiphany."

# PART THREE

## The Personal Becomes Political

Throughout most of recorded history lesbians have lived underground, in cooperation with the social contract binding them to invisibility. They have either passed as heterosexuals, lived together quietly in presumed spinsterhood, or otherwise suppressed their identities from public view. Few, if any, historical records exist showing any lesbian declaring herself openly prior to the twentieth century. Even then, the first people to challenge society's oppression of lesbians in the United States were heterosexual social reformers, and these spoke out against oppression of all homosexuals, both male and female.

Margaret Sanger, now chiefly remembered for her advocacy of birth control, was an early proponent of an end to the oppression of homosexuals. In 1913 Sanger hosted Edith Ellis, European sex researcher Havelock Ellis's lesbian wife, in the United States where she spoke openly, advocating lesbian relationships. Emma Goldman, the anarchist, going against the warnings of her comrade anarchists, spoke frequently and forcefully against injustices to American homosexuals.

And then, until 1929, the wall of silence around the subject of lesbianism rose again to be breached only by news of the obscenity trial against Radclyffe Hall's book *The Well of Loneliness*. Publication of the book was finally allowed in America where it sold millions of copies, but was seldom discussed. The subject of lesbianism again became taboo until after the second World War.

The results of World War II were twofold. Women and minorities who had found employment both in the military and the booming wartime industry entered the peacetime economy with raised expectations of continued economic and social options. At the same time, under the Truman administration, the cold war began—with its purges of lesbians and male homosexuals, along with communists and alleged "fellow travelers" from government, government-related employment, educational institutions, and the media. "Commie-pinko-pervert" became one word for the enemy of Americanism. (This despite the fact that homosexuals tend to span the spectrum of political opinion from conservative to radical. Few lesbians, only about 6 percent in Bell and Weinberg's findings, identify themselves as radical.)[1]

By 1951, Senator Joseph McCarthy, riding on the wave of repression that had already been building, was able to make a career of the persecution of "perverts and subversives." The year of Senator McCarthy's infamous Wheeling, West Virginia, speech on alleged communists in government also marked the founding of the Mattachine Society, the first postwar American homosexual rights organization. Although mostly a male organization, a few lesbians were members.

It was not until 1955, at the peak of the great fear aroused by McCarthy and his predecessors, that lesbians themselves organized their own group under the banner of Daughters of Bilitis (DOB). DOB, reflecting the era, at first proposed only modest goals designed to help the lesbian "fit" better into mainstream society and to change her seventeen-hundred-year-old image as a pseudomale. By the mid-sixties, DOB had chapters in many American cities and its goals had been expanded. Lesbians had begun to assert that they, as human beings in a free society allegedly espousing dedication to the civil rights of all people, were just as entitled as any other Americans to basic human and civil rights and to the legal protections necessary to ensure them.

In the sixties, the organizing that surrounded the struggle for black rights and the protest against the Vietnam war led to two phenomena that influenced the emergence of the lesbian rights movement as it exists today. The women's movement, dormant for many decades, resurfaced under the banner of the National Organization for Women

(NOW) and its more radical counterparts; and gay leftists from the antiwar protests began, in the early seventies, to organize under the banner of the Gay Liberation Front (GLF). Lesbian activists found ideological homes in both movements. They also found that they were unwelcome in the first—NOW—and second-class citizens in the second—GLF.

From this experience a lesbian consciousness and theory of feminism arose, asserting that the roots of both the oppression of women and the oppression of homosexuals are to be found in "sexism"—that host of attitudes stemming from the mainstream patriarchal assumption that men are superior to women and that certain roles are "normal" to each gender.

Lesbians, after intense struggle, were able to show their heterosexual sisters that the source of their oppressions was the same and that many of their concerns overlapped, especially the primary issue of the women's movement: freedom to control one's destiny as a person equal to any other. Lesbian feminists argued that integral to this must be the freedom of a woman to control her body, including its sexuality. By the late seventies, most women's rights organizations included on their agendas civil rights for gay people, and lesbians were welcomed into the women's movement with a degree of warmth at all levels.

Similar progress was not made in the traditionally male-led gay movement where many lesbians find they still must fight sexism to establish positions of equality. In some male gay rights circles, a nascent backlash against feminist demands began to become noticeable to some lesbians by the late 1970s. Reports one, "I think it goes along with this whole 'me first' movement we're experiencing in society. A couple of years ago I could have had a relatively peaceful discussion with most activist men on issues of feminism—why I resented being called a girl and so forth. Lately, I sense a real antagonism. It's as if some men figure they've made enough concessions to feminism and have gotten into thinking that it's okay to be sexist. Now I get told straight out, 'Yes, I'm sexist. So what?' and then they'll go out of their way to call me a 'girl'" In some largely middle-class and often conservative circles, men now assert their "right" to be sexist. It is symptomatic of the backlash feminists have observed in mainstream society.

## A CHANGING WORLD

The world has changed dramatically over the last quarter-century for the American lesbian. Lesbian activism, with roots in the homophile movement of the early fifties and DOB, and toughened by its contacts with both the women's and gay liberation movements, is now a vibrant movement in its own right. No longer is the word *lesbian* unmentionable. No longer is the lesbian's invisibility complete. No longer need she be quite so isolated as she was twenty, ten, or even five years ago. Indeed, many women's first lesbian experiences are now taking place in context of the movement, rather than in America's lesbian underground.

Where once the lesbian's role models were to be found in pornographic books or texts on abnormal psychology, they are now available to her in many aspects of public life. In a move inconceivable even a few years ago, an open lesbian state legislator, Elaine Noble, campaigned in 1978 for a United States Senate seat with the endorsement of one of the most powerful political figures in the country, the Speaker of the House of Representatives. Fifty-two thousand Massachusetts citizens cast their votes for her.

Once the lesbian's primary social meeting place was the gay bar, but now she has a variety of organizations and clubs geared to her special interests in many regions of the country. Instead of living out a life in an underground subculture, she has access to an emerging counterculture, with its own lesbian music, poetry, literature, publications, and services.

# 12

# The Dream

What we wanted was to see a world where women would be free from any stigma because of their love. We saw a world where loving women was not a sign of shame. We saw a world where young women would not have to put themselves in a purgatory of questioning their worthwhileness, a world where there would be fewer suicides, fewer traumas, a world where women would not be put away because they loved women.

We envisioned a world where younger lesbians could come out into a place of support, where a crime-syndicate-run bar in a back-alley would no longer be the place where she had to go to meet other women.

We envisioned a world where a woman could love women and be judged on her merits on her job, in the courts, in her relations with others, and not on her love.

We saw a world that someday would affirm that love between women was as positive and beautiful as we knew it to be. A world where love would not be measured by gender, but by its qualities of compassion, its depth of passion, its wealth of aliveness.—*A lesbian rights activist*

In 1955 a small cluster of women gathered semisecretly to form the first American lesbian rights organization, many feared arrest, and few were willing to give their true names. They called their organization the Daughters of Bilitis, a comfortable name reminiscent of just one more women's civic group akin to the Daughters of the American Revolution.

Twenty years later an eighteen-year-old woman from Twin Falls, Idaho, hitchhiked through the Nevada desert, over the Sierra Nevada Mountains, and into the green farm valleys of California to San Francisco, where the dream of lesbian rights had found its first expression. By 1975 that city was known, even in remote regions of rural America, as the Mecca of homosexuality. Explained Carla, ''I knew I would never make it in Idaho. As far as I knew, I was the only lesbian in town. I didn't know much, but I knew that I would find something in San Francisco that was better than where I was. I went there in search of myself, in search of other people like me, in search of my tribe. As a high school student I had read reports about the Gay Liberation Front in *Time* and *Newsweek*. Once in a while there were even photos, photos of women who were lesbians. They mentioned demonstrations by thousands of gay people, things like Gay Pride Day. I felt that if I went to San Francisco I would find myself.

"I guess I had a fantasy about what San Francisco would be like—gay people on every street corner or something. When I got there I was in a state of shock, first, I guess, because it was the biggest city I'd ever been in. And second, because I didn't see any gay people, just regular people, all of whom seemed to have a place to go, something to do. I didn't know where to start, what to do. I didn't know one place from another. I didn't even know there were gay districts. My best chances, I guessed, would be to go to Haight-Ashbury. I figured if that had been the big hippie district I might find something there.

"It was nearly deserted. The hippie thing was over. It was just like any other place except for a couple of run-down head shops. I wandered around quite a bit looking for someone, something gay.

"I must have looked pretty scared. A black guy came up and asked me what I was looking for. You can't imagine my apprehension. I had never talked to a black person in my life before. I just blurted it out, 'I'm looking for Gay Liberation.' He laughed at me, 'Well, you've found it, baby.' He told me he was gay and suddenly it all became real for me. I think if I had any racial prejudices, they all vanished the minute he said he was gay.

"He took me under his wing for a few days, introducing me around and telling me where things were. Eventually, I ended up downtown at the offices of the Daughters of Bilitis and they had a whole list of resources. I met the first lesbian I had ever seen there in that Market Street office. Finally, it was as if I had come home."

In an interview three years later, Carla recalled a coming out experience vastly different from that of many of her older peers. Asked if she had ever experienced any guilt about her lesbianism, or any feelings that it was something she should reject, she responded, amazed at the question, ''Guilt? Why should I feel any guilt? Being gay is the most wonderful part of my life. I'm proud to be a lesbian!''

## LESBIAN HOMOPHOBIA

Some Meccas are located in time, rather than in some geographic place. A lesbian in New York recalled, ''I'd lived in Manhattan for the last fifteen years, in the Village. Right through Stonewall, right through gay liberation, women's liberation, everything. But I had never gone to a gay bar, not to mention a gay organization meeting. I'd seen the newspaper stories, the television coverage, the parades, all of it. They frightened me. The boldness of them, the way many of them dressed, the radicalness. All of those images kept me away.

''But when Anita Bryant won in Florida in 1977 I was totally blown away. It made me madder than hell. I didn't know what to do about it, but I knew I had to do something. There was a lot of talk about International Women's Year and the meeting they were having for it in Houston that November. I decided to become involved in one of the support groups for IWY—not as a lesbian, just as a concerned woman. It was my way of finding a safe place to begin exploring the gay rights movement. I went to Houston as an observer. What I was there to observe, of course, were the lesbians.

''It was an explosive experience for me. In those few days my consciousness took a leap into a totally different place from where it had ever been before.

''I learned that I had a lot of homophobia. This went back two or three years to when I was trying to come out, trying to meet someone else who was gay. I needed some role models to come out by. And certainly I hadn't seen them in any of the gay parades or demonstrations. I didn't see myself as a butch, so I didn't feel I needed to learn how to be butch because that wouldn't be me any more than being straight was me. I didn't know how to be a lesbian, how to act. I needed some kind of role model and the only visible gay women I saw were the butches. You could walk down the streets and point them out, 'There's a dyke, there's a dyke.' Of course, if they're not butch, you can't point them out, you can't find them even if you know they are there. So I was angry because I didn't have any role models.

"And I was angry at the dykes because I felt like I wanted to feel good about being gay and they didn't look like they felt very good about themselves. You would see them walking down the streets in their army fatigues, in rags practically, and they just looked very unhappy. Their faces looked troubled. And I thought to myself, 'How am I supposed to feel good about that?'

"Of course, my sister was fine like that. She looked like that all the time dressed in her jeans and blue workshirts, but that was *her*. That's the way she's always been. And she's not gay. I didn't understand the discontinuity of that at first—it's okay to look butch if you're straight, but if you're gay it's not okay.

"So at Houston I remember going into the room of nondelegate lesbians. There were a lot of dykes who had obviously traveled a long way to get there and who had traveled hard. They had sleeping bags with them and they didn't look like they had eaten very much for a long time. And they were what I thought of as butches. I walked into the room and they were having a meeting. They were hassling back and forth, arguing radical things that didn't make any sense to me. I just automatically turned off. I just shut them out and wouldn't have anything to do with them.

"But when I got back to my hotel room I really had to confront myself. These women were the backbone of the lesbian movement. If the conference was going to pass a lesbian rights resolution it would be because of the labors of these women. And here they needed support and I was dumping on them. I was dumping on them because they made me feel sad. And these were the women who did hard work to get to the conference and were poor and didn't have anything to live on while they were there and I wanted to kick them out.

"And then on the next day the conference was supposed to vote on the sexual preference resolution. All those delegates—two thousand of them—manicured, hair-dressed, pants-suited, and skirted. A hush came over the hall. Betty Friedan, the woman who a few years ago tried to get lesbians kicked out of the women's movement, supported the gay resolution. And Ellie Smeal, head of NOW, took the microphone. I don't think I will ever forget the effect her words had on me:

I rise because I know that this is a profound human issue. The double standards—one for women, one for men, one for heterosexuals, another for homosexuals—these double standards work to keep women in their place. We must be free. We must be free to develop all of our potentials. And we must not oppress any part of our society, or of womanhood. Human rights are indivisible. When we march together toward equality, we will march as homosexuals, heterosexuals, minority women and majority women, rich and poor. We will all go together, as full human beings.[1]

"And it struck home. I realized that what had been keeping me away from my sisters was my own homophobia and I began to feel very bad about it and realized that was something, this homophobia of mine, that I would really have to look at. That is my kind of homophobia. Those people just look funny. That's where I have to grow.

"When I got back to New York I decided I had to face up to it. I joined the National Gay Task Force and began volunteering some of my time. I still feel strangely about some of the women I meet there, but I cannot forget that moment at Houston—when we march together toward equality, we will all march together, rich and poor, gay and straight, black and white, dressed in army fatigues or high heels. It was my coming out."

## MERGING THE PERSONAL AND POLITICAL

There is a second coming out which many consider essential if basic civil and human rights are to be secured for lesbians: the public declaration of affectional preference. The reasoning behind this argument is that gay people, without this public declaration, remain invisible—unlike racial minorities who are physically visible (when people choose to look) as a substantial segment of the American populace. Without this public coming out, no one can be certain that gay people are a sizable minority. Few people are aware of the reality of the social contributions made by closeted lesbians in public office, in schoolrooms, in hospitals, everywhere—as mothers, sisters, daughters, friends. The argument is made that were all lesbians to turn lavender overnight, America would be shocked into accepting them as part of the mainstream and the stereotypes so convenient to those who challenge gay rights today would be eliminated.

As a woman enters the lesbian movement, even on the fringes, increasing pressure is exerted on her to come out publicly. This pressure is also an internal one, as one woman explains, "I know things would be better for all gay people if women such as myself would come out publicly. I wish I could. One thing is certain, however. That would be the end of my career. No multimillion-dollar corporation is likely to want a lesbian company president.'' The decision to come out publicly is an intensely personal one in which a woman must confront her fears of losing her livelihood. Though there are many public ways of coming out—on the job, to the family, to friends—none seems so public as sitting for a newspaper interview, talking to a church group in support of gay rights legislation, or marching in a gay rights demonstration. This is a kind of public coming out that cannot be covered up later, cannot be retracted, cannot be erased from the historical record. It is irrevocable. In this kind of coming out the lesbian may feel she is releasing the most private and sacred parts of her life into an arena that she cannot control. She fears the public response and she fears what might happen as a result of her action in five, ten, or twenty years when times may change and jobs be closed to lesbians. She is not confident that what limited security she has in her present position will be protected in the distant future after a public coming out.

The kind of coming out that the drive for gay rights seems to compel appears to be a step from which there is no return. The lesbian is often terrified of taking that step. Yet many a lesbian does take this public step, either out of compassion for her sisters, or as a step toward enhancing her own self-esteem. The challenge is before her. ''Will you be on a panel at the high school? Will you march in the demonstration with us? Will you speak on a television program?''

Explains one woman, ''I'd been involved in the background of the gay rights movement for a few years. Everyone in the group knew I was gay. My family knew I was gay. My clients knew I was gay. I was almost as far 'out' as a person could be. But I had always backed off from that final step. Occasionally they tried to volunteer me for a newspaper interview. I could see the headlines splashed across the front page the next day, 'LESBIAN GYNECOLOGIST COMES OUT.'

''There were all sorts of reasons why I should come out publicly: the movement needed more professional people in visible positions, true; I would be setting a positive role model for women, true. All of what they said was true.

''Finally I just got tired of saying no. I decided to make my first public coming out at a gay professional caucus. It was a program on lesbian health problems. I was a natural for the panel. And, I supposed, I could always back out. After all, I didn't *have* to say I was a lesbian if I didn't want to.

"And there I was on the podium in front of about fifty people, most of them strangers to me. The moment of choice had arrived for me. I knew that I had to do it if I was going to be able to live with myself.

"I introduced myself and then I said it straight out: 'I am a lesbian gynecologist and have had an extensive practice in the field of lesbian health problems.' The audience applauded that statement. And I continued, 'This is the first time I have ever declared my affectional preference publicly.' It brought down the house. It was an instantaneous and tangible feeling of tremendous emotional support for me. It was as if they were taking me into their hearts. You could feel the love in that room. They talk of sisterhood and brotherhood in the movement. At that moment I experienced what that really is.

"From there on I grew less shy about talking about my lesbianism publicly. I had passed a personal test of courage and felt better for it.

"The big surprise came later: there were no headlines. It was then that I realized how true it is that society presumes you're heterosexual. The first public coming out is only the first. Every time I talk to a group they presume I'm straight. So I make my statement over and over. There is no single coming out, there's only the terror of confronting that first test of courage."

For many thousands of lesbians, their first public coming out is at a demonstration or gay pride march. Despite the fact that some of these marches draw tens of thousands of participants and that participation does not mean that all who march are gay, the decision to join is still a conflict-ridden one for many lesbians. Generally, such marches draw younger women, those with less invested in careers or other significant symbols of security which could be jeopardized.

Perhaps because of the conflicts surrounding the decision to join such demonstrations, the woman who *does* participate for the first time feels an exuberance often incomparable to any of her past experiences. Says one woman, "I was marching in San Francisco. There were a quarter of a million of us! It was my first march. I never felt such a feeling of strength, of, well—pride—before in my life. There we were. All of us. It was as if nothing could stop our tide, our demand for equal rights."

For some women, their first epiphanal experience with pride in their lesbianism is satisfying in itself. For a few, it is much more than this. It is a conversion in the truest sense. And the new convert, like one emerging from a religious or other conversion, must share the experience, must proselytize her newfound joyous revelation, must explore the dimensions of her experience in the context of social and historical reality.

From the corps of the converted are drawn some of those who move on to devote their lives to the movement for social change. They will provide the radical social experiments that are out of step with the contemporary world and in step with dreams of a more humane future. They are the radical lesbian activists.

In the words of one woman, ''Suddenly, I saw what could be. I saw what we could create. I had to go and help build it—a new world, a better place for those who follow us.''

# 13

# Radical Experiments

Disaffected from the male-dominated left, tossed out by the women's movement, relegated to serving coffee at Gay Liberation Front meetings, a new breed of lesbian began to emerge in the early seventies: the radical lesbian.

The women who initiated what has since been called lesbian feminism saw in both their oppression as women and their oppression as gays the potential for a revolutionary movement that would be different from any preceding it: a movement that could make the world a more egalitarian place, where all people could struggle together in peaceful cooperation, to the benefit of all, the oppression of none.

The government apparently shared this image. Women's groups, especially those espousing radical feminism and lesbian feminism, were infiltrated by a variety of government investigatory agencies, most notably the FBI. Undoubtedly, some of these groups were included in the FBI's Cointelpro plan, a plan to disrupt and disperse "subversive" organizations and their leaders.

The radical lesbian and radical feminist challenged not only the operant assumptions of this country—patriarchy and capitalism—but those of their radical and leftist male contemporaries as well. They had seen oppression of women by the male left: "We want grass, booze, and broads," "A woman's place is lying down." They had learned that Marxist-Leninist analysis, when taken into the social laboratory of the world, condemned homosexuals as criminals.

They had seen in the women's rights movement its antagonism toward lesbianism and its reformist tendencies. Ti-Grace Atkinson summarized many radical feminists' sentiments in a press release announcing her resignation from the chair of the New York chapter of the National Organization for Women (NOW) in 1968:

The leader of NOW, in the discussion of feminist goals, said, ''I want to get women into positions of power.''

Some of the rest of us saw this statement as representative of the opposite side to our differences. We said, each in our own way, ''We want to destroy the positions of power. To alter the condition of women involves the shifting of over half the population. We complain about the unequal power relationships between men and women. To change that relationship requires a redefinition within humanity. We want to get rid of the positions of power, not get up into those positions. The fight against unequal power relationships between men and women necessitates fighting unequal power every place: between men and women (for feminists especially), but also between men and men, and women and women, between black and white, rich and poor.''

Lesbian feminists had seen in the gay liberation fronts the desire for no further social change than that which would give gay males a bigger piece of what seemed to them a rotten patriarchal pie, whether capitalist or socialist.

Lesbian feminists also saw a need to retreat from the fray of these contemporary movements to explore and analyze their own experience and to develop theories of social change that would address *their* issues. They called themselves ''separatists,'' separate from both the women's movement and the gay movement. The separatists imperative was a phenomenon whose time had come, as it had, earlier, for the black movement, and lesbians formed separatist groups in several American cities. The best-known of these came to be the Furies collective which published a monthly newspaper by that name in Washington, D. C. Within the pages of *Furies,* radical lesbian feminists addressed the issues of patriarchy, their own experiences of class discrimination, and their researches into previously suppressed lesbian history (*herstory,* they called it, in rebellion to the patriarchal bias of the English language). *Furies* was one of the early philosophical homes for many lesbians who emerged later in the vanguard of the lesbian feminist movement as writers, organizers, publishers, and theoreticians. Perhaps the best-known of these today are Rita Mae Brown and Charlotte Bunch.

Within their separatist groups lesbians confronted issues of class struggle and racism and worked not only to provide a theoretical framework for a feminist revolution, but also to develop alternative institutions embodying their ideals.

These feminists were not the first to suggest a massive shakeup of social institutions going far beyond demands for equality. Feminists of the 1800s had preceded them in advocating the abolition of marriage, challenging the nuclear family as an institution, and attacking traditional notions of romantic love. By the end of the nineteenth century, however, many of the radical feminist voices had joined the more moderate American drive for women's suffrage, and then been silenced by it. Suffrage, by World War I, had become the final goal and symbol of the women's movement. When suffrage was won, the movement diffused. It didn't take long for women to discover that suffrage had done little to change their lives for the better. Women remained second-class citizens, but the movement, having achieved its goal, was no longer ready for continued fight.

Lesbian feminists noted this historical lesson and concluded that the movement needed a body of theory and analysis which would outlast the winning of legislative reforms. This analysis goes on today in the publication *Quest,* a quarterly journal launched in 1974 by Alexa Freeman, Beverly Manick, Mary-Helen Mautner, Gerri Traina, Charlotte Bunch, Nancy Hartsock, Jane Dolkart, and others. The publication, while encompassing some of the analysis of lesbian feminism, now describes itself as a "nonaligned feminist forum for long term political analysis," providing "a forum for development of feminist theory and practice."[1]

Fundamental to early lesbian feminist analysis was the thesis that gender is the basis of class division. Women were, in a political sense, a class: the oppressed class. Men were also a class: the oppressors. Men were also seen as the class responsible for creating social institutions and defining social goals and expectations. It was reasoned that the oppressor created these to buttress his power and to keep the oppressed class in its position of servitude. Seen from this perspective, all social institutions were up for challenge by the radical feminist theoretician: divisions of labor, religion, the economic system, marriage, the family, love.

## THE LESBIAN FEMINIST COLLECTIVE

Within their laboratories of separatism, lesbian feminists

experimented with collectivism as a way of life, forming various collective ventures in several cities. Perhaps the oldest surviving of these experiments is the Atlanta Lesþian Feminist Alliance, affectionately called ALFA, formed in 1972 "under a set of circumstances that birthed many of the lesbian feminist organizations in the United States: Atlanta Women's Liberation was too straight and the Gay Liberation Front was too male."[2] In the collective context, the first institution to be challenged by lesbian feminists was the nature of organizations themselves which, they observed, are generally run in a hierarchical fashion: a leader at the top, a subgroup of secondary leaders, and a mass of followers. This, they reasoned, was a patriarchal institution that insured continued oppression by institutionalizing inequality. And, so, hierarchical structure was the first institution to be renounced.

Explains one radical lesbian about her early-seventies experience with a group of lesbian feminists intent on operating a women's bookstore: "We saw that there was all kinds of work involved in running the place, but that mainly it divided into two kinds: shitwork and so-called creative work. As women in other organizations, we'd always been used to being handed the shitwork—men got the creative work. We saw right away that we had to get rid of that division of labor because it tended to favor those of us who had more class privilege. If you've been to college you're supposed to be 'better' at creative work. If all of us who were 'better' at creative work—like deciding what books to order, writing the newsletter or whatever, did only that, then a group of less privileged women would be left with what was left: shitwork. The same old thing that was going on in patriarchal institutions.

"We decided to share the shitwork equally, thinking that would give greater opportunities for everyone to do the suposedly 'creative' work.

"That was a great idea, but it didn't solve the problem. We found that those women who had greater privilege also tended to be leaders of the group, even though we weren't supposed to have leaders. It was as if we were creating a hierarchy and authoritarian structure without calling it that.

"We decided next that all decisions would have to be arrived at by consensus of all of us together. Wonderful. We had meetings that lasted for hours and hours while we hassled over the finest points of everything. But what we noticed again was that the privileged women were more articulate and everyone tended to go along with what they said. Some women did not speak at all. So here again was the hierarchy.

"What we did then was borrow a system we'd heard about from some sisters in New York. This is where you give each woman ten poker chips, or match sticks, or whatever. Each time a woman speaks, she throws one chip in the pot. When she runs out of chips, she can't speak anymore. Well, there were great periods of silence at first as the same old people used up all their chips, but this system helped a lot. After a couple of months we found that all women were participating more equally in the discussion and that those who weren't used to talking or being 'influential,' had a lot of important things to say. We learned together, all of us from all the others.

"Then when we had a consensus, we really had one, and had the benefit of everyone's ideas and views. I think we got over a lot of the problems of the hierarchical structure and a lot of the class divisions which we were really struggling with at first."

The bookstore, located in a relatively isolated southern community, eventually closed because members of the collective moved to other cities.

Not all collectives met with even this degree of success. Indeed, many seemed to founder, especially those which involved large numbers of women or which tried to devote some energies to reformist political efforts and media outreach. Commented one woman, "You can't run a lobbying group or a political campaign by consensus. Someone calls, something has to be done immediately. You can't assemble a dozen people and argue about what to do or say. Someone has to be able to make decisions fast."

Some experimenters resolved the decision-making question by having rotating leaders or spokeswomen who were responsible, in times when immediate decisions were needed, for making them. Equality of opportunity and responsibility in this arena was ensured because every woman in the group was eventually in the position of leader. It was a conflict between the collective experiment and a hierarchiacally structured outside world, and the compromise was a quasi-executive board selected by lot.

Both types of collective experiment—that in which decisions are reached by consensus of the entire group, such as Olivia Records, and that with rotating quasi-executive committees, such as a few local NOW groups—still survive. Other collectives like ALFA, have resigned themselves to what they describe as ''an informal heirarchy of power'' that ''exists around those who do the work,'' but maintain that although it ''has had its ups and downs . . . its importance to the community is proven by its continued existence and large membership.''[3]

The concepts of organizational structure were perhaps the easiest for the radical feminists to resolve.

## PERSONAL RELATIONSHIPS

Marriage has been under attack by feminists since the nineteenth century. Traditionally, the basis for the attack has been three-fold. Marriage has been compared to involuntary servitude, which indeed it was under common law, when women were held to be the property of men. Marriage has also been seen as an institution that maintains an available and cheap labor force accessible when needed to sustain a capitalist economy. And marriage, even when undertaken voluntarily in an egalitarian framework, has been viewed as a cop-out to the revolution. To be a ''real'' feminist, the rhetoric held, a woman must devote her primary energies to other women, and not to the nurture and care of man, her oppressor.

This third attack, renewed by radical feminists of the seventies, was widely misinterpreted as a statement that no woman could be a true feminist unless she was a lesbian. By ths time, however, in the radical circles calling for every woman to be a lesbian, the word *lesbian* had a different meaning from the tradition-bound ''woman who sleeps with other women.'' A lesbian, in the new terminology, was simply a woman-identified woman; it did not matter with whom she slept, but only to which class—male or female—she devoted her energies. When a few radical spokeswomen proclaimed that all feminists had to be lesbians, they were using the word in those terms, not in the traditional terms.

Attacking the institution of marriage as a kind of trade made by women for a degree of heterosexist privilege had little direct effect on the lives of most lesbians. Radical lesbians went to the heart of the matter by carrying the marriage theorem one step further: monogamy was also an oppressive institution. Jeri Dilno, administrative coordinator for the Gay Center for Social Services in San Diego, explains the antimonogamy argument cogently: "Two of the societal functions of marriage are child rearing and identification of heirs. An important by-product of these functions is the containment and control of sexual activity—thus monogamy. To assure the perpetuation of this system, young people are carefully trained to fill roles that are defined for them by gender. For women, this biological destiny provides us access to a single, narrow part of our personhood . . . dependent on 'the other' for most of our external needs. In playing this role, we have denied our independent self."[4]

Many lesbians, she explains, are experimenting with alternate relationships styles, including celibacy, multiple relationships, and so-called open marriages. Dilno's description of the value of multiple relationships echoes that of many radical feminists, "This pattern of living requires a woman to place herself as the top priority for her attention and energy. Being selfish in this way is a radical stance for a well-trained nurturer to take." Her description of lesbians' complaints about monogamous relationships is echoed widely in radical critiques. "Women in these nontraditional relationships," says Dilno, "spoke of prior experiences in monogamous unions . . . They discussed disadvantages that had led them to try other ways of relating. A tendency to become 'lost' in the other person was a common complaint. An overwhelming sense of dependency . . . (either on their partner or being directed toward themselves) was a strong reason for the choice to experiment. Many women felt limited by jealousy, fear, and/or uncertainty in extending themselves beyond the traditional [monogamous] relationship. A feeling of lost opportunity for personal growth led these women to make the decision to try something other than a monogamous relationship."[5]

Dilno's perception of the monogamy versus nonmonogamy issue as an area of conflict in lesbian circles is also correct: "Younger lesbians are sometimes critical of older lesbians, seeing them as static, without growth in their relationships. The lesbians of small towns do not always understand the political radicalism that churns in large metropolitan areas like New York City, San Francisco, Boston, etc. The one issue that seems to divide and threaten more than any other is the definition of the lesbian relationship. Is monogamy a cop-out to the system? Is the relationship of women with each other a political statement?''[6]

To those who regard relationships as political statements, some radical lesbians have assured their audiences, monogamy is just one of many relics of heterosexism that has to be abandoned along the way to revolution.

Radical theorists have also challenged love, proposing that it, and the supposedly emotionally dependent relationships that stemmed from it, were symptomatic of the captive/captor syndrome. In close and painful confinement, such as that endured by kidnap victims, the victim comes to identify with and even "love" his or her captor as a kind of emotional survival mechanism. Reduced to complete dependency on the captor, the victim retreats into the emotions of childhood, when parents, also captors of a sort, were "loved." Women, it has been argued, as the oppressed class, were held in such a situation by their captors—men—resulting in "love" and its delusions of romanticism.

Commented one radical lesbian on romanticism: "About a year ago I went out to dinner with this woman friend. We were trying a relationship we thought was going to be viable. We were sitting in a restaurant eating dinner and she mentioned to me, 'Gee, this is really romantic.' Well, I just wasn't into that head set. I was eating dinner and sharing the energy with a person I wanted to be with and it could have been anywhere, I wasn't enjoying the material aspects of it.

"There is a manipulation in the whole flowers, candy, candlelight syndrome and the whole Lenox china advertising thing. You see that real intimate dinner looking over New York City with all the lights and that is supposed to be romantic. I'd like to put that in a nonmaterial environment. To me, romanticism is more or less a tool which has kept women from knowing their condition, which has kept women oppressed. I really feel that we've been brainwashed into putting a lot of energy into the material trappings of a relationship and not the emotional and spiritual in the sense of working together and sisterhood."

Lesbians, of course, weren't thought to be "in love" with their oppressor—the male class—but love in its own right, like romanticism, was seen as a dangerous delusion nevertheless, an institution created by patriarchy to keep women down. Instead of love, coupledness, and monogamy, the desired attributes for the radical lesbian feminist were sisterhood, comradeship, and class loyalty. Anything less was a drain on the feminist revolution and was, according to some, counterrevolutionary.

## SPIRITUAL QUESTS

By the midseventies, some lesbian feminists, angered by the traditional patriarchal and hierarchical church institutions which they viewed as having oppressed women for centuries, had merged the abolition of romantic love and their own dedication to self-definition with a quest for a different and "spiritual" environment, more meaningful than that found in the simple (but ofttimes dull) dedication of comrades working together in sisterhood. From this trend reemerged the study of ancient religions, especially those worshipping female goddesses. Women researchers, with some historical justification, found that goddess worship had preceded patriarchy thousands of years ago. The goddess, they learned, had been called by many names in many cultures: Isis, Demeter, Athena, Diana, Artemis, Astarte, Ishtar. Her worship, they determined, with somewhat less historical justification, was the "Old Religion," "Wicce," "Wicca," or witchcraft. Goddess worship soon became identified with Wicca, and, largely through the inspiration of Z Budapest a Los Angeles lesbian witch, Wicce covens became the resolution to many feminist's quests for a spirituality that would mesh with their political beliefs. (Budapest has tried to have her coven, the Susan B. Anthony Coven Number One, recognized as a legitimate religious organization in the state of California. The courts have turned her down.)

Explained Wicce advocates Susan Rennie and Kirsten Grimstad about the rising interest in witchcraft, "Feminists are unearthing a female-centered religion whose ethical system and practices are far more humane and life-affirming than the patriarchal religions which usurped it. A comparison of the values and goals of feminism with the beliefs and practices of this matrifocal belief system immediately illuminates the attraction it has for feminists looking to enlarge the spiritual dimensions of their lives . . . The women's movement is rediscovering and exploring women's connectedness with natural rhythms and life cycles. Wicce is a religion of nature in its purest sense

. . . The women's movement rejects oppressive heirarchical structures and seeks to create institutions which embody egalitarianism and sharing. There are no social distinctions within the Craft . . . the women's movement espouses active social change. Conventional religions, both eastern and western, tend to support the status quo by focusing on other-worldly matters. Wicce, by contrast, is very much concerned with the quality of life in *this* world (always an incentive to rebellion) . . . The women's movement is based on a vision of personal freedom and self-definition . . . Witches take absolute responsibility for their own destinies . . . Wicce *requires* self-definition. There is no elite, priestly class to define and interpret orthodoxy. There *is* no orthodoxy . . . Within the coven all wicceans are equal . . . The women's movement emphasizes the celebration of our bodies and it rejects the mind-body dualism which characterizes masculinist culture . . . Wicceans celebrate the physical senses and despise the physical asceticism which is idealized in patriarchal religions . . . The women's movement seeks to infuse culture with the life-giving and life-affirming female principle. It should hardly be surprising that feminists are attracted to wicce . . .

"The women's movement has reawakened interest in the healing skills and homeopathic expertise which were traditionally in the hands of women. Witches *were* the healers, and their healing powers derived from their deep and profound affinity with and understanding of the natural world."[7]

Intriguingly, the mixture of political radicalism with experimentation in spiritual quests was also a phenomenon of some elements of the nineteenth-century feminist movement. Elizabeth Cady Stanton preceded her sisters by nearly a century in questioning the patriarchal assumptions of Christianity by publishing *The Woman's Bible* in the 1890s (since reissued for contemporary feminists). Victoria Woodhull and her sister Tennessee Claflin were two other nineteenth-century feminists who questioned the patriarchal religion of their era. Along with their advocacy of the then most radical feminist notions—free love, abortion, birth control, and women's right to organize labor unions—they advocated spiritualism. In 1873 Woodhull, at the peak of her feminist career, was elected president of the American Association of Spiritualists—a kind of Z Budapest of her day.

## ECONOMIC SURVIVAL

Yet another controversial issue addressed by lesbian feminists was the issue of economic survival. Arguments here centered around the dualistic notion that one was either actively resisting oppression or was part of the problem. How, then, could a *real* feminist work for an oppressive institution and not claim that she was part of the problem? If not willing to work for patriarchal, heterosexist, capitalist institutions, how was she to finance the essentials of the feminist revolution: food, clothes, and printing presses?

Theorists reached a stumbling block here. In contrast to some of those still working within the male-identified leftist movement, none, apparently, advocated violent appropriation of property. Instead, certain compromises were accepted. First, women, unless able to survive on welfare (an unlikely proposition), could work in the establishment, but should give to the movement all the money they earned above what they needed to subsist on. Second, women could create money-making (capitalist) enterprises that were not oppressive by applying the principles of feminism to their business operations.

The first such endeavors included feminist publications like *Lesbian Tide* (still publishing) and *Furies* (now defunct); publishing houses like Diana Press, and Daughters, Inc.; recording companies such as Olivia, still run as a nonheirarchical collective; and book stores, which have had, as a rule, short lives. These endeavors have had two advantages: they could be laboratories for further practical experimentation with feminist theory, and they could nurture the movement by providing propaganda and cultural alternatives to the male-establishment media. Not all of these were self-sustaining economically, and many continue to be financed by women working in the capitalist marketplace. Perhaps the most revolutionary of these experiments is the publication *Lesbian Connection,* which, because many of the women who compose its potential market are not able to afford a subscription price, offers itself free, subsisting totally on donations.

While many enterprises have failed, many have become self-sustaining. Thus the conflict between radical feminist theory and pragmatic reality has created an abundant and vitalizing counterculture which today includes dozens of rural, nearly self-sustaining lesbian communes, urban coffee houses and social centers, social events, schools, art studios, and retreats, in addition to media-related enterprises.

# 14

# The Extremist Fringe

Lesbian feminists theorists have propounded no single ideology. No spokeswoman has even insisted—beyond the moment of passionate discourse—that there was one "correct" feminist party line. All have upheld the ideals of pluralism in their public speeches. But in the late seventies, in the bars, on the streets, in the coffee houses, and in the lesbian feminist counterculture, a rigid orthodoxy began to creep into public life and take a stranglehold on the neck of the movement. The orthodoxy centers around two issues: separatism and relationship styles.

The separatism of the new orthodoxy differs from that which was advocated by the early lesbian feminists as a means of centering and gathering strength for the struggle. The separatism of the orthodox extremist requires complete dissociation from men and all male institutions, incuding most forms of employment in the mainstream economy. Those who do not adhere to this separatist formula are ostracized. The result is a subculture of isolation perpetuating itself by its own stridency and creating erraticisms typical of other closed societies and institutions.

By the new orthodoxy the lesbian is judged by her peers and tossed into one of two classes: the politically correct (PC in latter-seventies jargon) or the politically incorrect (PI). Creative efforts are evaluated in the same vein. Those who have put long years of work into the lesbian movement are either shouted down if they are currently viewed as PI, or followed by contingents of lesbian groupies if they are politically "correct."

## LATTER-DAY LESBIAN FASCISM

The PI-PC dichotomy has led, in many circles, to a latter-day lesbian fascism. Comments one native of a Midwestern city, "Everyone in this damned town is so concerned about keeping cool, keeping politically correct, and women are dying here. Dying from lack of care, lack of human contact, lack of humanity. Where do we take our depressions, our loneliness, our madnesses when everyone is too occupied by being cool and correct?

"I have seen it. One woman was struggling with her depression. She went to the bars and sat in the corner. No one said hello. She went to the parties, and no one even asked her name. Where else was she to go, but to her 'sisters'? They didn't want to hear her story. They would have had to blow that cool to extend a smile, to reach out and hug her. She finally took her loneliness to a bottle of cyanide."

Comments a woman from southern California, "We had arranged for a feminist performer at the coffee house here, something we do once a month. The place is supposed to be a women's place, our place, where we all help and volunteer. One of the women on the steering committee—what they call the collective that actually manages the coffee house—canceled the performance. When we asked her why, she told us she knew the performer, that the performer wasn't 'politically correct'. This was supposed to be a women's space. I began to wonder which women? If we censor one sister, who will we censor next?"

And, on the PC side, one woman from the Midwest explained, "We had one of the movement 'stars' in town. Now that she's famous and getting rich she doesn't look like a lesbian. She's copping out to the system. I suggest we take a look at what kind of 'stars' we're creating. We don't need 'stars' who get rich and then buy into the system. If she comes to your town, don't buy a ticket to hear her." The "star," ironically, was Rita Mae Brown, one of the earliest lesbian feminist theorists. (Brown, before signing a lucrative contract with Bantam for her novel, the lesbian best-seller *Rubyfruit Jungle,* had complained in a San Francisco newspaper interview that groupies followed her home and sat outside her New York apartment. Among its other attributes, latter-day lesbian fascism is fickle.)

Boycott, censor, cold-shoulder, these are the sentiments of latter-day lesbian fascism. Its most obvious victims are those who have emerged as leaders, organizers, and achievers, especially those who have attained a degree of recognition outside their own community. Many leaders are strong enough to sustain such attacks from women they once regarded as their sisters. Others, supported by no tradition or experience of leadership, are not.

Explains one woman who was responsible for organizing—in a city of half a million which had had no gay rights activity until the midseventies—its first gay political group, its first women's studies program at a local university, and a host of other efforts: "I had spent about three years totally devoting my energies to the movement. I admit I had built this image of myself as a kind of community leader with all these people around who really seemed supportive of me. I was their big spokesperson. Whenever they needed someone, they came to me and I helped them. And it went to my head, being at the vanguard of creating a movement.

"I had put out all of this stuff for all of these people, and then I did one little thing they didn't approve of, that they didn't even understand, and they were willing to just throw me out. I was renounced absolutely and dashed to the ground for being such a bitch.

"I had a terrible time with that and I became really insecure. And there I was alone, totally abandoned by these people who had worked with me and supported me, who I had come to think of as friends. And I'm still working on deciding exactly who I am. Obviously, not who they thought I was.

"I've been trying to figure out what it is about this whole movement subculture that makes for such rigidity, that never sees any side except the side it wants to see."

This woman, whose great sin was beginning a monogamous relationship, has since left the community. She now devotes her free time to the Green Peace organization, a save-the-whales group. The organizations she founded continue without her, but the talents and skills she has for organization and strategy have been lost to them and to the community that abandoned her.

Explains another victim, "I was very 'in' with everyone. There was one woman who was a kind of cult leader in a radical therapy group. I was one of this women's string of lovers—she had about five she told me about. And I thought that was okay, that it was wrong to want to hold her, to need support from her.

"Because I was with this woman I had a lot of friends, her friends, or followers, I should say. We carried on like that for about four years and I guess I began to think that some of those women were my friends too.

"One day, she dropped me. Dropped me cold. She just said, 'I don't ever want to see you again, get out.' That was it. I tried everything, calling her, begging her, whatever I could. Then I realized that she meant it. When I tried calling all those 'friends' we had made, everyone was too busy to listen. Not one of them, despite all their talk about sisterhood, friendship, support groups. When she dropped me I was dropped by all her friends, dropped like a cold cod by each of them.

"I was suddenly, after four years, totally and absolutely alone and devastated. I wanted to kill myself. Finally, a straight guy I knew, and not too closely at that, saw my pain and got me to his therapist.

"It saved my life. Now, after a few months of therapy, I've been able to see how fucked that whole way of life I was living was, to begin to put that kind of 'sisterhood' into perspective—it's no sisterhood when they shit on you.

"I'm beginning to rediscover my own identity, my own values. I'm a refuge from the 'movement.'"

Many women, perhaps made of sterner stuff, or perhaps expecting less from a movement that is rapidly institutionalizing, have been nearly broken by experiences such as those above, but have emerged with even greater personal strength to promote social change. One of these is Elaine Noble, the first openly gay person to be elected to state office. Reflecting on her two terms as a state representative in Massachusetts, she explained, "Basically, what I have experienced is that because I was considered the gay politician, I had not only more work, but got more flack, more criticism, more heartache from the gay community than from the people who elected me . . .

"In one siege with harassment, the people who were doing it were gay women who had it out for me. They had one guy who was not gay, who was just crazy. They shot through my apartment windows and my car windows. Have you ever had the sensation when you start to perspire and your lips get numb and you feel like you're going to faint? That's the feeling I had when I saw their pictures. I thought I was going to pass out because I assumed it would be somebody I had offended. But I had never met these people before in my life . . .

"I guess more than anything I'm just exhausted and very, very tired and probably disillusioned because I really tried the best I could and it wasn't good enough for the gay community. To be honest, I don't know what 'good enough' is . . .

"I think the level of self-hate right now among gay people is so damned high that if, when you start trying to work in the community in a sane manner and you ask, 'What are you doing constructively?', it has a self-hate backlash. They can't hit the straight world, they can't swing at the straight world, so they swing at the person who's nearest them."[1]

Undeterred, Noble continued in public life, becoming the first openly gay person to run for the United States Senate, with the backing of many of her party's political leaders. Support from movement women was mixed, however. Harassment from her own 'sisters' continued.

## WOMEN SEARCHING

Less obvious, but more pervasive, are the effects of this latter-day lesbian fascism on women who are not leaders, women who are simply searching for some of the "sisterhood" that was at the core of the lesbian feminist dream. What they often find, rather than the warmth of "sisterhood," is the coldness of instant, anonymous sexuality that is more reminiscent of a large subgroup of the gay male culture than of lesbians.

Says one thirty-five-year-old lesbian, a native San Franciscan familiar with the lesbian underground, subculture, and counter culture as they have developed there over the past twenty years: "In the last couple of years some of the bars have become like a sexual meatrack. It's a kind of renaissance of lesbians, but only because there are more women out, more women available everywhere—for sex. Not love. No involvements wanted. No emotional attachments. It is hurtful for me with those types of women because I start to invest myself and get nothing back. So I'm prefering to be single now than to be involved with people who come and go with such swiftness, who are afraid of hanging in there and even playing.

"There's a casualness about the women I meet now, about going to bed not even with a promise of being together again. It's just saying 'Hello, goodbye, and don't give me any of your stuff, don't give me any of your tears. Don't lay your trips on me. I don't want any melodrama. Just let's play and then goodbye.' I've had that and it saddens me.

"They care about you on one level—what you do at work, what other women you know, who you've slept with—but it doesn't go any deeper. There's no deep affection. There's no nurturing, no contact made other than 'I'll see you for a date, but I don't need you.' It's not human. It's being cool, retaining a distance. It is a restraint in the affection of many people out there and I'm just not that capable of being there.

"I don't want to become jaded. I won't create the cynicism that some of these women have created, that everything is self-centered, that love is crazy, that all there is is coming and going in the night.

"I will hang in there with my old friends, the ones I've known for ten or twenty years, hang in until this thing passes, before going back out into it. It's not real."

Another woman, a long-time observer of the New York scene, puts it differently: "All you hear about is cruising, sex, one-night stands, open relationships, multiple relationships. I went to a bar once and thought I'd gone to a men's bar by mistake. All I heard was women actually bragging about the numbers of women they'd 'had.' Sure, that's great sexual openness, but when you strip it of all the rhetoric, what's going on is that these women are just picking up values from a group of gay men, from the gay male bar scene, and calling it feminism.

"There's a lot of talk about how 'hot' a particular woman looks. That's male jargon for making a woman just another dehumanized sexual object. They proclaim they're real feminists, but what I see is a bunch of women taking up the same male values that have oppressed women for centuries, except now we're busy oppressing each other."

Monogamy, once a predominant role model for relationships in the lesbian subculture and underground, has vanished from the new closed culture. Comments one woman, "I went into my third lesbian relationship and was really scared that it would end up like the previous two, just another in a series of repetitive spirals—serial monogamy. We talked a lot about open relationships, how everyone says that's supposed to be more healthy. We still haven't settled the issue. We sort of agree to have monogamous agreements for three months, or six months, and then renew them.

"Monogamy, of course, is very 'PI,' but both of us felt we couldn't cope with open relationships at the time. Jealousy, possessiveness, a feeling of being threatened or rejected, all of those 'PI' emotions would have interfered in our primary relationship with each other.

"But when we began to have relationship problems during the first year, we looked around for other couples to see how they handled them. We knew dozens and dozens of movement women, and none of them had been together even as long as we had. There wasn't anyone to talk to about how relationships work, what kinds of things to expect, what kinds of problems develop, how to keep a relationship going. All we got were messages that if everything wasn't perfect, we shouldn't waste time being together.

"Finally, we went to counseling to a closeted therapist whom we found out about. She'd been with her lover for twelve years. Wow, did that put a different perspective on things for us. Just knowing that it was possible to sustain a long-term relationship was important to us.

"At least then we had the option, at least there was one voice—although not a 'politically correct' voice—saying that long-term relationships were not a priori places where you repressed each other's individuality. If we'd stayed where we were, without that option, the only option we would have would be to split up, start over again with someone else, or just treat sex as if there wasn't any emotional component to it, sort of like jerking off with a partner."

Latter-day lesbian fascism, like any closed movement, carries within it the seeds of its own destruction. Its ability to produce social change is sapped by continuous debate over which variant of the ideological fad of the moment is politically correct, and thus it spirals in on itself, doomed to implosion and extinction. Squabbles over the right of lesbian transsexuals to be present at lesbian conventions all but disrupted two major conferences in the midseventies, and splintered one chapter of the Daughters of Bilitis. Standards of political correctness, evaluated by one's position not only as PI or PC but as a "real" lesbian, have disrupted fundraising ventures by excluding supposedly heterosexual women. The notion of lesbian separatism itself, taken to extremes, has even brought some groups to occasional exclusion of lesbian mothers with male children.

It is possible, as Sally Gearhart, a spokeswoman from a tradition now called "cultural feminism," suggests, that lesbian fascism may affect even feminists' quests for a new spirituality, "that in our attempt to share energy we will institutionalize our rituals or approach some 'party line' of women's spirituality. If any one of us ever feels uneasy or 'spiritually incorrect' (and the tiny ways that that can happen are infinite), then it's time to look hard at what we're doing, at the assumptions we're making, at the expectations we're putting on each other; it's time to examine our selves for differences among us—most obviously the differences of class—that will divide us and make our spirituality seem mighty like an old-fashioned power trip."[2]

The quest for political, or spiritual, correctness is like a funnel cloud, spiraling inward, each spiral excluding more and more women, until, finally, none will be left but a few enclaves of would-be demagogues talking to no one but themselves.

# 15

# Changing Times

I remember hanging out around the bars in 1948. They were dreadful, fearful places, as were our lives. We were so scared we didn't even use our real names and certainly never used last names. There were dozens of nicknames—Tex, Mom, Boss, Brandy—but you seldom learned who these women were.

Walk into a bar today and ask someone's name today and you get it. Her real name. Her real job. Her reality.—*Roberta, sixty-eight years old, known as "Legs" to some.*

It used to be that if you knew someone from the bar scene, maybe even you were friends, and if you saw them later somewhere outside—on the street or at work, you looked the other way. You ignored them. It was a code of life, not to blow someone's cover by smiling at them in public. Today there's hardly any of that. There's more openness. You walk by someone you have met, you say hello.—*Louise*

Nineteen eighty marks a quarter-century of lesbian rights activism, a time frame that has encompassed tremendous changes in all aspects of American life and culture. According to law, racial and ethnic minorities, and women, are guaranteed greater access to the American pie. Gay people, however, still have few legal protections. In the so-called liberation decades, legal equality was not established for lesbians. The trend of the eighties appears to be toward greater separation between rich and poor, and diminution in the size and status of the middle class as it is driven closer to the ranks of poverty by inflation. It is the type of socioeconomic trend that is least sympathetic toward minorities. In view of these realities, it is difficult to foresee how the lesbian subculture will develop during the near future, but a review of the changes it has undergone in the near past is a stepping-off place where certain themes of change may be found, themes perhaps predictive of what is ahead.

The first phase of the lesbian movement, predating the recent resurgence of the women's movement, marked the beginning of the end of false conceptions about lesbianism. These conceptions had had two sources: myth, and a handful of scientific studies of captive homosexual populations—prisoners or psychiatric patients, mostly male. With the founding of the Daughters of Bilitis (DOB) in 1955 it became possible to study lesbians, and noncaptive ones at that. DOB fostered and encouraged such studies, many of which were published in its journal, *The Ladder,* the first American lesbian publication. From these roots came later studies which were to shatter the myths that lesbians were exactly like male homosexuals and that, as a population, they were mentally unstable. As lesbians began to organize for social change in the late fifties and early sixties, their self-perceptions began to change as well. By the end of the sixties, fear, which had gripped lesbians in an iron vise, had diminished, allowing for a more public humanity, in which an identity found in a bar was not necessarily obliterated on the street. This experience was the lesbian subculture's primary inheritance from the first half of the quarter century of struggle for lesbian liberation.

## EFFECTS OF THE WOMEN'S MOVEMENT

The lesbian movement of the seventies, tied closely and synergistically with the women's movement, produced an explosion of changes affecting lesbians' lives. Many lesbians today credit the women's movement with having improved the quality of their lives more than any other phenomenon. Explains one woman, "I'd always felt discriminated against because I was gay. I didn't think anyone knew about it—I made sure they didn't—but when it came time for promotions or raises, I knew I wasn't getting my fair share. So I thought someone in the company somehow had found out about me. I didn't put up much of a fight. I just worked harder. But the women's movement sparked a whole new consciousness for me: I was being discriminated against because of my gender and because I was single. Look at the facts. A single woman had an awfully hard time in the fifties and sixties getting much of anything—credit, housing, insurance, whatever. And a woman in any circumstance didn't get much of anything unless she was tied to a man who helped her up the ladder.

"So hell, whatever discrimination I had wasn't because I was queer—no one knew what I did at home in bed—it came from being single and female."

The changes fostered by the women's movement—equal employment opportunity, the drive for equal pay for equal work, repeal of gender-discriminatory laws in many areas, as well as status-discriminatory laws that based a woman's options on her marital status—have produced the most tangible benefits to individual lesbians. Lesbians recognize this. As Fleener reports, when her sample was asked if the women's movement had affected their lives, an overwhelming 95 percent said that the women's movement had made it easier for lesbians.[1]

Lesbians, both open and closeted, had contributed to these changes both through reformist strategies and by radical explorations of a woman's role and position. Lesbian-feminist visibility and analysis promoted questioning of mainstream presumptions about women in a vigorous attack on gender-role stereotyping. Once lesbian feminists successfully showed their heterosexual sisters that they were equally women and that they, as women independent from gender-role norms, had significant contributions to make to the women's movement, the synergy moved into full swing. Women could be sexually independent from men: weren't lesbians? Women could function in egalitarian relationships free from gender-role stereotypes: didn't lesbians? Female autonomy was the major threat to patriarchal institutions: weren't assertive, achieving women always branded as lesbians?

Commented Gloria Steinem in a statement prepared for *Our Right to Love,* "Just by working and surviving as women without the protection of some status vis-a-vis a man, lesbians may force institutions into some acceptance of women on their own. And this pioneering act helps break a barrier for all autonomous women."[2]

Increasing lesbian activism in support of lesbian struggle against archaic sex laws highlighted key ideological points of the women's movement. Were women free if they were not free to control their own bodies, including their sexuality? Did children absolutely need male role models to grow up as healthy adults? Increasingly, the courts are finding that they do not and are granting child custody to openly lesbian mothers when they are the more capable parent. Such victories have been few—and mothers are still counseled by responsible attorneys to make whatever private compromises can be made rather than to go public—but nonetheless, they have raised fundamental questions about gender roles and gender-role modeling.

The openness of lesbian feminists brought changes to the consciousness of nonlesbian women as well. The positive assertion of the fact that women, not queers, could love other women, confronted heterosexual women with their own feelings about themselves. Summarized Shere Hite, "If we [as women] want to grow strong, we must learn to love, respect, honor, and be attentive to and interested in other women . . . Any woman who feels actual horror or revulsion at the thought of kissing or embracing or having physical relations with another woman should reexamine her feelings and attitudes not only about other women, but about *herself*."[3]

## EFFECTS OF THE LESBIAN MOVEMENT

While working both alone and with other movements in the last decade, lesbians have seen measurable changes in the institutions that affect their lives. From only a handful of groups in which lesbians could meet and work with each other, have blossomed nearly one thousand in the fifty states, roughly divided equally between lesbian services offered through women's organizations, gay rights groups open to lesbians, university-affiliated groups, religious organizations, and specifically lesbian-oriented groups. Nearly 100 feminist or gay bookstores offer a variety of books, periodicals, and records. Where there was once only a single lesbian publication, *The Ladder*, now there are about fifty lesbian media outlets, including recording companies, radio and television programs, and film collectives.

While bars were once the only place one lesbian could expect to meet another, now there are coffee houses, organizations, and other environments. There are also a handful of privately owned dating and meeting services, the most successful of which is *The Wishing Well*, a publication begun in 1974. By 1978 this service, which enabled lesbians to meet through brief descriptions in the quarterly newsletter followed by letters between the interested parties, had more than one thousand subscribers, most in search of relationship partners. (This subscription rate may not seem high, but it brought the newsletter into the top-ten circulation rate of exclusively lesbian publications.) An analysis of a typical issue showed that most listings came from the greater San Francisco Bay Area (the publication is based in rural California) and that the largest number of listings were written by women between the ages of twenty and twenty-nine, the same age group of those most active in the region's lesbian-feminist movement counterculture.

Lesbianism as a topic has gone public. Little more than a decade ago a woman could have spent her life without ever having heard the word mentioned, much less having considered that she herself might be a lesbian.

Thousands of lesbians today can be marshaled for gay pride demonstrations in major cities. Because of their political power, more than a dozen open lesbians now hold appointive positions in various state and local governments. Lesbians' rights as single women are protected almost everywhere. Meanwhile, their rights as gay people are protected in thousands of federal civil service jobs and by several municipal jurisdictions. Their aspirations toward full equality under the law are advocated by more than one hundred major national associations, from the National Education Association to the Young Women's Christian Association and the Girl Scouts of America.

The lesbian movement has produced a degree of social change that its founders did not imagine possible a quarter of a century ago. Areas of measurable change are two: points of contact with the lesbian subculture are more available in more regions of the country, and are often characterized by a new context of pride and self-affirmation; in addition, the lesbian's self-identity is changing, becoming more positive and self-affirming.

It is perhaps too early to project long-range effects of these changes on the lives of America's lesbians or on society as a whole. Lesbians have always managed, one way or another, to get by. There has always been a lesbian underground in America. The full effects of the reality of a lesbian counterculture and a public lesbian presence are not yet measurable. While the majority of lesbians feels that the women's movement has produced positive changes in their lives, fewer perceive the changes brought specifically by the lesbian or gay rights movements.[4] Most lesbians remain underground or on the fringes of their gay sisters' public presence. It is as if many lesbians are waiting out the tide of social change before emerging to see if it will be safe "out there," as some advocates of their rights claim.

Says one woman, a public school teacher, "I cannot come out. It is as simple as that. If I stay in the closet, I keep my job." She, like many, is on the fringes of the public movement, a member, through a post office box, of two national gay organizations, participating in their functions only when they are private. Her sentiments are typical of many women who found a niche of economic security before the current wave of lesbian and gay pride demonstrations.

Explains another, of a common sentiment, "I don't relate to life as a lesbian. I relate to life as a human being, a female human. My concerns are many and varied. The last thing I want to do to myself is put myself into some little box neatly labeled and packaged as 'lesbian.'"

Many younger women, whose first connection with the lesbian underground was most likely through a gay organization, also have a savvy "wait and see" attitude. Comments one, a college student, "I'm not ready to risk the chance of getting a decent job by being too public. I'll go march in a gay pride day parade, but that's actually a fairly safe thing to do. I don't see any need to wear any label that says 'dyke activist.' That's foolish."

## LIFESTYLE CHANGES

A comparison of the Bell and Weinberg and Fleener studies of lesbians' lives shows that changes in lifestyles, despite the rhetoric of gay liberation and lesbian feminism, are actually few. Both samples were drawn primarily from the greater San Francisco Bay Area. Bell and Weinberg's lesbians were interviewed in 1970 (though the results of their study were not published until 1978) before the contemporary wave of gay liberation. Fleener's lesbians were surveyed in 1976, well into the peak of the lesbian-feminist movement. Demographically, the two samples differ significantly by age. Bell and Weinberg's lesbians averaged between thirty-two and thirty-five years old, while Fleener's averaged twenty-six years old. Additionally the researchers, even while probing the same areas of experience, asked slightly different questions (Bell and Weinberg's suffer somewhat from being more male-directed than Fleener's). Despite these differences, the areas that can be compared between the two studies are illuminating.

The chief differences between the samples were in two areas: membership in gay rights organizations and levels of self-acceptance. Approximately 18 percent of the Bell and Weinberg sample reported that they belonged to gay organizations.[5] Fleener reports more than twice as many, 41 percent, belonged to a gay or lesbian organization. Nearly 60 percent, she reports, were personally involved in the women's movement (Bell and Weinberg did not report on lesbians' affiliations with the women's movement). While Fleener reports that 32 percent said that the gay liberation movement had not changed their lives, 47 percent reported that the movement had given them more pride in themselves, a fact corroborated by responses to the question that asked how they felt about being gay. None reported that they felt their lesbianism was either wrong, immoral, or dirty. Only a few, 7 percent, reported that they didn't know how they felt, a possible indicator of lack of self-acceptance. The remainder reported either that they took lesbianism ''for granted,'' or that they were ''proud of it and love it.''[6] Bell and Weinberg, using a different measure, found a far lower level of self-acceptance among their sample.[7]

Interestingly, the manifestation of gay pride in the Fleener sample did not extend as far as coming out of the closet. Fifty-four percent of her sample couples reported that neither of their parents knew they were gay, a comparable level of interfamilial openness with parents found by Bell and Weinberg six years earlier.[8]

Despite the rhetoric surrounding ''open'' and ''multiple'' relationships in urban lesbian movement circles, the sexual habits of the pre- and postliberation samples did not differ noticeably. In fact, the Bell and Weinberg sample tended to be more sexually promiscuous and to have had more lesbian sexual partners than did the Fleener sample. This, however, was probably a factor of age rather than other phenomena because when the portion of the Fleener sample corresponding to the average age of Bell and Weinberg's sample is selected out, numbers of sexual partners were approximately the same. Additionally, numbers of sexual contacts increased with age in the Fleener sample and there were no indications that younger lesbians tended to be more promiscuous than their older peers.

The Fleener study also shattered another key point of lesbian movement rhetoric. Although Fleener reports that 28 percent viewed monogamy with disfavor, chiefly because it is allegedly a "sexist" value, 86 percent of her sample involved in coupled relationships were in fact living monogamously—only 14 percent actually practiced so-called open relationships.[9] This is approximately the same percent reported by several observers in the heterosexually married female population.

Bell and Weinberg postulate that homosexuals can be divided into five "types" or subgroups which they characterized as: closed-couple, open-couple, functional, dysfunctional, and asexual. Thirty-eight percent of their female sample fell into the closed-couple sub-group and 24 percent into the open-couple subgroup. Bell and Weinberg's open-couple percentage was almost double that of the Fleener sample when the same selection criteria were applied to it. Bell and Weinberg found that closed couples—those that were pre-dominantly monogamous in their relationships—reported a higher degree of self-acceptance than did open couples. They also reported fewer sexual problems, and a greater degree of happiness than their open-coupled counterparts.[10]

An intriguing question for further research would be whether self-acceptance is causal in creating closed, or predominantly monoga-mous, couples. A causal relationship might be postulated from the comparison to the Fleener sample which showed more self-acceptance *and* a higher percent of closed couples.

Other tentative comparisons between Bell and Weinberg's sub-groups and the Fleener sample can be made. The third most populous subgroup in Bell and Weinberg's study were asexual women. These, the researchers found, had a high degree of self-acceptance and tended to be older than the average respondent. This tendency is also present in the Fleener report. Her older women tended to be single, self-accepting, and asexual.[11]

Bell and Weinberg found that about 14 percent of their lesbians fell into the subgroup they labeled as "functional." These were those women with a high level of self-acceptance who lived what might be described as a "swinging single" lifestyle. This percentage had not changed six years later when the Bell and Weinberg selection criteria were applied to the Fleener sample.[12]

reported a high degree of regret about their homosexuality, totaled approximatley 8 percent of their lesbian sample.[13] This category seems to have shrunk in the Fleener sample, although no exact comparison can be made because additional qualifications for membership in this subgroup—low feelings about sex appeal, particularly —were absent from the Fleener questionnaire.

If comparisons between the two samples can be made within the context of six years of active gay and lesbian liberation movements, then it would appear that lesbians today are more self-accepting and tend to form monogamous relationships more frequently. There is also reason to believe that the asexuality noted in Bell and Weinberg may be, because of its ties to age, a remnant of the preliberation experience, one that may be likely to diminish in future years.

Lesbian liberation, along with gay liberation and the women's movement, has done much to improve the outside realities impacting on lesbians' lives. Although the legislative reforms sought by some lesbian rights activists may be a long time in coming, changes already on the books—in psychiatric manuals, in political life, and in the media—guarantee that the spiritual contribution of the movement, lesbian pride and self-affirmation, once found, will never be lost.

This psychic dimension is perhaps the most significant change affecting the vast majority of American lesbians now, and it may remain so even in a future when and if the complete agenda of legislative and social reforms proposed by lesbian rights activists has been exhausted.

As "Legs" summarized, "They can take away gay rights laws. They can shove me back in the closet. They can jail me. They can even give me all the technical freedoms I could dream of or demand. But none of that affects the thing that is inside me—my personal sense of value and worth. Once you get that feeling, you will never lose it, and, believe me, there's *nothing* that even comes close to it."

# CONCLUSION

## Beyond Liberation: The Implications for Society

While America sits wordlessly in front of her television sets, computer technologists prepare plans for a television-centered world that would all but eliminate our need to leave our homes for banking, shopping, voting, and even learning. Meanwhile, we see less of our neighbors, talk less with our friends, and silently approach the state of walking, talking, rootless monads increasingly frustrated by, but otherwise not feeling, outside reality.

The technology surrounding us is developing more rapidly than we can keep track of it. While this book was written, not only had an uproar about artificial insemination of lesbians been running its course, but test-tube babies had brought images of horror to John Birch Society members as their publication warned them that "the Lesbians propose that 200,000 of these births take place in New York City to cause a profound change in the political climate there."[1] Meanwhile, discussions of the potential for cloning human beings have stirred national debate. The first few chapters of the manuscript of this book were typed on something called "paper." By mid-manuscript, the office supply store sold only something called "substance," abbreviated "sub.," and available in various weights and qualities.

Americans are tending to become more mobile as air fares drop and new national boundaries are opened to our tourist and business trade.

Planes are so crowded and airfields so overloaded that many cities are planning super-airports miles away from their city limits to accommodate the tide of travelers to and from the megalopoli of the future.

Data about our world is so vast, even at the level of our local communities, that it is difficult to locate, much less place into comprehensible context.

Future studies' scenarios have been modeled for the possibilities of American and world life in the next quarter century and beyond. Among the more grim are those postulating economic chaos, hyperinflation, and an economy centered on three groups: an upper crust of technocrats, systems analysts, and planners running a robotized system of production, a second class of people employed in the service and entertainment sector, and a third, permanent, underclass of unemployed, seemingly nonessential people.

Nineteen eighty-four is upon us and George Orwell's book is not far from wrong. Increasing *isolation* has brought us from the days of a decade ago when a community threatened by natural disaster came together in mutual assistance to a time when armed guards must be called out to prevent looting; *mobility* is so entrenched that corporate men (and a few women) are now international people, nearly stateless; *change* accelerates in geometric leaps which most of us cannot follow, to which few of us can adapt. No sooner has our system of law adjusted to cope with a medical technology that can maintain a comatose "dead" person "alive," than it must cope with the legal paternity rights of an artificially inseminated woman's child or a test-tube baby. Thousands of children have grown up in cities where they have never seen the Milky Way through the smog. An entire generation exists that has never seen a cow or steer except in photos, or perhaps on a trip to the zoo, or, even more rare, a trip to countryside beef-raising factories.

Americans are sensing these changes, which they might not yet (or ever) fully comprehend. In increasing thousands they join cults promising to transform them, to give them an experience of feeling, and, although unadvertized, a sense of *belonging*. No longer are children alone fleeing to such cults (perhaps they, more perceptive than adults, were the first to realize the cults' benefits); droves of adults are signing up for Erhardt Seminars Training (est), Scientology, Transcendental Meditation, and more traditionally Christian-oriented groups led by born-again ministers. All these groups have given their members a refuge from isolation, a place where they are more than numbers on a computer data card. Cult followers are given a special language, so that the true believer, from among millions of others, may find instant kinship with another of her or his cult. Secret political societies like the Ku Klux Klan offer a similar remedy to isolation—"The wonderful thing about our organization is that no matter where the Marines send us we're only a phone call away from the Klan."[2] Even homosexual males have followed the trend with a gay Nazi group in Los Angeles and The Advocate Experience which draws heavily from est.

These groups appear to be America's way of coping with the realities of the strange world it faces in the last two decades of the century. They are in many ways reminiscent of the lesbian subculture in hiding that has coped, through past decades, with similar problems: isolation, mobility, and change. The lesbian subculture in hiding functions much the same way as the cult and secret society, with its own words and rituals of recognition, tight bonds of trust, and codes of behavior which ensure that this trust is maintained. Periods of repression have forced the subculture underground, weakened some of the links between the extended families that comprise it. Liberal times have allowed it to strengthen itself, to experiment with different ways of relating to people—economically, socially, and spiritually.

What distinguishes the lesbian subculture in hiding from the cult phenomenon of what others describe as the "me first" decade, is the fact that the former has always been leaderless. The subculture was an underground railway toward companionship and safety for some, but much like the underground railway of the slavery era, it has been centered neither around a single leader, nor around a hierarchical or authoritarian structure: it has always been a network of friends in extended families, helping sisters (and brothers) in need.

The fate of leadership-oriented, hierarchical, and authoritarian cults has left America with adequate lessons, from the People's Temple slayings in Guyana, to the last pangs of the hierarchical and authoritarian-oriented Synanon experiment. Leadership cults, hierarchical cults, authoritarian organizations are *not* a long-term solution for Americans confronted by future shock. They are often end solutions, where the end is brutal and inhumane.

This, perhaps, is the greatest lesson the lesbian subculture in hiding offers to America—a lesson of contrast between the nurturing, nonhierarchical, antiauthoritarian networks of extended families and their cult antitheses.

## LESBIAN FUTURES

The dream of lesbian liberation has not really changed much over the last two and a half decades. The dream has always centered around the concept that a lesbian should be free to fulfill her full potential in any arena she may choose—political, artistic, or professional, as mother or as worker—without having to fear that exposure of her private life will ruin all that she has built for herself. The dream has always been future-oriented, a dream that future generations of lesbians be able to grow up free to explore their affectional preferences without experiencing the agonies of those who went before them and struggled with values internalized from a homophobic society—values that said *lesbian* means bad, sick, evil, less competent.

The last quarter-century has seen vast change on the landscape of lesbian life. Respected institutions no longer regard a lesbian as mentally ill. She herself has learned that her love is a positive part of her life. Many of the sources of lesbians' economic oppression have been removed—laws that discriminated against her because she was female and single.

The lesbian movement, as it enters the last years of the century, is only one facet of a nation on the apex of vast social change. America's middle class is being squeezed out of existence by inflation and decreased real earnings. Liberal programs and ideologies of the sixties are no longer adequate to serve a nation that is an integral part of an international economic system. There is almost universal fear of economic collapse as cities default or teeter on the brink of bankruptcy. It is a classic environment for backlash politics, as were the depression years when attempts were made to rescind such advances as the women's movement had made.

In 1977 the antigay backlash found a charismatic leader in the person of Anita Bryant who, if let free to create social policy, would send all lesbians to prison for twenty-year terms, ban them from access to public accommodations, and exclude them from almost the entire economic life of the country.

To date, the Bryant backlash and its extremism have benefited gay people more than harmed them. If lesbianism was a nontopic before 1977, it is now out in the open. It is no longer the unmentionable crime against nature. While backlash demagogues like Bryant, Phyllis Schlafly, and John Briggs argue that homosexuality, and even a woman's role in society, are moral issues—just as backlash demagogues of the antiabolitionist movement argued about slavery more than a century ago—they bring a social awareness of far more fundamental concerns of the body politic. These concerns are two: Where is the dividing line between moral issues and human rights issues? Can the civil rights of a minority be allowed to be determined by public vote, as they have been in Miami, St. Paul, Eugene, Seattle, and the state of California? Both are issues that will eventually find their resolutions in the United States Supreme Court.

Concurrently, the backlash against the women's movement as a whole continues, personified by Schlafly and others who would deny women equal rights under law and would seek to restore women to the servitude of unwanted pregnancy by declaring that abortion is, from the unidentified moment of conception onward, murder.

Along with these backlash movements, in the late seventies a political coalition forging itself around an ultraconservative base appeared to be gaining enough political power to forestall, if not yet repeal, many of the liberal advances made in earlier decades.

The future of lesbian rights, in view of these realities, is tenuous. Lesbians' future opportunities are tied not only to the gay rights movement, but to the women's movement as well. Indications are that for lasting social reforms fulfilling the dreams of lesbian liberation, lesbians will have to come out and discuss their lifestyles with their friends, families, coworkers and bosses. This has not yet occurred in any large measure. Most heterosexuals even after nearly three decades of gay rights agitation, still say they do not know a single lesbian personally—even though their daughter or sister might be one. Although more and more women *are* coming out, most lesbians still fear alienating their families and are too dependent on their jobs to take such a large risk.

The future of women's rights, in the short term, appears to be tied to the ability of women's rights advocates to out-organize their opponents in the political arena. They are fighting not only a grass roots backlash, but powerful institutional opposition from some organized religious groups, including the hierarchy of the Roman Catholic Church and the increasingly powerful Church of Jesus Christ of Latter-Day Saints (Mormon). In addition, those allies they might be expected to call on—friends in the trade union movement and among minority groups—are increasingly engaged in fighting off the advances of their own opponents. Maintaining and improving the civil rights of women in the current climate is a titanic struggle and its short-term prospects appear dim.

## HOPE FOR THE FUTURE

Even should the backlash personified by Bryant and Schlafly succeed in its worst form—that of a renewed McCarthy era—the lesbian-feminist and gay rights movements have already achieved significant changes that cannot be destroyed. Chief among these is the lesbian's new self-image, an affirmation of her value, rather than a degradation of it. This feeling of self-acceptance and pride has ramifications for America's lesbian daughters that have yet to be fully explored.

Its chief field of action is in America's lesbian underground, the subculture in hiding.

Prior to the last quarter-century, the lesbian subculture consisted of friendship cliques—extended families—that occasionally had interlocking connections with other extended families in different parts of the country. Yet this subculture in hiding was largely a closed subculture, especially among extended families having the most to protect—closeted lesbians in public offices and in public service positions. Such groups remained relatively isolated from the interconnectedness characterizing the subculture's mainstream. Today, the attitudes of many of these women have changed. Many of them have become integrated into the lesbian underground network. Such women, in public office, in the professions, in the world of entertainment, in professional athletics, and in the media, have a growing perception of themselves as healthy, proud women. And while remaining closeted, they are able to extend help to their sisters in need and to the gay and feminist movements. It is unlikely that these women will return to their once self-imposed isolation.

America's lesbian underground has additionally been strengthened by those women who have spent time in the lesbian movement and returned to other fields of attention, out of public view. These women also are unlikely to turn their backs on the needs of their sisters. Explains a woman who was part of a campus gay rights group during her years at law school, "I'm kind of closety now. You can't expect to go into court and win cases for your clients if all the judge is thinking about is 'What's this queer doing in my court?' But I do take lesbian cases and my clients know I'm gay, so they are comfortable. I also take referrals from other attorneys who know I'm gay. Some people have told me I should come out publicly now that I'm an attorney. I just laugh at them and tell them, 'Hell no, I can do a lot more for my sisters right here, right where I am, in my own kind of closet!'" Her sentiments are shared by many women whose early adult lives were affected by the lesbian-feminist and gay rights movements.

And those questions that have been raised in the mainstream by lesbian feminists and heterosexual feminists as well—questions about sex-role stereotyping, gender and sexual identity, parenting, and intimate relationships—will not be forgotten. They are questions which have raised concepts that may not yet have found full acceptance—just as the concept of zero, a revolution in its own time, was not fully accepted for many years—but which, like the concept of zero, are unlikely to be ignored.

It is clear that the conditions of lesbian life will never again be as they were before 1955. The lesbian underground of today is a vastly changed terrain, a far more expansive place to be. And the closet too has changed. Even if it remains a necessary refuge from a hostile society, it is no longer a deadly place: windows have been opened to it, filling it with fresh currents of air; within it, women may grow, live, and love. They may even thrive.

# End Notes

## Introduction

1. Spencer Rich, "Profile Shows Big Rise in Fatherless Families," *Washington Post,* March 15, 1978.

2. Associated Press, "Record 30.4 Million Families Have at Least Two Wage Earners," *Washington Post,* July 25, 1978.

3. Associated Press, "Single-Woman American Households Are Increasing, Census Reports," *Washington Post,* August, 14, 1978.

4. California Senate, Judiciary Committee, testimony of state senator Jerry Smith, October 25, 1978.

5. Harvey Cox, "Why Young Americans Are Buying Oriental Religions," *Psychology Today,* July 1977, p. 39.

6. "Articles of Incorporation" (Kingman, Ariz.: Happiness of Womanhood, Inc., December 28, 1970).

7. Jacquie Davison, "Ten Point Platform," (Kingman, Ariz.: Happiness of Womanhood, Inc., 1971).

8. Phyllis Schlafly, "The Right To Be A Woman," *The Phyllis Schlafly Report,* November, 1972, p. 4.

9. Phyllis Schlafly, *The Power of the Positive Woman* (New Rochelle, N.Y.: Arlington House Publishers, 1977), p. 166.

10. "Lesbians & Radicals Dominate IWY," *Eagle Forum,* July, 1977. *Eagle Forum* is the mimeographed one-sheet newsletter that accompanies the monthly *Phyllis Schlafly Report.* As Schlafly is president of Eagle Forum, it is presumed that the newsletter reflects, if not her writing, at least her opinions.

11. Ken Kelly, "Playboy Interview: Anita Bryant," *Playboy,* May, 1978, p. 244.

12. Mike Thompson, "The Miami Vote: Important Lessons for Conservatives," *Battle Line,* June – July, 1977. Thompson, chairman of the Florida Conservative Union during the Bryant campaign, also directed the campaign's media activities.

13. Phyllis Schlafly, "Statement of Non-Candidacy," *Eagle Forum,* December, 1977.

14. "How California Voters See Sexual Preference and Occupation," *The Advocate,* June 14, 1978. This article described the publicly released findings of an early 1978 poll conducted by the Public Response Associate, Inc.

15. Dolores Klaich, *Woman + Woman, Attitudes Toward Lesbianism,* (New York; William Morrow & Co., 1975), p. 130.

16. Dolores Klaich, p. 145.

17. Jim Peron, "Homosexuality and the Miracle Workers," report for Evangelicals Concerned, Chicago, 1978. Also see Sasha Gregory Lewis, "Right Watch," *The Advocate,* October 4, 1978. As this book was going to press, Edward Rowe, executive director of Anita Bryant Ministries, in response to a letter from this author, prepared and released an official policy statement on "Deliverance from Homosexuality," which, approved by both Ms. Bryant and her husband Bob Greene, now represents the Ministries' position. In essence, the statement recognizes the fact that "salvation" from homosexuality is by no means an instantaneous process, and that the end result of deliverance would be a reorientation to a heterosexual lifestyle. Quoting from the end of the statement, "To be 'saved' does not mean that a person is sinless. What it does mean is that he possesses a new life, a new hope, a new expectation, a new fellowship, a new walk. He does not live under legalism, but rather under a gracious, loving, patient God who wants to fulfill a great purpose through him. Righteous living and good conduct are tremendously important to God—but still the failing Christian is not struck down instantly when he sins. The outward evidence of his salvation is not so much his *sinlessness* as the *direction* of his life. He is headed toward better conduct, more abundant living, spiritual maturity, and greater service for the Lord who redeemed him (1 Peter 1:18-19)." The complete three-page statement is available from the Ministries at P.O. Box 40-2608, Miami Beach, Fl., 33140.

18. Charlotte Wolff, *Love Between Women,* (New York: St. Martin's Press, 1971), p. 209.

19. Catherine Barnett, "Prop. 6: Nazism or Godsend?" Santa Rosa, Calif. *Press Democrat,* Sept. 21, 1978.

20. Jonathan Katz, *Gay American History: Lesbians and Gay Men in the U.S.A.* (New York: Thomas Y. Crowell Co., 1976), pp. 127-128.

21. Virginia Vida, ed., *Our Right to Love: A Lesbian Resource Book* (Englewood Cliffs, N.J.: Prentice-Hall, 1978), pp. 35-36.

22. Jonathan Katz, pp. 166-167.

23. Virginia Vida, pp. 91-92.

24. Virginia Vida, pp. 206-207.

25. Interview with this author. Also see pp. 37-40 of *Sappho Was a Right On Woman* by Sydney Abbot and Barbara Love (New York: Stein & Day, 1972) for an excellent description of various ways society works to keep lesbians invisible.

# Part One

# Rites of Passage

1. Paul Watzlawick, *How Real is Real? Confusion, Disinformation, Communication* (New York: Random House, Vintage Books, 1976), pp. 63-64

## Chapter 1: The Lesbian Identity

1. Charlotte Wolff, *Love Between Women* (New York: St. Martin's Press, 1971), p. 208.

2. Marilyn G. Fleener, "The Lesbian Lifestyle" (report presented to the Western Social Science Association, April, 1977), p. 14.

3. Fleener, p. 14.

4. Alan P. Bell, Martin S. Weinberg, *Homosexualities: A Study of Diversity Among Men & Women,* (New York: Simon & Schuster, 1978), p. 313. The Bell and Weinberg study is among the first to have a sufficient pool of lesbians of two races (black and white) to make comparisons between them. The statistical information reported in the body of *Sunday's Women* has combined the findings into one figure. Where there are significant differences between races, they are noted.

5. Bell and Weinberg, p. 338. In this instance, only white lesbians in the sample attempted to stop being homosexual through heterosexual marriage. None of the eleven black women reporting an attempt to stop being homosexual tried heterosexual marriage.

6. Bell and Weinberg, p. 388. These data refer to the duration of the women's first marriage. About a quarter of the women studied reported being married two or more times.

7. Wolff, p. 209.

8. Bell and Weinberg, pp. 374-386. Forty-eight percent of the white women reported that they were "not homosexual" before they were married the first time; only 23 percent of the black women made this report.

9. Wolff, p. 210. Wolff comments that she found no significant difference in the number of heterosexual partners between the lesbians and the heterosexual control group.

10. Fleener, p. 12.

11. Bell and Weinberg, p. 286.

12. Bell and Weinberg, p. 287.

## Chapter 2: The Transformation from Butch to Dyke

1. Dolores Klaich, *Woman + Woman, Attitudes Toward Lesbianism* (New York: William Morrow & Co., 1975), p. 151.

2. Merlin Stone, *When God Was a Woman* (New York: Harcourt Brace Jovanovich, Harvest edition, 1978). Stone's book is an excellent resource on the extant history of matriarchal cultures.

3. Rossell Hope Robbins, *The Encyclopedia of Witchcraft and Demonology* (New York: Crown Publishers, 1959), p. 287. While the title and presentation of this book make it seem like one of the many poorly researched and largely fictitious accounts of witchcraft, it is actually one of the best researched books available on the subject. The only area of doubt now being cast on the work is that Robbins hypothesized that the activities of alleged witches were largely the creations of witch-hunters. Some contemporary feminist writers argue that the phenomena of witchcraft over the last two thousand years did in fact exist among groups of women adhering to ancient beliefs in goddess worship.

# END NOTES

4. Robbins, p. 468.

5. Nancy Byron and Charlotte Bunch, eds., *Women Remembered: A Collection of Biographies From the Furies* (Baltimore: Diana Press, 1974), pp. 44-45.

6. Susan Baker, "Anne Bonny & Mary Read," in *Women Remembered*, Nancy Byron and Charlotte Bunch, eds., p. 86.

7. Jonathan Katz, *Gay American History: Lesbians and Gay Men in the U.S.A.* (New York: Thomas Y. Crowell Co., 1976), pp. 232-238.

8. Richard von Krafft-Ebing, *Psychopathia Sexualis*, trans. Franklin S. Klaf (New York: Bantam Books, 1969), pp. 315-317.

9. Arno Karlen, *Sexuality and Homosexuality A New View:* (New York: W.W. Norton & Co., 1971), pp. 545-546. Karlen's description is based primarily on two studies performed by women, one, "The Concept of the Lesbian, a Minority in Reverse," by sociologist Suzanne Prosin, published in the lesbian publication *The Ladder* in 1962, and the second, "A Study of a Public Lesbian Community," an unpublished thesis by Ethel Sawyer, Washington University, St. Louis, Missouri, 1965.

10. Marilyn G. Fleener, "The Lesbian Lifestyle," (report presented to the Western Social Science Association, April, 1977), p. 13. The direct reference refers to Fleener's finding that 98 percent of her sample denied they live butch/femme roles. The remaining data are taken from unpublished data drawn from the original responses to the Fleener questionnaire. These were not included in her report and were summarized by this writer. In future notes, references to the summaries of Fleener's data, in contrast to the specific data mentioned in her report, will be referenced "Fleener Data." The Fleener report was based on survey responses from 162 women, twenty-two of which were responses to her pilot questionnaire. The Fleener Data, however, do not include these pilot questionnaire responses.

11. The quality of lesbian sexual encounters has been a topic of widespread debate. Wolff states that lesbian sexual encounters differed from women's heterosexual encounters in "the rare occurrence of frigidity" among lesbians (*Love Between Women* [New York: St. Martin's Press, 1971], p. 149). Unfortunately, her work offers little documentation to substantiate this claim except a table of responses titled "Orgasms In Role Of," where only 13 percent report "no orgasm" (p. 214). Fleener's report found that 87 percent experience orgasm with a woman "most of the time" or "every time" (p. 12). The Kinsey data are more difficult to interpret. They report on "incidences of sexual difficulties" of women, finding that "approximately one-third to two-fifths noted occasional difficulty in maintaining affection for their partner, a lack of orgasm in the partner, or concerns about their own sexual adequacy." Reporting on the "severity of sexual difficulties," the Kinsey report notes that "difficulty finding a suitable partner" was very much a problem for the greatest numbers. Next most often mentioned was insufficient sexual frequency. Fewer had had problems with lack of orgasm . . . these difficulties were described as very much of a problem only by small numbers, less than 10 percent of either race (Alan P. Bell and Martin S. Weinberg, *Homosexualities: A Study of Diversity Among Men and Women* [New York: Simon & Schuster, 1978], p. 119). As clinician Nancy Toder notes in "Sexual Problems of Lesbians," the myth that "all lesbians have great sex all the time," is "one of the most popular and destructive myths in the lesbian community" because it prevents lesbians who do have problems from seeking help and because it creates an image that is impossible to maintain in every

sexual encounter (in Virginia Vida, ed., *Our Right to Love: A Lesbian Resource Book* [Englewood Cliffs, N.J.: Prentice-Hall, 1978], pp. 105-113).

**Chapter 3: Making Connections**

1. *Gaia's Guide,* 1978 (115 New Montgomery Street, San Francisco, Ca. 94105). This directory is updated and published yearly.

2. Alan P. Bell and Martin S. Weinberg, *Homosexualities: A Study of The Diversity Among Men and Women* (New York: Simon & Schuster, 1978), p. 412.

3. Marilyn G. Fleener, "The Lesbian Lifestyle," (report presented to the Western Social Science Association, April, 1977), p. 15.

4. Fleener, p. 15.

5. Bell and Weinberg, p. 412.

6. Dolores Klaich, *Woman + Woman: Attitudes Toward Lesbianism* (New York: William Morrow & Co., 1975), p. 184. Klaich makes a very strong argument that the reason *The Well of Loneliness* was suppressed was not so much because of its content, but because author Radclyffe Hall was so open about her own lesbianism.

7. Barbara McDowell and Hana Umlauf, eds., *The Good Housekeeping Woman's Almanac by the Editors of the World Almanac* (New York: Newspaper Enterprise Association, 1977), p. 453.

8. Jonathan Katz, *Gay American History: Lesbians and Gay Men in the U.S.A* (New York: Thomas Y. Crowell Co., 1976), pp. 227-228.

9. E. Carrington Boggan, Marilyn G. Haft, Charles Lester, and John P. Rupp, *The Rights of Gay People: The Basic ACLU Guide to a Gay Person's Rights* (New York: Avon Books, Discus edition, 1975), p. 46.

10. McDowell and Umlauf, p. 457. This source claims that equal opportunity for women in the armed forces became a reality in 1967. Several court cases, however, were needed to enforce the technical equality granted women in 1967's Public Law 90-130. It was not until 1973, according to this source, that a Supreme Court decision granted families of enlisted women equal benefits with men.

11. "Gay Vets Can Upgrade Discharges," *The Advocate,* October 4, 1978. Unless the policy is extended, vets have only until January 1, 1980, to make use of this option. Gay vets should seek counseling from a qualified civilian military counselor before undertaking this process. On December 6, 1978, the U.S. Court of Appeals in the District of Columbia ruled that the Pentagon cannot discharge homosexuals from the military without offering specific reasons in addition to their homosexuality, on the basis of findings that not all homosexuals in the armed services are discharged ("Service Dismissal of Homosexuals Limited by Court," Kenneth Bredemier, *Washington Post,* December 7, 1978). The Department of Defense, of course, could appeal this ruling to the Supreme Court. If the appelate court ruling stands, it essentially means the military must not only prove homosexuality before making a discharge, but must prove, in each case, that the individual's affectional preference somehow had an adverse affect on the performance of her or his duties.

12. *Lesbian Connection,* P.O. Box 811, East Lansing, Mi. 48823 (3:1 April, 1977). Forty-one percent of those who had previous military experience said they would not recommend it to other women.

13. Nancy Goldman, ''The Changing Role of Women in the Armed Forces,'' in *Changing Women in a Changing Society,* ed. Joan Huber (Chicago: University of Chicago Press, 1973), p. 133.

14. Vito Russo, ''Pat Bond, the Word Is Out WAC,'' *Christopher Street* 2:11 (May 1978).

## Chapter 4: A Subculture in Hiding

1. Alan P. Bell and Martin S. Weinberg, *Homosexualities: A Study of the Diversity Among Men and Women* (New York: Simon & Schuster, 1978), pp. 30-32.

## Chapter 5: Relationship Experiments

1. Alan P. Bell and Martin S. Weinberg, *Homosexualities: A Study of the Diversity Among Men and Women* (New York: Simon & Schuster, 1978), p. 317. The second most frequently cited change under this category was ''more afraid to get involved again''; ranking third were 10 percent who responded they had learned something about how to keep a relationship going. Responding to a question about ''positive changes in self'' as a result of the first affair were 35 percent who said their first affair gave them a greater sense of maturity. Nearly a third reported that they felt they had become better, or more complete, people. About a third reported they had gained self-confidence or self-acceptance through their first affair.

2. Bell and Weinberg, p. 313. About 60 percent of the total lesbian sample reported living together during their first affair, but there was a significant difference between white and black respondents: 65 percent of the whites and 41 percent of the blacks reported living together during their first affair. There is no apparent explanation in related data for this difference.

3. Bell and Weinberg, p. 314. The Kinsey researchers put a limit on their questions regarding the duration of first affairs of ''more than five years,'' to which about 12 percent responded affirmatively. During the course of research for this book, the author met two couples in their forties and fifties for whom their current affair was the first. In the first case the affair had lasted thirteen years and in the second case the affair had lasted thirty-two years.

4. Bell and Weinberg, p. 98.

5. Bell and Weinberg, p. 315. Interestingly, the ''romantic involvement'' did not seem to mean a sexual involvement. This was a separate category named by somewhat less than 3 percent of the respondents.

6. Fleener Data (see Chapter 2, note 10). Tabulated data from the Fleener survey found that more than a third of the women between twenty-one and forty had experienced all-female threesomes. Fleener's questionnaire did not solicit a response to why the threesomes had taken place, but some deductions from responses to her other questions may be indicative. Most threesomes appeared to have been undertaken by women with a sexually adventurous nature: those who had reported between ten and twenty or more than twenty sexual relationships with women. The second highest category of women who had experienced threesomes were those who advocated so-called open or nonmonagamous relationships. The remainder, about 8 percent of the total in this age group who had experienced threesomes, were not sexually adventurous,

nor did they advocate or practice open relationships. This may indicate that the nature of their threesomes was a ritual of partnership-ending. Such an assumption, of course, is only an hypothesis that must be documented by further research.

7. Bell and Weinberg, p. 315. More than twice as many of the black lesbians (11 percent) reported the reason for the breakup of their first affair as ''forced apart by others,'' than did white respondents (5 percent).

8. M. A. Karr, ''Who the Hell is Carmelita Pope?'', *The Advocate,* December 13, 1978.

9. Bell and Weinberg, pp. 457, 427.

10. Bell and Weinberg, p. 317.

11. Bell and Weinberg, p. 319.

# Part Two

# The Lesbian Couple in a Heterosexual World

1. Alan P. Bell and Martin S. Weinberg, *Homosexualities: A Study of Diversity Among Men and Women* (New York: Simon & Schuster, 1978), p. 322.

### Chapter 6: The Closeted Couple

1. E. Carrington Boggan, Marilyn G. Haft, Charles Lester, and John P. Rupp, *The Rights of Gay People: The Basic ACLU Guide To A Gay Person's Rights* (New York: Avon Books, Discus edition, 1975), pp. 212-235.

2. Alan P. Bell and Martin S. Weinberg, *Homosexualities: A Study of Diversity Among Men and Women* (New York: Simon & Schuster, 1978), pp. 295-297.

3. Bell and Weinberg, pp. 361, 362, 426.

### Chapter 7: Breaking Free

1. Alan P. Bell and Martin S. Weinberg, *Homosexualities: A Study of Diversity Among Men and Women* (New York: Simon & Schuster, 1978), pp. 342-343.

### Chapter 8: Parents and "In-Laws"

1. Marilyn G. Fleener, ''The Lesbian Lifestyle'' (report presented to the Western Social Science Association, April, 1977), p. 8.

2. Fleener Data (see Chapter 2, note 10).

3. Press release, Public Response Associates, San Francisco, Ca., May 25, 1978.

4. Press release, Public Response Associates.

5. Bell and Weinberg, p. 463.

6. Press release, Public Response Associates.

7. Fleener Data.

8. Parents of Gays organizations in several states. Their addresses are available from the National Gay Task Force, 80 Fifth Ave., New York, N.Y.

# END NOTES

9. Alan P. Bell and Martin S. Weinberg, *Homosexualities: A Study of Diversity Among Men and Women* (New York: Simon & Schuster, 1978), p. 315.

10. Fleener Data.

11. Fleener Data.

12. Fleener Data.

13. Fleener Data.

## Chapter 9: Lesbian Families

1. Randy Shilts, "L.M.D.F.'s 'Apple Pie' Battles," *The Advocate*, October 22, 1975. The address of the Lesbian Mother's National Defense Fund and of *Mom's Apple Pie* is 2446 Lorentz Place North, Seattle, Wa., 98109.

2. Elenore G. Pred, ed., "Studies and Surveys," *The Advocate*, May 31, 1978.

3. "A Display of Homophobia in Appeals Court," *The Advocate*, March 12, 1975.

4. Randy Shilts.

5. Alan P. Bell and Martin S. Weinberg, *Homosexualities: A Study of Diversity Among Men and Women* (New York: Simon & Schuster, 1978), p. 374.

6. Charlotte Wolff, *Love Between Women* (New York: St. Martin's Press, 1971), p. 210.

7. Randy Shilts.

8. Bell and Weinberg, p. 392; Wolff, p. 210 (Wolff apparently only solicited information on children from lesbians who had been or were currently married); Fleener Data; "Ambitious Amazons," in *Lesbian Connection*, March, 1978.

9. Fleener Data (see Chapter 2, note 10); Randy Shilts.

10. Randy Shilts.

11. Bell and Weinberg, p. 392-393.

12. An excellent resource for lesbian mothers who are considering discussing their lesbianism with their children is Betty Berzon's article, "Sharing Your Lesbian Identity With Your Children," in *Our Right to Love*, Virginia Vida, ed. (Englewood Cliffs, N.J.: Prentice-Hall, 1978), pp. 69-74.

13. Bell and Weinberg, p. 394.

14. Fleener Data.

15. Fleener Data.

16. Marilyn G. Fleener, "The Lesbian Lifestyle" (report presented to the Western Social Science Association, April, 1977), p. 16.

17. According to an October 1, 1978, Reuters dispatch, it took the British Medical Association about one year from the time the issue of artificial insemination for lesbians was raised in the media to advise doctors that "it is not unethical to help lesbians have babies by artificial insemination," despite the fact that "several politicians had demanded curbs on what they called 'this horrific practice.'" Artificial insemination for lesbian couples, meanwhile, had been quietly available in the San Francisco Bay Area for about one year according to three doctors interviewed by a local reporter. None of the doctors interviewed could determine how extensive the practice is, but one, a lesbian who asked to remain anonymous, stated that she expected the practice to increase as artificial insemination becomes more available ("Artificial Insemination Available, Quietly, to Lesbians in Bay Area," Judie Telfer, San Jose *Mercury News*, December 17, 1978.)

### Chapter 10: Living with the Law

1. An excellent guide to how to handle property arrangements should be the first gift made to the new lesbian couple (or commune). It is easy to read and includes sample agreements which can be copied and used. The book is *Sex, Living Together and The Law: A Legal Guide for Unmarried Couples (and Groups)* by attorneys Carmen Masey and Ralph Warner (Courtyard Books, Nolo Press, 1974, Box 544, Occidental, Ca., 95465). For more serious (or wealthy) readers looking for legal loopholes to achieve financial benefits from their unmarried state, William L. Blaine and John Bishop's *Practical Guide for the Unmarried Couple* might also be valuable (Sun River Press, Two Continents Publishing, 1976, 30 East 42 Street, New York, N.Y. 10017).

2. Fleener Data (see Chapter 2, note 10).

3. Ted Vollmer, ''Lesbian Ordered to Pay 'Wife' Monthly Support,'' *Los Angeles Times,* June 7, 1978.

### Chapter 11: Role-Free Living

1. Alan P. Bell and Martin S. Weinberg, *Homosexualities: A Study of Diversity Among Men and Women* (New York: Simon & Schuster, 1978), p. 324-325.

2. Bell and Weinberg, p. 323.

3. Bell and Weinberg, p. 323.

4. Bell and Weinberg, p. 323.

5. Bell and Weinberg, p. 322.

6. Fleener Data (see Chapter 2, note 10).

7. Bell and Weinberg, p. 320.

8. Fleener Data.

9. Fleener Data.

10. Fleener Data.

11. Fleener Data.

# Part Three

# The Personal Becomes Political

1. Alan P. Bell and Martin S. Weinberg: *Homosexualities: A Study of Diversity Among Men and Women* (New York: Simon & Schuster, 1978), p. 368. More than 82 percent of the lesbian respondents denied that their homosexuality had affected them politically in any way. Interestingly, when asked about the effects of their homosexuality on liberalism, 15 percent of the white lesbians responded that it made them *less* liberal, while 11 percent of the black lesbians reported that it made them *more* liberal.

### Chapter 12: The Dream

1. Maureen Oddone, ''Breakthrough in Houston, Women's Movement Throws Support Behind Gay Rights,'' *The Advocate,* January 11, 1978.

**Chapter 13: Radical Experiments**

1. *Quest: A Feminist Quarterly,* P.O. Box 8843, Washington, D.C., 20003. Business manager Arleen Rogan notes that about 83 percent of the publication's readership, according to its last reader survey, are lesbians.

2. Vicki Garbriner and Susan Wells, "Nurturing a Lesbian Organization," in Virginia Vida, ed., *Our Right to Love: A Lesbian Resource Book* (Englewood Cliffs, N.J.: Prentice-Hall, 1978), pp. 134-138.

3. Garbriner and Wells, pp. 134-138.

4. Jeri Dilno, "Monogamy and Alternate Life-Styles," in Virginia Vida, pp. 56-59.

5. Jeri Dilno, pp. 56-59.

6. Jeri Dilno, pp. 56-59.

7. Susan Rennie and Kirsten Grimstad, eds. *The New Woman's Survival Sourcebook* (New York: Alfred A. Knopf, 1975), pp. 197-198. This book's section on spirituality gives a wide sampling of the varieties of spiritual endeavors being undertaken by feminists.

**Chapter 14: The Extremist Fringe**

1. Sasha Gregory Lewis, "Rep. Elaine Noble, Reaching a Turning Point After Three Years," *The Advocate,* January 25, 1978.

2. Sally Miller Gearhart, "The Spiritual Dimension: Death and Resurrection of a Hallelujah Dyke," in Virginia Vida, ed., *Our Right to Love: A Lesbian Resource Book* (Englewood Cliffs, N.J.: Prentice-Hall, 1978), p. 192.

**Chapter 15: Changing Times**

1. Marilyn G. Fleener, "The Lesbian Lifestyle," (report presented to the Western Social Science Association, April, 1977), p. 15.

2. Gloria Steinem, "The Politics of Supporting Lesbianism," in Virginia Vida, ed., *Our Right to Love: A Lesbian Resource Book* (Englewood Cliffs, N.J.: Prentice-Hall, 1978), p. 267.

3. Shere Hite, *The Hite Report* (New York: Macmillan, 1976), quoted in Virginia Vida, p. 280.

4. Fleener, p. 14. Fleener comments, "A few had not heard of the Gay Movement and a very few were worried about it and it threatened them."

5. Alan P. Bell and Martin S. Weinberg, *Homosexualities: A Study of Diversity Among Men and Women* (New York: Simon & Schuster, 1978), p. 414. A significant difference existed between white and black lesbians' membership. While 21 percent of the whites reported belonging to a homophile organization, only 8 percent of the black women did.

6. Fleener, pp. 13-15.

7. Bell and Weinberg, p. 438.

8. Fleener Data (see Chapter 2, note 10); Bell and Weinberg, p. 295.

9. Fleener, p. 11.

10. Bell and Weinberg, pp. 219-221.

11. Bell and Weinberg, p. 481; Fleener Data.
12. Bell and Weinberg, p. 480.
13. Bell and Weinberg, p. 480.

# Conclusion

Beyond Liberation: The Implications for Society

1. Jean C. Blasdale, ''The Left: Babies For Lesbians?'' *The Review of the NEWS,* October 4, 1978. Many people do not know that this right-leaning magazine is one of the more moderate publications of the John Birch Society.

2. Roger Rapoport, ''The Marine Corps Builds Men,'' *New Times,* May 27, 1977.

# Sources and Resources

There are many available studies of lesbians. The studies used in this book, however, were selected because they represented the largest samples of lesbians ever studied. The Bell and Weinberg sample was 293, the Fleener sample was 162, and the final Wolff sample was 106. It was felt that these studies, because of their sample size, would tend to be reliable indicators of certain phenomena among the lesbian population as a whole, even though they were all, by necessity, drawn from regions where gay organizations and bars existed.

These studies were also chosen because of the large amount of statistical material presented in tabular form in the Bell and Weinberg and Wolff reports, and as raw survey responses in the Fleener material.

The best and most respected bibliography of gay materials is prepared annually by the Task Force on Gay Liberation of the American Library Association. Previous editions have cost $.25; however, the price of future editions may increase. Interested persons should send a self-addressed, stamped postcard to Ms. Barbara Gittings, P.O. Box 2383, Philadelphia, Pa., 19103, for price information.

Those interested specifically in the lesbian liberation movement will find the book *Our Right to Love, a Lesbian Resource Book*, edited by Virginia Vida of the National Gay Task Force (Prentice-Hall, 1978), an excellent source of information. Additionally, it has the advantage of presenting some of the diversity within the lesbian movement. Its appendix includes a somewhat comprehensive listing of gay organizations and publications.

Lesbians interested in a generally politically neutral view of America's lesbian subculture, unique in its presentation of comments and letters from lesbians in rural and mid-America, will enjoy *Lesbian Connection*, a more-or-less regular monthly publication of the Ambitious Amazons. It is free to lesbians who cannot afford the cost. Otherwise, it is priced at $1.00 per issue. The address is P.O. Box 811, East Lansing, Mi., 48823.

# Index